PARENTING
IN PRIVILEGE
OR PERIL

PARENTING

IN PRIVILEGE
OR PERIL

HOW SOCIAL INEQUALITY ENABLES
OR DERAILS THE AMERICAN DREAM

Pamela R. Bennett
Amy Lutz
Lakshmi Jayaram

TEACHERS COLLEGE PRESS

TEACHERS COLLEGE | COLUMBIA UNIVERSITY
NEW YORK AND LONDON

Published by Teachers College Press,® 1234 Amsterdam Avenue, New York, NY 10027

Copyright © 2021 by Pamela R. Bennett, Amy Lutz, and Lakshmi Jayaram

Front cover illustration by shuoshu / iStock by Getty Images.

Library of Congress Cataloging-in-Publication Data is available at loc.gov

ISBN 978-0-8077-6601-9 (paper)
ISBN 978-0-8077-6602-6 (hardcover)
ISBN 978-0-8077-7990-3 (ebook)

Printed on acid-free paper
Manufactured in the United States of America

Contents

Acknowledgments

We give our deepest appreciation to the parents and school personnel from the two schools in our study; without their participation and assistance this research would not have been possible. We are grateful to James McPartland, Athena Tapales, and Allen Ruby for their support, particularly in the early stages of our work. We thank Dalia Abdelhady, Karl L. Alexander, Myrtis Alexander, Joan Bennett, Andrew J. Cherlin, Caitlin Cross-Barnet, Marjorie DeVault, Katrina M. McDonald, Sandra McGee, anonymous reviewers, and the late Melvin L. Kohn for helpful comments on various aspects of the manuscript. We benefitted from research, translation, and transcription assistance from Mindelyn Buford II, Janet Carmona, Sandra Lutz, Matthew Messel, Roseann Presutti, Emily Singletary, and Karyn Stewart. Editing assistance came from Michael Barnet, Jessica Hausauer, and Maura M. McGee. While at the Russell Sage Foundation, we benefitted from support from Suzanne Nichols, Claire Gabriel, John Lee, and Galo Falchettore. We thank Kelly Bogart, Katrina Fiacchi, and Laura Walsh for assistance with the references. We are grateful for the opportunity to work with Carol Sargent, who illuminated and guided us through the book-publishing process. Sincere thanks to Teachers College Press and in particular our editor, Brian Ellerbeck, for believing in our project. Special thanks to the late Doris Entwisle for her mentorship, guidance, and early support. She is greatly missed.

The research reported in this book was made possible, in part, by a grant from the National Academy of Education/Spencer Foundation Postdoctoral Fellowship (Advanced Research Studies #200100304) to the Center for Social Organization of Schools and Department of Sociology at the Johns Hopkins University. Additional support came from grants from the American Sociological Association Fund for the Advancement of the Discipline, the Poverty & Race Research Action Council, Syracuse University, the College of Humanities, Arts, and Social Sciences at UMBC, and the Russell Sage Foundation through its Visiting Scholars Program. The views expressed are those of the authors and do not necessarily reflect the views of any grantor.

Pamela Bennett: To stay within our contractual word limit, I shall offer my acknowledgments via Senryu:

To my friends and family,
You've put up with much.
This is finally done. Wee!

Seriously, though, anyone who writes for a living knows well the highs and lows of it. During the time I spent working on this book, I was fortunate to have many wonderful, interesting, and patient people touch my life—supportive mentors and colleagues (Yu Xie, Katharine Donato, Andrew Beveridge, Katrina McDonald, Beverly Silver, Doris Entwistle, and Mel Kohn), old and new friends, and my dear, insanely funny family. In each of those categories are people I wish I were more in touch with. If you think for a moment that I'm referring to you, I am! My deepest appreciation and love are for my aunts, Myrtis Alexander and Joan Bennett, whose sacrifices and care during my childhood and early adulthood made my education and social mobility possible.

Amy Lutz: I thank my family for their love and support. My mother, Sandy Lutz, has been particularly supportive of this work, transcribing interviews and reading chapters. My husband, Andrew Ford, and my daughters, Lucy Ford and Sonja Ford, have been a constant source of joy and meaning in my life. I also thank my colleagues and former colleagues at Syracuse University, particularly Marjorie DeVault, Chris Himes, and Yingyi Ma, as well as Peggy Austin and Candi Patterson in the Center for Policy Research. Further thanks go to my long-time mentor, Richard Alba, whose work has encouraged me to think about the American mainstream.

Lakshmi Jayaram: My profound thanks go to my parents, Uma and K. Ramakrishna, who instilled a love of learning in me and modeled the power of education to uplift. I am forever grateful to my husband, Jayanth Jayaram, for his enduring belief in me and steadfast devotion to our family. Our children—Jennani, Naveen, and Saathvik—inspire me each day, and renew my energy to apply my research to the improvement of social contexts for children everywhere.

Introduction

The American dream that has lured tens of millions of all nations to our shores in the past century has not been a dream of merely material plenty, though that has doubtless counted heavily. It has been much more than that. It has been a dream of being able to grow to fullest development as a man and woman, unhampered by the barriers which had slowly been erected in older civilizations, unrepressed by social orders which had developed for the benefit of classes rather than for the simple human being of any and every class.

—James Truslow Adams, who is widely believed to have coined the term *American dream* (1931, 405)

Because of our tolerance for inequality, even the quintessential American dream has been shown to be a myth.

—Joseph Stiglitz, Nobel Prize–winning economist (2015, 106)

There is no shortage of debate about "the American dream"—what it entails, who has access to it, whether it is real or merely a device for protecting an economic system that serves a privileged few. Among the specific forms the dream can take, that which encompasses upward social mobility is what most people think of when they encounter the term (Cullen 2003). Educational attainment is critical to achieving the American dream because of its relationship to social class position. The correlation between educational credentials and earnings is strong and has grown stronger over time. Among young adults in 2007, for example, those holding bachelor's degrees earned 55% more than their counterparts who had only high school diplomas (Planty et al. 2009). By 2017, the earnings premium for holding a bachelor's degree had risen to 62% (McFarland et al. 2019).

Debates about the American dream are increasingly about who earns college degrees. The strong relationship between educational credentials and later adult outcomes is matched by a strong gradient along socioeconomic family background with respect to college degree attainment. Among a nationally representative cohort of students who were in 9th grade in 2002, only 14% of low-SES students completed a bachelor's degree by 2012. In contrast, 29% of their middle-SES peers completed a bachelor's degree, as did 60% of students from high-SES families (Kena et al. 2015). Few should be surprised to learn, then, that one third of children from the lowest income category remain in that category as adults, a figure that exceeds the corresponding value for the United Kingdom (30.6%), France (29.2%), Italy (27.3%), and Sweden (26.7%).[1] Rather than experience social mobility, those described by this statistic experience social reproduction: the inheritance of social class position generation to generation.

Understanding the reasons for social reproduction at the bottom of the social class hierarchy has been a longstanding objective of social scientists. Scholars, policymakers, and the media persistently have sought answers in the ways parenting practices of disadvantaged families differ from those of more advantaged ones. The dominant perspective on social reproduction in the United States, through the specific mechanism of parenting, argues that families of different social classes raise their children according to distinct cultural logics (e.g., Lareau [2003] 2011; Friedman 2013; Hamilton 2016; Calarco 2018). However, there is evidence to suggest that class differences in parenting practices may stem from class differences in resources (Chin and Phillips 2004; Bennett, Lutz, and Jayaram 2012). Thus, a fundamental question about social reproduction is unresolved: What are the underlying sources of class differences in parenting practices?

We engage with this debate motivated by our interest in inequality and social mobility. That interest leads us to make three decisions that define the scope of our investigation. One, rather than study parenting *writ large*, we focus on parenting practices that impact children's educational opportunities, performance, and achievement—that is, educationally relevant parenting practices, which make them also mobility-relevant parenting practices. Two, we reframe the question to one centered on known sources of social class inequality, which implicates parents' social contexts. Macroeconomic inequality plays out in America in ways that embed middle-class and working-class families in different neighborhoods, schools, and social networks. Within those contexts are resources and conditions that facilitate and constrain the enactment of educationally relevant parenting practices. Therefore, we ask: *How do resources and social contexts mediate the relationship between social class and educationally relevant parenting practices?* Three, much of the research on social class and parenting focuses on parents of preschool- and elementary-school-aged children (e.g., Lareau [2003] 2011; Kusserow 2004; Calarco 2018; c.f., see Hamilton 2016). In contrast, we study parents of adolescents during their transition from middle to high school, which we view as a key juncture in their journey toward upward or downward social mobility.

SOCIAL CONTEXTS MATTER

The contention that social contexts matter is a hallmark of sociology. Indeed, "the idea that individuals are affected by and respond to their social surroundings is fundamental to sociology as a discipline" (Marshall [1994] 1998, 435). This sociological insight has influenced how we understand the lives of young people. It is now well understood that adolescent development is shaped by the social contexts in which young people live. But that was not always the case. During the early 1990s, Richard Jessor took stock of the approaches that psychologists used to study adolescent development. In his influential paper, Jessor (1993) described a turn toward contending with the "socially organized environment of human action," borrowing concepts and insights from sociology and other disciplines (117). The new way of thinking about adolescent development conceptualized young people as simultaneously occupying three overlapping social contexts—their families, which was long part of the discipline's focus, but also their schools and neighborhoods, all of which were encased in a larger structural environment shaped by economic, political, and cultural factors. This new conceptualization produced a wealth of knowledge, regarding both how social contexts facilitate and frustrate the achievement of positive outcomes among young people and their transitions into adulthood, but also insights into group disparities in those achievements and transitions.[2]

Adolescents are not the focus of our research, however. Their parents are. Yet, social contexts are as relevant to how and why adults engage in social action as they are to adolescent development. Therefore, we situate parents in social contexts that inform parenting practices. Figure I.1 illustrates that, like adolescents, parents simultaneously contend with three social contexts—the neighborhoods in which they live, the schools their children attend, and the social networks in which they are embedded, encompassing not only family members (as in the case of Jessor's model for adolescents), but friends, acquaintances, coworkers, and other social relations.

Centering our disciplinary knowledge about the importance of social contexts can yield insights into why parents employ the parenting practices they do. Systematic attention to parents' social contexts also can make visible the underlying sources of class differences in parenting practices, particularly those that relate to young people's educational achievement and social mobility. The reasons are twofold. First, the United States is characterized by a high level of economic inequality (Stiglitz 2012). Economic inequality translates into working- and middle-class families having, on average, very different financial resources with which to raise their children. Second, financial resources and social contexts are intimately linked in America due to economic residential segregation. The separation of families into different neighborhoods based on their income is not at all a neutral social fact because the presence and quality of services and social institutions, including

Figure I.1. Social Contexts of Parenting

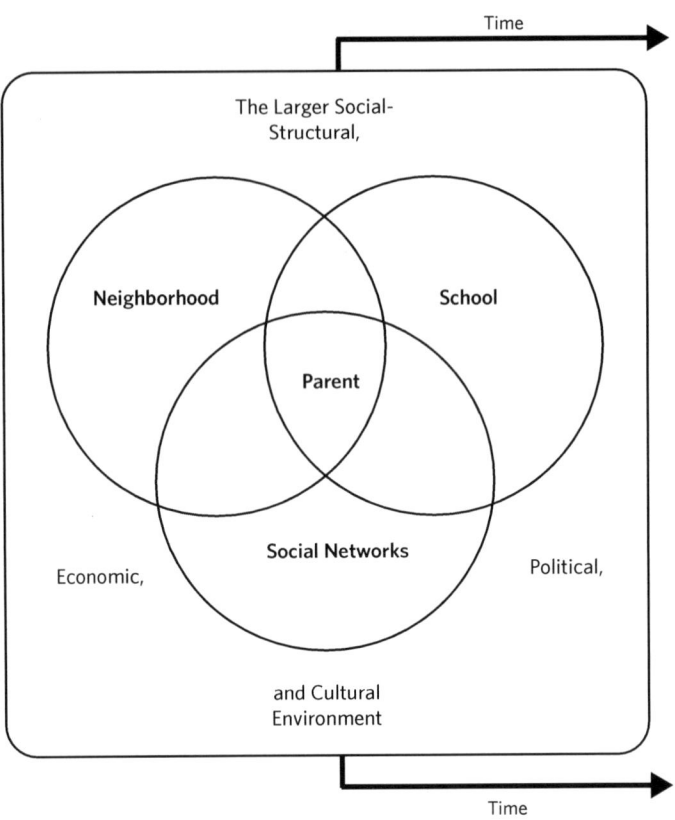

Adolescent's Educational Trajectory

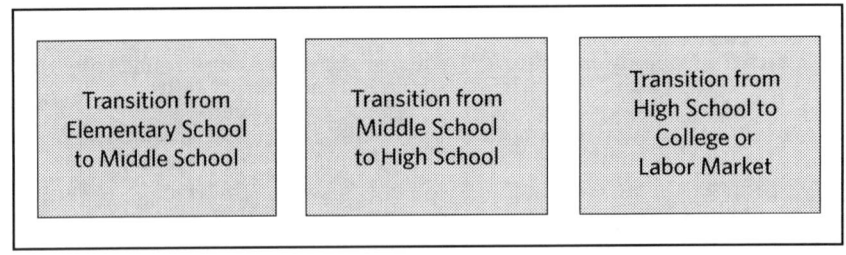

Source: Authors' adaptation of Figure 2 in Jessor (1993).

schools, are unequally distributed across residential space, generating class differences in what economist George C. Galster and historian Sean P. Killen (1995) call "geographies of opportunity." What's more, social networks are economically segregated, even though they are capable of transcending geographic and social boundaries. Collectively, these social patterns in how life is organized in America mean that middle- and working-class families tend to occupy very different kinds of physical and social spaces (Massey 1999; Reardon and Bischoff 2011). Attention to differences in the financial resources and social contexts of working- and middle-class families makes clear how class differences in parenting practices may be powerfully shaped by factors beyond class culture; indeed, they are shaped by what sociologist Barry Wellman (1983) calls "the social distribution of possibilities"—"the unequal availability of resources such as information, wealth, and influences as well as the structures through which people may have access to these resources" (163). If social contexts important to parenting vary by class, then that variation should inform us about why class differences in parenting practices exist, how they might be addressed, and how and why they are related to the perpetuation of advantage and disadvantage across generations.

CULTURE, CONDITIONS, AND CONSTRAINTS: THEMES AND VARIATION IN EXPLANATIONS FOR SOCIAL REPRODUCTION

Explanations for why children grow up to occupy the same social class position as their parents can be grouped into at least three types—those that focus on sociocultural factors, those that emphasize social conditions, and those that center on social constraints. Differences between types of explanations are important because they have implications for where the public should direct effort and resources intended to address the problem of social reproduction in America. Sociocultural explanations tend to view the problem primarily through a cultural lens, locating the causes of social reproduction within family dynamics, which has made for a long and complex history in the social sciences of using cultural perspectives to explain why some groups get ahead while others do not (see O'Connor 2001). Although sociocultural approaches recognize the influence of other factors, they give priority to the role of cultural elements such as values, attitudes, frames, and dispositions. In contrast, sociostructural approaches view social reproduction as a problem rooted in the social conditions in which poor and working-class families live relative to their more advantaged counterparts. Cultural elements can play a role in sociostructural explanations, too, but sociostructural approaches emphasize how cultural elements change as social conditions change (see, for example, Kohn [1969] 1977). Finally, social constraint explanations begin with the premise that substantial cultural overlap exists between disadvantaged and advantaged families, and emphasize the structural barriers that poor and working-class families face in their pursuit of goals and enactment of values that they share with their middle-class counterparts—goals and values that are constitutive of American identity (see, for example, Liebow [1967] on racial differences).

The explanations for class differences in parenting practices provided in *Parenting in Privilege or Peril* are of the third type. We arrive at them having taken an integrated approach to investigating our research question, one that allows the influence of cultural elements, structural forces, and their combination to emerge. Such an approach allowed us to explicitly recognize that social behavior often sits at the intersection of values, perspectives, and interpretations about what *should* occur—or what sociologist Melvin Kohn ([1969] 1977, 7) calls "conceptions of the desirable"—and the *ability* to actualize those conceptions.

To investigate class differences in parents' "conceptions of the desirable," we explored parents' values, orientations, and expectations, as well as their narratives regarding parenting and their children's schooling. To investigate class differences in whether and how parents actualized their conceptions, we situated parents in their neighborhoods, social networks, and their children's schools. We paid attention to how class disparities characterize each context and endeavored to treat those contexts interactively by showing how they relate to one another in facilitating or constraining parenting practices.

Our approach pays off with a set of findings that we hope will inform the debate on social reproduction. First, like other studies, ours shows that working- and middle-class parents are engaged in a common project to raise healthy and well-adjusted children. In contrast to other studies, however, ours shows that working- and middle-class parents share an expectation that their children will continue their educations beyond high school in order to build a satisfying career and earn a stable income. Second, we document substantial class differences in the resources that working- and middle-class parents bring to their common project, as well as differences in the neighborhood, school, and social network contexts in which their parenting takes place. Whereas the resources and social contexts of middle-class parents combine to create an environment of relative security, those of working-class parents form an environment of precarity. Our analyses of how those divergent conditions relate to parenting practices make clear why attempts to achieve their shared parenting goals demand from working-class parents something altogether different than that required of their middle-class counterparts. The relative security of middle-class parents and the precarity of their working-class peers give rise to different parenting strategies that we call *strategic parenting* and *defensive parenting*, respectively.

Middle-class families in our study engaged in strategic parenting—the use of adolescence as a period in which to consciously optimize their children's experiences and to develop in them the qualities and skills needed to go off to college, such as autonomy, organizational skills, management of multiple commitments, and the ability to safely move about metropolitan areas on their own. Strategic parenting is predicated on having options. The financial and social resources of the middle-class parents in this study availed them of myriad options: what high school to send their children to, which activities to enroll them in, even which math teacher would instruct them. Middle-class parents select among their options in an effort to provide their children with the very best resources and experiences to further their development. Although our concept of strategic parenting is broadly consistent with the "concerted cultivation" cultural logic developed by Annette Lareau ([2003] 2011), if we imagined that logic applied to early adolescence rather than to elementary-school-aged children, our explanation for middle-class parenting differs fundamentally from the cultural one she offers. We illustrate how strategic parenting is facilitated by the financial resources middle-class families possess, the resources in their social networks, the safety of their neighborhoods, and the quality of their children's schools. Those resources and contexts create for middle-class families a world vastly different from that of working-class families.

In the case of the working-class families in this study, their reality was simply this: Their children lived and learned in places with too little opportunity and too much danger. In response, working-class parents engaged in defensive parenting—a two-pronged strategy that combined the pursuit of social mobility for children with an almost frantic use of harm-mitigating interventions to protect adolescents from threats in their neighborhoods and schools that had the potential to inflict mortal and psychological damage and to derail their prospects for mobility (e.g., physical and sexual assault, teenage childbearing, drug or gang involvement, violence at school, inadequate education, and challenging school policies and personnel).

That working-class parents engaged in a parenting strategy in which protecting children features prominently might suggest that safety was their primary concern. Such a finding would mirror results of prior studies that found that the provision of care and safety is the foremost objective of poor and working-class parents. But that is not what our data show. We find that working-class parents set their gaze upon and actively pursue social mobility for their children. Indeed, ensuring that their children enter adulthood unscathed is a component of their mobility strategy; for safety is a necessary, but insufficient, condition for social mobility.

Defensive parenting overlaps somewhat with, but is distinct from, parenting strategies that Frank Furstenberg and colleagues call "preventive family management strategies" (Furstenberg et al. 1999; Furstenberg 2001). Although a goal of both defensive and preventive strategies is to shield children from harm, the strategies differ in how parents seek to achieve that goal. At its core, preventive parenting involves keeping children and adolescents away from the outside world as much as possible by keeping them at home or in after-school programs. In contrast, defensive parenting reflects an acceptance among parents that their children will interact with the world around them and therefore be exposed to challenging neighborhood and school conditions. Working-class parents recognize that their children will encounter people who may do them harm. And they recognize that, given the immaturity that accompanies adolescence, their teens may make poor decisions that may bring lasting consequences. In light of their children's exposure to potential harms, working-class parents defend against those harms through vigilant monitoring, preparation, and, when necessary, intervention. They monitor their children's whereabouts, activities, and peer groups, their adolescents' romantic relationships, clothing, emerging sexuality, and the circumstances surrounding their sexual debut. Some even monitor their adolescents' interactions with school personnel and intervene in school decisions that they believe to be wrong, actions thought to be the purview of middle-class parents. Working-class parents also teach their children how to be savvy observers of their surroundings. In short, working-class parents seek to protect their children from physical and social threats by monitoring their behavior and the behavior of others in relation to their children, as well as preparing their children for the variety of encounters they may have with the outside world, all while pursuing their mobility goals.

DEFENSIVE AND STRATEGIC PARENTING: AN ILLUSTRATION

On any given day of the school year, parents scribble initials in their children's academic planners, sign permission slips, send notes or email to teachers, phone them, or meet with them during parent–teacher conferences. Parents and teachers coordinate in ways intended to benefit students. But when conflict arises between parents and school personnel or between parents and school policies, parents must decide what, if anything, to do. The prevailing perspective on social class and parenting suggests that parents are likely to respond based on cultural logics rooted in their social class backgrounds. We, too, anticipate class differences in parents' responses, but not for the reasons many have come to accept.

Polly and Nancy illustrate the primary social class difference in parenting this study uncovers. Polly, a White working-class mother, engaged in *defensive parenting*, the use of harm-mitigating interventions to protect her daughter from a school decision she feared would threaten her daughter's education, well-being, and chances for mobility. In contrast, Nancy, a White middle-class mother, displayed *strategic parenting* by challenging a school decision so that she might obtain for her son one of the most valuable resources in her school district, an *elite public education*. Together, they exemplify the essential finding of this study—that the divergent strategies employed by working- and middle-class parents have less to do with differences in class culture than with the dramatically unequal social contexts in which parents pursue the American dream.

Defensive Parenting: Polly's Story

Polly, a sales clerk at a national pet store chain, disagreed with efforts to socially promote her daughter, Robin, to 9th grade. At the end of 8th grade, Robin had not earned grades and standardized test scores high enough to graduate from middle school. She was asked to participate in a summer program to prepare her for high school in the fall. On the first day of the program, Robin failed diagnostic exams, returned home upset, and shared the news with her mother. Polly then contacted the teacher, who explained that it was unlikely that the program would adequately prepare Robin for 9th grade. Yet, participating in the program would automatically qualify Robin to move on to her zoned high school where she would enter a special class that combined 8th- and 9th-grade studies. Robin could then reintegrate with her peers in 10th grade. Despite the potential for Robin to catch up to her peers, Robin's teacher advised Polly to have Robin repeat 8th grade given her low diagnostic scores.

Not only did Polly agree with Robin's teacher, but she also had a second reason for resisting the school district's plans for Robin: She wanted to avoid sending Robin to their neighborhood high school because of ongoing violence there, which had culminated in the school district classifying the school as "persistently dangerous." However, school district policy required students of Robin's age to attend high school, creating a conflict between the school district and what Polly had come to believe was best for her daughter. Polly recalled that her reaction to the policy was "No! You're not going to do that to my child." She engaged in numerous trips to school and discussions with teachers, administrators, and even the school board until she convinced everyone that it was in Robin's best interest to repeat 8th grade. Robin finished her second year in 8th grade with a higher GPA and admission to a charter high school that Polly was pleased with, thereby avoiding the dangerous zoned high school. Polly recounted:

> Well, she went to summer school. She went *one* day and the teacher said, "Listen, you don't know anything that you're gonna need to know to go into 9th grade." . . . And they still wanted to push her forward. The school district itself wanted to push her forward. [They] had already enrolled her in [high school]. . . . It took a whole lot of phone calls, a lot of bull, you know, [but] they finally sent her back [to 8th grade].

Polly credits the middle school with helping her overcome the school district's policy:

If it wasn't for them keeping on helping me and telling me what to do, how to do it, [Robin] probably would have been stuck in [high school] and heaven knows how she would be doing now. She certainly wouldn't be [attending the charter high school], doing as good as she is if she would've went that route, 'cause she wasn't ready for 9th grade.

Strategic Parenting: Nancy's Story

Nancy, a health-care consultant, also experienced a conflict with her child's school. Nancy's son, Miles, applied to two of the city's most elite magnet programs for high school. He was waitlisted at one and admitted to the other. Nancy's oldest son graduated from the school that waitlisted Miles, and she and her husband preferred this school due to their relationship with its teachers and its small class sizes. Nancy was confused by the school's waitlist decision, given that Miles had strong academic and conduct records; therefore, she sought to find out more about it. She spoke with several teachers, sent emails to other school personnel, and attended school council meetings. She learned that there was another criterion for admission that her son had not satisfied, namely, a sufficient attendance record. During the school year, two of Miles's relatives passed away in different states, causing him to miss several days of school to attend funerals. It felt unfair to Nancy that those absences were held against him. As she stated: "We just felt that a simple inquiry should have identified that these were not routine absences. . . . Several of Miles's teachers have intervened and also felt like it was not a fair decision."

Nancy also learned that there were institutional and administrative complexities at play; the school that waitlisted Miles was experiencing a space shortage and sought to downsize. Additionally, many of the admissions decisions had been made by an outgoing principal, but the interim principal was not empowered to change them. Although the interim principal and Miles's middle school teachers agreed that an error had been made, there was no clear way to correct it. Therefore, Miles attended the other elite magnet school to which he had applied.

Both Polly and Nancy responded to school decisions they disagreed with; one parent engaged in defensive parenting whereas the other employed strategic parenting. Desperate to prevent Robin from taking a path she feared would lead to low educational and occupational achievement, Polly defended her daughter against the school district's social promotion policy in order to preserve her mobility prospects. And because the neighborhood high school to which the policy would have sent Robin was a dangerous place, Polly simultaneously defended her daughter's well-being by seeking to prevent her from attending a school in which she could be harmed. Nancy intervened in the waitlist decision not to safeguard Miles's opportunities for mobility or to ensure that he attended a safe school, as both were already assured. Although her intervention was unsuccessful, it illustrates that Nancy sought to optimize her son's high school experiences by pursuing the *best* option for him among a myriad of very good ones. What is of interest is not which strategy of action is more effective, but rather how and why working-class parents use their agency to struggle against various physical and social threats to their children's prospects for mobility, in contrast to middle-class parents who are secure enough in their resources and social contexts to select among very good options in an effort to obtain not only what they feel is good for their children, but what they deem to be optimal or the best.

In *Parenting in Privilege or Peril*, we reveal the sociostructural sources of class differences in parenting practices. We show how and why working-class parents engage in defensive parenting, while middle-class parents engage in strategic parenting, two approaches that characterize social class differences in the parenting practices of families in this study. We argue, and our data show, that these differences are rooted primarily in inequalities in the financial resources that working- and middle-class families possess and the unequal social contexts those resources make available in which to raise their children —contexts characterized by precarity for the former and relative security for the latter. Our conclusions encourage a shift in thinking about how to address the problem of social reproduction at the bottom of the social class hierarchy in America—from one that seeks to change parents to one that endeavors to improve their resources and social contexts. The book closes with a discussion of policy recommendations for helping working-class parents achieve the American dream that they, like their middle-class counterparts, seek. Below we describe the data that inform our conclusions then present an overview of the book.

DATA

We gathered, assembled, and analyzed a multitude of data. The centerpiece of our data set comprises transcripts from 50 semistructured interviews with a diverse group of parents during which they talked with us about their parenting and their child's schooling. Four other components of the data reflect our focus on parents' social contexts and resources that facilitate or constrain educationally relevant parenting practices. Specifically, (1) census and local police data supplement parents' descriptions of their neighborhoods, (2) school climate data describe the environments of the schools their adolescents attended, (3) social network data provide information on parents' social resources as well as a social context in which they make decisions, and (4) sociodemographic survey data describe parents' human and financial resources. Together, our multipart data set provides information on respondents' parenting practices and perspectives on parenting, the resources they bring to the parenting endeavor, and the social contexts in which their parenting occurs. Below, we outline the procedures used to recruit parents into the study and describe each component of the data set in greater detail. The final section describes how the book unfolds.

Recruitment of Parents and Collection of Sociodemographic Survey Data

From 2004 to 2006, we recruited and collected data from parents whose children attended two middle schools in a large northeastern city, in order to produce a diverse sample. One school comprises predominantly working-class families and the other mainly middle-class families, although both schools are racially and ethnically diverse. The former, which we call Augusta Middle School, is a neighborhood-zoned school situated in a racially and ethnically diverse community.[3] The middle-class school, which we call McKinley Middle School, is a citywide magnet school that competitively selects students based on test scores and academic evaluations.[4]

Although all middle-class parents were recruited from the magnet school, not all working-class parents were recruited from the zoned school. Four working-class respondents came from the magnet school. However, the realities of class segregation in residential space, and thus school catchment areas, made it impossible to recruit middle-class respondents from the neighborhood-zoned school. Nevertheless, our sampling strategy has some benefits. By drawing working- and middle-class families from mostly separate schools, we avoided imposing limits on class differences that might arise from sampling from a single school (see Chin and Phillips 2004). Our recruitment strategy produced a diverse sample, but without the potential drawback of constraints on class variation. Moreover, use of a citywide magnet school gave us access to middle-class families in the city, which allowed us to avoid introducing an urban–suburban divide mapped along class lines.[5]

With the schools selected, we recruited families into the study via a multistep process. First, we introduced the study at parent meetings at each school. Following these in-person introductions, and with the cooperation of each school, we sent letters to all parents of 8th-grade students that described the study and invited their participation. In total, 87 parents indicated their interest and completed a sociodemographic survey. With it, we collected background information about each family, including a roster of household members, financial resources, education and occupation of caregiver(s), as well as self-reported race and ethnicity.

Informed by respondents' answers to the survey, we employed a purposeful sampling strategy to select individuals for in-person interviews. Our goal was to select a diverse sample of parents with respect to race, class, and immigrant generation rather than a sample representative of the schools from which they were recruited. Interview respondents (i.e., those in the analytical sample) vary in social class (working class and middle class), race/ethnicity (White, Black, Latino,[6] Asian, and multiracial), and immigrant background (native born, immigrant, and mixed status). The analytical sample comprises 28 working-class and 22 middle-class parents.

While recognizing the robust debate around the question of how to measure social class, the approach we adopt is in service of analyzing the "ways in which unequal life conditions and individual attributes generate salient effects in the lives of individuals" (Wright 2008, 336). Such an approach is consistent with a measure of class that is reflective of the "relationship of people to income-generating resources" (331). Consequently, a bachelor's degree held by at least one parent or caregiver serves as our measure of middle-class status. This measure is consistent with a focus on skills and expertise (Weber 1947), and is intricately related to other indicators traditionally used to measure social class. Possession of postsecondary educational credentials affects, for example, access to and placement in the occupational structure (Blau and Duncan 1967; Collins 1979). In our sample, at least one parent in all middle-class families had a professional or managerial occupation. Education also affects the wages and salaries one can command in the labor market. In our sample, more than half of working-class families reported earning less than $25,000 per year (or $33,136 in 2020 dollars), whereas a similar proportion of middle-class families reported earning more than $75,000 per year (or $99,408 in 2020 dollars) (Bureau of Labor Statistics 2021).[7]

If we categorize respondents by race/ethnicity, the analytical sample contains 17 White, 16 Black, 11 Latino, two Asian, and four interracial families (see Appendix A). If we categorize sets of parents by immigrant background, we have 40 native-born, four immigrant, and six families with mixed status (where one parent is an immigrant and the other is not) in the sample. Most respondents (78%) were born on the U.S. mainland; 12% were born in Puerto Rico, whereas 10% were born outside of the United States. The subsample of working-class parents is majority (but not totally) Black and Latino, while the subsample of middle-class parents is majority (but not totally) White. Ideally, we would have more White representation among the working class and more Black and Latino representation among the middle class. However, it is the case that Whites are disproportionately represented in the middle class and Blacks and Latinos are disproportionately represented in the working class. Thus, our sample reflects that reality. Nevertheless, our use of a diverse sample engenders confidence that the experiences of working- and middle-class families reported in this study are not limited to those of Blacks, Whites, and those who are native born. Therefore, this study contributes to the sparse but growing body of work on social class, parenting practices, and social mobility that incorporates the experiences of contemporary ethnic groups and immigrant populations (see also Chin and Phillips 2004; Dumais 2006).

Interview Data

We conducted in-depth, semistructured interviews designed to elicit respondents' perspectives on parenting, descriptions of their parenting practices, and discussion of their 8th-grade adolescents' schooling. To facilitate exploration of these topics, we developed a comprehensive interview guide informed by existing theories and empirical findings regarding cultural, social, and financial influences on parenting practices. Accordingly, we included questions about what respondents' typical weekdays and weekends are like, the type and frequency of communication with their child, their experiences with their child's school, and their child's structured activities. We included questions about the financial resources families had and those they expected to have as their children transitioned to high school and beyond. In addition, questions about respondents' parenting philosophies explore the extent to which their beliefs about parenting are transmitted across generations or are independently formed. Taken together, the questions we asked, with relevant probes, form an intensive interview instrument that yielded rich and detailed data about educationally relevant parenting practices, beliefs about those practices, parents' goals and motivations, along with the constraints and barriers parents face in their attempts to achieve their goals or enact the parenting practices they wish to use.

Interviews lasted between 2 and 4 hours. We interviewed the primary caregiver.[8] For those in two-parent families who indicated that they shared childrearing duties equally, the parents themselves determined who was interviewed. We interviewed respondents in their native language, whether English, Spanish, or Chinese (the latter with the help of a translator). All interviews were transcribed for analysis; those in Spanish also were translated to English.

School Climate Data

School climate data describe the learning environments of the schools that respondents' adolescents attended. We did not interview children. Rather, we adopted a school climate survey, which was completed by 8th-grade students in each school.[9] The survey covers topics such as students' sense of safety at school, frequency of certain kinds of events at school (e.g., disruptions during class), and whether students feel teachers and staff care about them.

Neighborhood Data

To analyze class differences in the neighborhood contexts in which parenting occurs, we combined census data and local crime data to create statistical portraits of the neighborhoods in which parents lived. We used census tracts to approximate neighborhoods and used respondents' addresses to identify those tracts. We attached crime rates to census tracts based on data from the city police department. Together, these data allow us to describe the sociodemographic composition of respondents' neighborhoods and depict levels of (reported) criminal activity. Information from parents provide insight into what it is like to live and raise children in their neighborhoods.

Social Network Data

Like schools and neighborhoods, social networks are a social context that shapes parenting behavior through the resources that inhere in parents' ties to others. We gathered information on parents' networks using the tools and procedures of social network analysis. We collected egocentric network data for each parent in our study through name and position generators. Name and position generators are used to define the areas of parents' lives about which we sought information. Whereas name generators produce a list of individuals a respondent knows or interacts with in particular domains of life, position generators describe the social positions within the occupational hierarchy to which respondents have social ties. Prior work suggests that name and position generators yield distinct measures of social networks (van der Gaag, Snijders, and Flap 2008). Therefore, unlike most studies of social networks, we use both types of generators to obtain a fuller view of the social resources to which parents have access in their networks.

OVERVIEW OF THE BOOK

The next chapter begins presentation of the book's empirical foundation. The first two chapters analyze class differences in parents' social contexts; the next three chapters analyze their educationally related parenting practices and the ways they are shaped by social contexts; and the two that follow examine parents' expectations for their children's futures and parenting practices beyond those tied directly to education. The empirical chapters are followed by a conclusion.

In Chapter 1, "Worlds Vastly Different," we describe the neighborhoods in which working-class and middle-class parents lived and the schools their children attended. Working- and middle-class parents mostly resided in different neighborhoods, which reflects rising levels of residential segregation by income among families with children (Owens 2016). The residential contexts of middle- and working-class parents differed in their sociodemographic composition, but they were even more distinct in their levels of violence and criminal activity. Whereas the neighborhoods and schools of working-class parents contained threats to children's well-being and social mobility, middle-class parents lived in neighborhoods and their children attended schools that, for the most part, were safe and pleasant spaces in which to raise children. The contextual precarity of working-class families, in contrast to the contextual security of their middle-class counterparts, comes into immediate view in this first empirical chapter.

In Chapter 2, "Networks to Get Ahead and Networks to Get By," we analyze parents' social networks to understand how class differences in social ties, and the resources they contain, shape the practices that working- and middle-class parents adopt. To do so, we describe (a) the structure of parents' social networks, (b) the network resources middle- and working-class parents possess, (c) the types of network resources they actually used to pursue parenting objectives, and (d) the kinds of objectives for which parents relied upon their networks to help them achieve. We show that middle-class parents used their network resources primarily to help transmit middle-class status to their children by, for example, receiving from their networks contributions to their teen's college fund and critical school-related information, which reflects the ways their social networks were prepared to help them achieve this long-term goal even before their adolescents transitioned to high school. Although working-class parents aspired to send their children to college, their use of networks demonstrated their need to use network resources to not only support their mobility aspirations but to meet the immediate financial and material needs of their families. We argue that use of networks to meet basic needs likely puts downward pressure on working-class parents' ability to direct network resources toward realizing the college aspirations they hold for their children.

Chapter 3, "Navigating Adolescence in Unequal Contexts," describes how parents negotiate adolescence and their children's transition from middle to high school. We find that working- and middle-class parents used divergent approaches to manage this transition, and that those approaches are intimately connected to variation in the social contexts in which families are embedded. Primarily because of their difficult neighborhood and school conditions, working-class parents were preoccupied with keeping their children safe, even as they remained focused on pursuing their mobility goals. In the presence of frequent drug activity and other criminal conduct, working-class parents sought to protect their children from mortal and social threats that could wreak havoc on their physical and psychological well-being and derail their mobility prospects. In contrast, middle-class parents, in the context of safer neighborhoods and schools, sought out the best educational experiences for their children, developed in them a sense of autonomy, and taught them skills for navigating urban environments on their own, confident that their children would be able to pursue their mobility goals by leaving home for college.

Class differences in support for children's involvement in organized activities have become increasingly important and are the subject of Chapter 4, "Opportunities to Participate." Organized activities affect young people's development and commitment to school, academic performance, and college destinations. For this reason, participation in organized activities is recognized as a mechanism through which social inequality is perpetuated, and the sources of class differences in participation are hotly debated. Like other studies of this topic, we situate the class gap in activity participation within families, but in contrast to other studies, especially those that contribute to the prevailing cultural explanation, and in order to better understand how and why opportunities to participate vary by social class, we also situate the class gap in neighborhoods, schools, and the wider community in which the family is embedded. We find that social contexts and financial resources are implicated in both the size and nature of class gaps in participation, and that social institutions contribute to class differences in the *kinds* of activities in which children become involved. Moreover, working-class parents in our study articulated many of the same reasons for supporting their children's participation in organized activities as their middle-class counterparts. Where reasons for participation diverged for the two groups is connected to the precarity or security of their neighborhoods and their differential use of defensive and strategic parenting. Collectively, these findings point more toward a structural (i.e., contextual) explanation than a cultural one for class differences in children's participation in organized activities.

Just as young people's organized activities can have a critical impact on their development and opportunities for social mobility, so does the quality of the high schools they attend. Although school choice policies are prevalent in urban districts, parents and students are not required to participate in the process; instead, they can attend their neighborhood schools. In Chapter 5, "In Search of a Good School," we analyze parents' participation in the high school selection process to understand whether and how social class shapes their approaches to this important educational transition. We find nearly universal participation in the high school placement process among parents in this study; however, the objectives parents pursued varied widely by social class. Whereas middle-class parents pursued and obtained an *elite public education* for their children, and used their social networks to do so, working-class parents applied to a wider array of high school types to avoid their highly undesirable neighborhood school, one that was classified by the school district as "persistently dangerous." The divergent experiences of working- and middle-class parents in this study illustrate the consequences of precarity and security during the transition to high school. Free from safety concerns regarding their neighborhood school, middle-class parents could focus solely on the quality of their children's high schools. In contrast, the precarious social contexts of working-class parents required them to seek a high school that met their adolescents' educational needs as well as one that was safe, illustrating the ways working-class parents' pursuit of social mobility for their children necessitated simultaneous and explicit attention to safety.

Chapter 6, "Unequal Contexts and Parents' Educational and Occupational Expectations," analyzes the expectations parents held for their children's futures. We asked parents to describe how far in school they thought their children would go and the kinds of jobs or careers they thought their adolescents would have. We find that parents have optimistic outlooks for their children's futures, but the educational and occupational content of those outlooks varies by social class, as do parents' articulations of them. Additionally, working-class parents described an incessant worry that shadowed their daily efforts to realize their expectations, one that was well-informed by their neighborhood and school contexts—that a single poor decision made by their adolescents would have life-altering consequences. Although middle-class parents recognized the potential for adolescents to make mistakes, they did not view them as having lasting ramifications. That working-class parents were beset with worry that adolescent missteps would cast a long shadow over their children's lives, while middle-class parents were free from such concerns, demonstrates the precarious hold on mobility that working-class parents felt in contrast to the relative security of their middle-class counterparts.

Perhaps more than any other arena, parenting involves a reflection on one's personal biography weighed against mainstream norms. Parents can adopt the same (or similar) parenting practices that they were raised with, or they can employ different ones. Therefore, in Chapter 7, "The American Shift to Child-Centered Parenting," we examine how parents think about their parenting practices in light of current norms and their own upbringing. We asked respondents to describe whether and how they approached parenting similarly to and differently from their own parents, their co-parent (if present), and other people they knew. We inquired about parents' main sources of childrearing information and what they felt was most important for parenting an 8th-grader. And we asked parents to describe how their parenting changed as their children grew older. We found intergenerational change among both middle- and working-class parents, in that both groups described using more intensive, child-centered parenting practices, although the meaning of this shift varied by social class. We suggest that this shift is reflective of contemporary norms that continually are communicated to parents through the media, child-care professionals, government agencies, schools, and other socializing agents. This common shift to child-centered parenting reflects the influence of the *broader American cultural milieu* that parents in this study experience, as we all do, as part of our membership in American society.

In the Conclusion, we bring together the findings of the preceding chapters to present an integrated picture of what our study suggests about the sources of class differences in mobility-relevant parenting practices—namely, that such differences are intricately and inseparably linked to class differences in financial and social resources that middle- and working-class parents possess, along with the social contexts their respective resources afford them. Findings show that the resources of middle-class parents provide for them social contexts that are vastly different from those that working-class families inhabit, and those contexts necessitate different parenting strategies to facilitate children's social mobility.

Having achieved safety through the ability to purchase homes in safe neighborhoods and send their children to safe, high-quality schools, middle-class parents in this study were free to pursue the reproduction of their class status among the next generation. For them, safety operated in the background, facilitating their approach to parenting like clean air facilitates breathing—unseen and unnoticed until it is in short supply. In contrast, the challenging neighborhood and school environments in which working-class families in this study lived and learned necessitated a defense against myriad negative forces, not merely out of concern for children's well-being, but motivated by a desire to keep them on a path away from life-altering mistakes and experiences and toward a successful transition to high school, postsecondary education, and a job or occupation that brings with it upward social mobility. For working-class parents, the struggle to ensure basic safety was *inseparable* from their mobility goals and their strategies to help their children achieve those goals.

Having analyzed the resources, conditions, and constraints in the neighborhoods and schools of working- and middle-class parents, and having examined the size, structure, and resources contained in parents' social networks, we reach the following conclusion: The ways in which the mobility-relevant parenting practices of working-class families diverge from those of their middle-class counterparts map less along cultural lines and more along the objective realities that families face. Guided by our findings, we close the book with policy recommendations that hold the potential to reduce the impact of economic inequality on the social contexts in which working-class families raise their children and pursue the American dream.

CHAPTER 1

Worlds Vastly Different

The Neighborhood and School Contexts of Middle-Class and Working-Class Families

The primary objective of our research endeavor is to use an expansive analytical lens to investigate the sources of social class differences in educationally relevant parenting practices. We argue that parenting strategies are influenced not only by dynamics within the family, but by the social contexts in which families are embedded. Attention to the social context of parenting is especially important when one seeks to explain social class differences in parenting behavior, given that the United States is characterized by a high (and rising) level of economic inequality (Stiglitz 2012), which translates into middle-class and working-class families occupying very different physical and social spaces (Massey 1999; Reardon and Bischoff 2011). To begin our investigation, we examine the neighborhood and school contexts of working- and middle-class parents. We examine a third context, parents' social networks, in Chapter 2.

THE SCHOOL CONTEXTS IN WHICH MIDDLE-CLASS AND WORKING-CLASS CHILDREN LEARN

As described in the Introduction, we selected individuals to participate in our study with the goal of assembling a diverse group of working-class and middle-class parents to talk with us at length about their parenting practices and their children's schooling. Therefore, we collected data from parents whose children attended two middle schools located in a large northeastern city. At the time of our study, the schools each had between 700 and 1,100 students. One school comprised predominantly working-class and poor families, and the other mainly middle-class families, although both schools were racially and ethnically diverse, as shown in Table 1.1. The former, which we call "Augusta Middle School," is a neighborhood-zoned school. The multiracial, multiethnic neighborhoods that surround the school contain a mixture of residential and commercial properties. Community residents are a combination of people who are

Table 1.1. Characteristics of Schools at the Time of Recruitment

Characteristics	McKinley	Augusta
Percent White	46.8	7.7
Percent Black	30.3	32.9
Percent Latino	7.6	46.7
Percent Asian	14.6	12.6
Percent Other	0.7	0.1
Percent Who Qualified for Free or Reduced Lunch	39.9	80.6

working, unemployed, and out of the labor market. The school itself has an informal feel to it due in part to its functional architecture. Augusta has a small cafeteria but lacks an auditorium. However, with colorful murals painted on its walls and student-authored poetry on display, the school was made livelier than its architectural design suggested. Teachers and administrators were friendly to us when we visited, although parent meetings held on those days were sparsely attended.

The middle-class school is a magnet school that competitively selects students from the entire metropolitan area based on test scores and academic evaluations. The school, which we call "McKinley Middle School," had a student population about three-quarters that of Augusta. McKinley is centrally located in a popular area of the city that contains a mix of restaurants, other businesses, and tourism. The school has a rich architectural design and grandeur about it. Tall columns frame its doorway, and a bust of an important historical figure greets all who enter. Because of its central location, there is limited land surrounding the school; therefore, social and recreational space for students is in short supply. Despite the school's large cafeteria, students often eat their lunch outside. On one of the days we visited, music drifted through McKinley's hallways as the school's orchestra practiced in its large, neoclassical-style auditorium. Parent meetings at McKinley were very well attended. On an evening we were there, parents of 8th-graders alone filled the auditorium.

As ours is a study of parenting practices, we did not interview adolescents. However, students at Augusta and McKinley participated in school climate surveys, which we used to gain insight into school environments from students' perspectives. Eighth-grade students at both schools were surveyed about whether and at what frequency certain kinds of events took place at school, about whether they felt teachers and staff cared about students, and about their sense of safety while at school and en route to and from school. Results are displayed in Table 1.2.

Table 1.2. Assessments of School Climates by 8th-Grade Students at McKinley and Augusta

	McKinley Percent	Augusta Percent	Percentage Difference[1]
Eighth-graders who responded with "everyday" or "most days" to the following statements:			
Disposition Toward School			
I like this school.	61	37	66.7
Teacher, Staff, and Student Relations			
Teachers and staff make everyone feel included.	50	56	-10.6
Teachers and staff care about students at this school.	57	65	-12.3
Fearfulness and Student Disruption			
I am afraid when I am at this school.	9	12	-25.0
Students who misbehave take a lot of our class time.	42	73	-42.5
Eighth-graders who responded with "very safe" or "mostly safe" to the question, "At your school, how safe do you feel . . . "			
In classes	87	82	6.5
In hallways	85	73	17.1
In bathrooms	83	58	44.3
In the cafeteria	86	73	18.5
In the gymnasium	82	76	7.3
Outside the school	73	51	43.1
On your way to and from school	74	59	26.3

1. Values indicate how different the values for McKinley 8th-graders are from the values for Augusta 8th-graders.

The majority of 8th-graders at McKinley reported that teachers and staff cared about students and made everyone feel included. An even larger share of 8th-graders—two thirds of them—indicated that they liked McKinley. Similarly, the vast majority of 8th-graders at Augusta indicated that their teachers and staff cared about them and made everyone feel included. However, a much smaller percentage of students at Augusta than at McKinley liked their school (37% compared with 61%). Part of the reason for the difference may be that proportionally more students at Augusta than at McKinley reported that students who misbehaved routinely commanded a lot of class time (73% compared with 42%). Moreover, a larger percentage of 8th-graders at Augusta than at McKinley reported being afraid regularly while at school, although this was true for only a small percentage of students at either school (12% compared with 9%).

Consistent with the small percentage of students who felt unsafe at school, the majority of 8th-grade students in both schools reported feeling "mostly safe" or "very safe" inside their schools—in classes, cafeterias, hallways, bathrooms, and auditoriums—as well as beyond school doors—outside of school and on their way to and from school. There is a persistent difference, however, across schools. For every setting, a smaller percentage of students at Augusta than at McKinley reported feeling safe, especially in bathrooms and outside of school, spaces where students are less frequently under the direct supervision of faculty and staff.

Given that most McKinley students traveled outside their neighborhood to attend the magnet school, it is noteworthy that proportionally more of them than 8th-graders at Augusta felt safe en route to and from school. Perhaps the need to travel across town contributed to McKinley students' sense of safety because their parents dropped them off in the morning and picked them up in the afternoon, thus providing a comfortable and familiar commuting experience. However, this is not the full story, as some McKinley students used public transportation to go to school and, as sociologist Carla Shedd (2015) notes, travel outside of one's neighborhood to get to school can be "a theater of both sociability and violence" (16). For example, Erica, a middle-class African American preschool teacher, shared that she moved to her neighborhood in part because the location allows her daughter to take the bus to school[1]:

> I like where we live because . . . the [city] bus stops on the corner and she's in school in 15 minutes; that's one of the reasons why we moved here.

Erica is but one of several parents in our study who were comfortable with their adolescents taking the city bus to school. Parents' support for and, indeed, enthusiasm about their teens' ability to do so suggests that their experience with adolescents' traversing the city to attend a school outside of their neighborhood was not, for them, the problematic experience documented in other places (see Shedd 2015). Given that we did not interview adolescents, we cannot be certain why proportionally more students at McKinley than at Augusta felt safe during their daily commutes between home and school. However, we suspect that McKinley's location in the city's bustling cultural and business district contributed to its students' sense of safety, as the district is more affluent and experiences less crime than did the neighborhood in which Augusta is located.

THE RESIDENTIAL CONTEXTS OF MIDDLE-CLASS
AND WORKING-CLASS PARENTS

Parents in our study lived in 30 different neighborhoods in the city, with middle-class parents accounting for 20 neighborhoods and working-class parents accounting for 10 neighborhoods.[2] As these numbers indicate, working-class parents were more geographically concentrated than were their middle-class counterparts. What's more, all except one working-class parent resided in the center of the city, in contrast to middle-class parents, who lived in neighborhoods toward the city's periphery in nearly every direction. This residential pattern is, undoubtedly, a reflection of the geographic reach of the two schools from which we recruited parents, given that Augusta is a neighborhood school while McKinley draws students from across the city.

To create statistical portraits of the neighborhoods in which parents lived, we draw on data from two sources. Population and housing data come from the Census Bureau, whereas crime data come from the police department of the city in which our study takes place. Because we interviewed parents between 2004 and 2006, we use data from the 2000 Census, which provides population and housing data for small geographic areas that can be used to approximate neighborhoods. Data for most crimes are available from the city on a yearly basis. For that reason, and because crime data are commonly reported with 3-year averages to smooth year-to-year fluctuations, we average crime rates for the 3 years we were in the field. Rates of homicide and rape are exceptions, as reports of those crimes are available only for 2006.

To attach census and crime data to parents' neighborhoods, we matched their addresses to census tracts. Census tracts are "small, relatively permanent geographic entities within counties . . . that have between 2,500 and 8,000 residents and boundaries that follow visible features" (U.S. Census Bureau 1994, 10-1). They contain, on average, 4,000 persons. Block groups, as subunits of census tracts, are smaller geographic areas, and one reasonably could ask whether they are better approximates of neighborhoods than are census tracts. It is a question of some debate and ongoing discussion.[3] That the boundaries of census tracts and block groups rarely mirror the contours of neighborhood boundaries as residents conceive of them makes both geographic units less than ideal substitutes for neighborhoods (see, for example, Rich 2009). Nevertheless, we use census tracts for three reasons. One, they are widely regarded as reasonable approximates of neighborhoods and often are used in neighborhood research (White 1987; Logan 2014). Two, smaller geographic areas tend to be more homogeneous than larger ones. Therefore, census tracts will provide a more conservative depiction of class differences in neighborhood contexts than will block groups, making for a more conservative approach to our analysis. Three, we use census geography to provide statistical portraits of neighborhoods, but we pair them with "on-the-ground" depictions of what life is like in neighborhoods by utilizing narrative data from middle-class and working-class parents, thereby limiting the implications of our decision to use one census geographic unit over another.

Sociodemographic Portraits of Neighborhoods

Census and crime data show that the neighborhoods of middle-class and working-class parents differed dramatically in their sociodemographic composition and criminal activity. The neighborhoods of middle-class parents were less racially and ethnically diverse and more socioeconomically advantaged than those in which working-class parents lived. Middle-class parents also lived in places that exposed them to far less crime compared with where working-class parents and their children called home, as shown in Table 1.3.

With respect to race and ethnicity, the neighborhoods of middle-class parents were overwhelmingly Black–White racial contexts. In those neighborhoods, on average, fewer than 10% of residents identified with a racial or ethnic group other than Black or White. In contrast, the neighborhoods of working-class parents were places where White, Black, and Latino residents each constituted, on average, at least a quarter of the population. Surprisingly, the representations of Blacks and Asian Americans in middle- and working-class neighborhoods were roughly the same, which means that differences in racial and ethnic composition between the two groups of neighborhoods rested on their share of residents who were White and Latino. Whereas Latino residents constituted a mere 3.0% of residents in middle-class neighborhoods, they accounted for a quarter of the population of working-class neighborhoods. Thus, the residential context in which working-class parents in our study were raising their children was more reflective of the increasingly multiracial, multiethnic character of America than was the residential environment of middle-class parents (Donato et al. 2008; Massey and Capoferro 2008).

Interestingly, when asked to describe their neighborhoods, 40% of middle-class parents spoke specifically about racial and ethnic composition, and most described their neighborhoods as very diverse places. Erica, the African American preschool teacher previously mentioned, gave a description of her neighborhood that was fairly typical of middle-class parents in the study, pointing to a mixture of people with different racial identities and religious backgrounds:

> We live in an extremely multicultural neighborhood. There's Blacks, there's Whites, there's Asians, Muslims; there's everything. . . . So, culturally there's a lot going on.

Table 1.3. Selected Neighborhood Sociodemographic Characteristics and Rates of Crime by Social Class

Characteristic	Neighborhoods of Middle-Class Parents (N = 20)	Neighborhoods of Working-Class Parents (N = 10)	Middle Class Relative to Working Class (% Difference)[1]
Size			
Total Population	4,256	5,059	-15.9
Number of Households	1,853	1,673	10.7
Number of Housing Units	2,048	1,860	10.1
Sociodemographic Composition			
Demographics			
Percent Non-Hispanic White	56.9	32.0	77.5
Percent Non-Hispanic Black	33.4	35.2	-5.1
Percent Hispanic/Latino	3.0	25.0	-88.0
Percent Non-Hispanic Asian	5.8	6.3	-7.6
Percent Foreign Born	9.8	11.5	-14.8
Percent Linguistically Isolated	3.7	7.4	-49.8
Percent Aged 17 and Younger	17.3	32.5	-46.7
Percent Aged 24 and Younger	30.6	42.6	-28.2
Percent Female-Headed Families With Children	16.8	30.7	-45.4
Socioeconomic Status			
Percent Aged 25 Years+ with High School Diploma	25.6	33.3	-23.3
Percent Aged 25 Years+ with College Degree	18.0	5.7	217.1
Percent in Labor Market	60.1	53.9	11.5
Percent of Civilian Labor Force Employed	89.7	91.4	-1.9
Percent of Housing Units Occupied by Owners	52.8	63.5	-16.9
Median Value of Owner-Occupied Housing Units	$100,565	$47,320	112.5
Median Household Income	$36,975	$27,151	36.2
Per Capita Income in 1999	$22,154	$12,385	78.9
Percent Below Poverty Level	14.6	27.2	-46.6
Percent Struggling or Doing Poorly[2]	33.0	52.8	-37.5
Rates of Criminal Activity (Per 1,000 Persons)			
Violent Crimes			
Homicide	0.1	0.3	-54.3

(continued)

Table 1.3. Selected Neighborhood Sociodemographic Characteristics and Rates of Crime by Social Class *(continued)*

Characteristic	Neighborhoods of Middle-Class Parents (N = 20)	Neighborhoods of Working-Class Parents (N = 10)	Middle Class Relative to Working Class (% Difference)[1]
Rape	0.5	2.0	-75.1
Aggravated Assault	4.0	14.0	-71.4
Robbery	5.5	12.5	-55.8
Other Crimes			
Burglary	6.3	11.8	-47.2
Theft	27.2	42.8	-36.4
Vandalism and Criminal Mischief	13.0	30.1	-56.7
All Narcotics Arrests	4.9	16.8	-71.1
Sales of Narcotics	2.4	6.4	-62.8
Disorderly Conduct	2.4	11.4	-78.9
Harassment	3.0	4.1	-27.5
Loitering and Prowling	0.1	0.2	-43.2
Prostitution	0.4	0.7	-47.6
Abduction and Kidnapping	0.0	0.4	-97.4

1. Calculated as [(middle-class value/working-class value) x 100] – 100; 2. Families with income below the poverty line are characterized as "doing poorly" financially, while families that earn up to twice the poverty line are characterized as "struggling financially" (Social Explorer 2002 Table 185).

Sources: Sociodemographic data come from the 2000 U.S. Census. Crime data come from the local police department. Crime rates are authors' calculations of 3-year averages that cover years 2004 to 2006, except for homicide and rape, which are reported for 2006 only.

Similarly, Theresa, a White mother who works in management, stated that her neighborhood is "diverse in every sense of the word: economically, racially, [and with a] fair amount of gays and lesbians. . . ." And Gwen, a White psychologist, described her neighborhood as "a very diverse neighborhood." Continuing, she explained that "It's racially mixed. It's got lots of different kinds of people; a lot of biracial couples and gay people and lesbian people and it's just a little enclave of diversity."

Only two middle-class parents depicted their neighborhoods as majority White. Wendy, a White college professor, said her neighborhood "used to be all Italian [and is] still probably about 50% Italian." Olivia, a White school-teacher, described everybody in the neighborhood as "Italian, Catholic, or Irish," but indicated that the neighborhood was "finally getting some more mixture of people."

Apart from its racial and ethnic composition, a few middle-class parents described where they lived in terms of its political and economic climate. Mallory, a White ESL teacher who had lived in her neighborhood for 22 years, told us about the many changes that had occurred. Over the 2 decades she lived there, she watched it transform from a "blue-collar neighborhood" to one that was "very yuppie." Jacky, a White mother who works for herself, described her neighborhood as "super, super, super liberal"; as the place "you could move to if you were [a] mixed-race couple [or if] you were gay." She estimated that a third of her neighbors were gay, and described the collective response of neighborhood residents to finding graffiti that expressed a gay slur in a public place: "Everybody put rainbow flags up outside their house[s]." No middle-class parent offered a description of their neighborhood as one that was politically or socially conservative.

Working-class parents also described their neighborhoods as racially and ethnically diverse, although proportionally fewer of them (28.6%) commented on it. Sarah, an African American mother who works as a housekeeper, has lived in her neighborhood for 7 years and described it as "a multicultural neighborhood [with] all kinds of people in [it]." Polly, a White sales clerk, appreciated the "nice variety" in the neighborhood she had lived in for the past 18 months. While describing the kids that she encounters in the neighborhood, she noted, "You'll see Spanish. You'll see Black. You'll see White. And you'll see them getting along." Another working-class parent described her neighborhood as home to Haitians, Palestinians, Africans, and Puerto Ricans in addition to the other groups mentioned above. Although most parents who commented on the racial and ethnic diversity in their neighborhoods viewed it positively, one working-class parent saw things differently. Rather than viewing her diverse neighborhood as a place where myriad groups share the same space, Tamara, an African American working-class mother who had recently lost her part-time job at an international shipping company, observed patterns of association that concerned her: "It's a lot of separation, too. . . . When I say separation, it's like Spanish on one side, African American, Arab . . . Cambodian. There's a lot of separation. I don't like it."

Socioeconomically, the neighborhoods in which the middle-class parents in this study lived contained proportionally more college-educated residents, higher income, and greater wealth than the places working-class parents called home. Compared with working-class neighborhoods, middle-class neighborhoods had more than twice the share of residents with college degrees, which largely accounts for the fact that the median household income and rate of poverty in middle-class neighborhoods were, on average, 36.2% higher and 46.6% lower, respectively, than income and poverty levels in working-class neighborhoods. One way of capturing qualitatively how well people are doing financially is to relate their income to the official poverty line. Families whose income is below the poverty line are characterized as "doing poorly" financially, while families that earn up to twice the poverty line are characterized as "struggling financially" (Social Explorer 2002, Table 185). Using this framework, census data show that more than half of residents in working-class neighborhoods were struggling, whereas only a third of residents in middle-class neighborhoods were similarly situated.

Unexpectedly, we find that lower income and more poverty in working-class neighborhoods did not prevent residents from becoming homeowners to the same degree as residents in middle-class neighborhoods. Indeed, the neighborhoods in which working-class parents in this study lived, had, on average, rates of homeownership that exceeded those in middle-class neighborhoods by 10.7 percentage points (63.5% compared with 52.8%). Although homeownership is the primary means by which Americans accumulate wealth (Oliver and Shapiro 1995; Conley 1999), higher rates of homeownership do not necessarily translate into greater wealth in the context of class and racial segregation across neighborhoods. This is certainly the case for our respondents: The median value of homes in the neighborhoods of working-class parents in our sample was just over $47,000, while the median home value in the neighborhoods of middle-class parents was more than twice that at $100,565 (U.S. Census Bureau 2002).

Lastly, the neighborhoods of working- and middle-class parents differed in family and age structure. Proportionately, middle-class neighborhoods had about half as many female-headed families with children as working-class neighborhoods (16.8% compared with 30.7%), which likely contributed to differences in their neighborhood age structures. For example, the share of residents who were aged 24 years old and younger in the neighborhoods of working-class parents exceeded that in middle-class neighborhoods by 28.2%. The disparity is larger for the share of residents who were children and adolescents—a third of residents in working-class neighborhoods were 17 years old and younger, whereas fewer than a fifth of residents in middle-class neighborhoods were so young. Collectively, these figures suggest that working-class parents in our study were raising families in places where there were proportionally more young people who required adult supervision but fewer families with two parents to provide it.

There is reason to be concerned about children during their adolescent years. Research has long established a relationship between age and crime (at both the individual and aggregate levels). Indeed, criminologists Jeffery T. Ulmer and Darrell Steffensmeier (2014) write that "it is now a truism that age is one of the strongest factors associated with criminal behavior" (378), although the strength of the relationship varies by type of crime (Steffensmeier et al. 1989). The overall relationship between age and crime is curvilinear such that the likelihood of engaging in criminal activity increases into late adolescence and young adulthood, but declines over the remainder of the life course. Steffensmeier and colleagues (1989) explain that this patterning "reflect[s] the increased sources of criminogenic reinforcement experienced by young people" in contrast to the "powerful institutional pressures for conformity that accompany adulthood" (806–07). The large discrepancy between the share of adults and adolescents in working- compared with middle-class neighborhoods may help explain why working-class parents appear to be more concerned than are their middle-class counterparts that their children will be touched by crime or negatively influenced by neighborhood peers.

Class Differences in Exposure to Crime in Residential Space

Not only did the neighborhoods of middle- and working-class parents differ in their sociodemographic composition and economic resources, but they differed dramatically in rates of criminal activity, according to official police records.[4] Prominent in the accounts of working-class parents in our study are complaints about misbehavior among adolescents. One of the disadvantages of living in poor neighborhoods is exposure to a higher prevalence of crime and adolescent delinquency than one typically encounters in better-off neighborhoods; there is a positive correlation between the geographic concentration of disadvantage and crime (Park, Burgess, and McKenzie [1925] 1967; Shaw and McKay 1929; Loeber and Wikström 1993; Massey 1994; Peterson and Krivo 2010; Sampson 2012; Krivo et al. 2020). However, challenging neighborhood conditions are not the only causes of crime (Sampson, Morenoff, and Gannon-Rowley 2002). Sociologist Edwin Sutherland ([1924] 1955), a critic of theories of crime that focus only on low-income populations and neighborhoods, argued that criminal behavior is learned behavior, whether committed by youth in disadvantaged neighborhoods or executives in multinational corporations, meaning that patterns of association make a difference. He noted that "whether a person becomes a criminal or not is determined largely by the comparative frequency and intimacy of his contacts with [criminal or anti-criminal] behavior" (Sutherland 1940, 11). That is, individuals who have more frequent exposure to criminal behavior, motivations, and rationalizations relative to exposure to anti-criminal behavior, motivations, and rationalizations are likely to commit crime.

Given greater exposure to crime in their neighborhoods, working-class parents worried that their own children would be affected by crime or mentored into criminal activity by older adolescents. Indeed, Harding (2009, 2010) notes that young adolescents who live in poor neighborhoods are more likely than others to have older adolescents in their peer group. Younger teens also may be especially influenced by older youth, given that neighborhood violence makes for tightly knit peer groups that function in part to defend adolescents against threats and help them to feel safe (Harding 2010). Moreover, research indicates that unsupervised teens are more likely than others to engage in delinquent behavior (Galambos and Maggs 1991), consistent with the narratives of parents in this study.

For example, even though Paige, a White working-class mother who provided in-home child care, is generally pleased with where she lives, she raised concerns about neighborhood kids whom she described as "so nasty" that her son "won't go outside and play." Continuing, she noted:

> It's a good neighborhood. It's not a bad neighborhood. It's just the kids that are in it. I guess they have so much time on their hands that instead of going to swimming or going down to the rec [center] and playing basketball they just steal cars and get into mischief.

Similarly, Juliette, a Haitian immigrant who worked as a housekeeper, described her neighborhood as "not that bad." She appreciated that residents greet one another and that they hold block parties, which Juliette contributed to but did not attend. Nevertheless, she found the behavior of the kids in her neighborhood to be problematic and, partly for that reason, did not allow her daughters to associate with them:

> [The] kids, they fight and you never know what happens because in America, I have to tell you that so many kids, they 15, 16, 17 years old, they carry the gun and you don't know where they get the gun from. So, they [are] selling the drug. You don't know where they get the drug from, but they [are] 15, 16 years old, you know. They get kids. They [are] selling the drugs. They do so many thing[s] wrong.

Although middle-class respondents generally described their neighborhoods as safe places, several of them described troublesome adolescents in their neighborhoods. Sutherland's differential association theory of crime is as useful for understanding criminal behavior among the privileged as it is for making sense of such behavior among the disadvantaged. He notes that "the essentials of the process are the same for the two classes of criminals" (Sutherland 1940, 11).

Grace, an African American middle-class mother who worked as a paralegal, told us about kids in her neighborhood who purposely damaged young trees that had been newly planted by the city and who, she believed, keyed her car. She bluntly communicated her feelings when she referred to them as "kids on the block that I just wanna choke." Kira, a White middle-class, part-time entrepreneur, lived in her neighborhood for about 12 years and described it as "a lovely area." Yet, she and her neighbors were "unwound a little bit" after discovering that a popular neighborhood kid had sold drugs. She believed he was influenced by older peers "from the neighborhood that hang out." As she described it, "He got hooked up with some 20- and 21-year-old drug dealers. . . . It's really scary." Kira further pointed to other young people in the neighborhood whom she identified as a source of demand for drugs, a source not typically described in neighborhood research:

> You can go a few blocks away from us and there's apartments. Some of the other kids are from very wealthy families with a lot of money, and they have cars at their disposal. They have all the money they could want for drugs.

Although Sophia, a White middle-class mother, felt that her neighborhood was "basically decent," she cautioned that "everything is not as clean and nice as it might appear on the outside. There might be other things going on." She then recounted events that led to the death of an adolescent:

> We had a real bad tragedy in the neighborhood. There was a couple of teenagers that got into a fight, and the one kid was killed. And he was basically the one that was breaking up the fight. And it was fighting over a girl. And he wasn't really involved. He was the mediator trying to get them to come to terms . . . and he was the one that wound up getting stabbed and dying.

Although teenagers appear to be the source of undesirable and criminal activity in the neighborhoods of both working- and middle-class parents, crime is a function of more than age distribution and the absence of monitoring by adults (Sampson and Laub 1992; Sampson, Morenoff, and Gannon-Rowley 2002). Whatever the specific social forces that produced crime in the city in which our respondents lived, they combined to expose working-class parents and their children to more of it in their residential environments compared with their middle-class counterparts. As disturbing and tragic as they are, the incidents recounted by middle-class parents do not alter the fact that working-class parents in our study experienced levels of crime and violence that make those documented in middle-class neighborhoods pale in comparison.

The lower portion of Table 1.3 displays rates of crime per 1,000 persons. The table contains information on violent crimes, which pose serious risks to neighborhood residents, and nonviolent crimes, which undermine residents' quality of life.[5] During our fieldwork, the neighborhoods of middle-class parents experienced, on average, 54% fewer homicides and 56% fewer robberies than the neighborhoods of working-class parents. Differences for other violent crimes are even larger. The neighborhoods of middle-class parents had 75% and 71% fewer incidents of rape and aggravated assault, respectively, compared with those of working-class parents. Given the magnitude of these differences, it is not surprising that for each type of violent crime, average rates for the neighborhoods of working-class parents are higher than citywide rates, whereas rates for the neighborhoods of middle-class parents are lower.[6]

The picture changes little when we focus on nonviolent crimes. Indeed, it is worth calling attention to class differences in exposure to the particular type of nonviolent crime that seemed to worry working-class parents more than most others—the sale and consumption of illegal drugs. During the 3 years we were in the field, there were, on average, 16.8 arrests per 1,000 persons related to narcotics in the neighborhoods of working-class parents. By comparison, the neighborhoods of middle-class parents had 4.9 such arrests, a rate that is 71% lower than that for their working-class counterparts. The class gap in the sale of narcotics is somewhat smaller at 63%.

Whether it is because of the association between drug trafficking and violent crime (Goldstein 2003; cf. Chaiken and Chaiken 1990) or because prohibited selling of controlled substances often is done in public on the street, many working-class parents mentioned drugs as a particular problem in their neighborhoods. And although other crimes occur with some frequency, working-class parents and their children seemed continually exposed to illegal and sometimes dangerous activities associated with drugs. While describing the racial and ethnic diversity of the neighborhood she had lived in for almost 12 years, Patricia, an African American working-class mother who was unemployed at the time of our interview, stopped to note the presence of drug dealers:

> We got a couple families of them [referring to Palestinians] on the corner. But then, across from them, we got drug dealers. If you could only . . . exterminate them roaches, you know? 'Cause that's what they are.

Rita, a Latina working-class mother, worried about the impact that drug-related activities would have on her daughter: "Where we live . . . the neighborhood isn't too good. There are drugs. . . . She's always watching what happens on the street. There's a lot of people that like to use drugs, and that scares me." Gabriela, a Latina working-class immigrant who worked as a housekeeper, described the scene near her home, saying, "Where I live, people sell drugs. . . . In reality, my kids are the only ones that aren't on the street. It scares me. Yes, because it's a place there, around where I live, all drugs. Every corner." Not only was Gabriela fearful of drug activities near her home; she was frustrated by what she perceived as a lack of will by the police to do anything about it:

> Seriously. I lived in Los Angeles for a long time. But I never, never had to deal with a state [like] where I live [now]. It's impossible to believe that the police can't do anything. Kids from school walk by; they get

out of school and there's drugs sold on every corner. It's impossible; not fair.

Proximity to drug-related activity was one reason why Layla, a Latina working-class mother, attempted to make her twin daughters savvy observers of the neighborhood they had lived in for 10 years. That her work as a court advocate took her away from home during the afternoons and evenings created challenges to keeping her girls safe:

> The neighborhood has gone down, more dangerous. Drug selling on the corners. . . . You got to watch more than before, and if we can get out, I will be happy to get out. . . . It's OK because they [other neighborhood residents] know my kids since they [were] born, and everybody knows them. Like I said, you always got to be on top of your kids to let 'em know what's going on. You gotta let 'em know what drugs [are] about. You got to let 'em know what the kids are about, you know? So, you always gotta be talkin'. I'm constantly talking to my girls. It's like, "Don't you know he's on drugs? Look! He's standing on the corner and I don't want you on the corner." This is a constant thing. We just can't stop.

Barbara, an African American working-class mother who was unemployed at the time we spoke with her, was so concerned about the prevalence of drug dealing in her neighborhood that she did not allow her children to play outside:

> They sellin' drugs on my street. I mean, I can't even let my kids go out in the front. It's like we're looking for somewhere else to move. . . . You're not goin' to have peace of mind everywhere you go, I know, but we're not just goin' to sit there and look out my front window and see the [drug] transactions goin' on. It's ridiculous. And I didn't grow up around that and I don't want my kids to have to deal with that. So, usually my kids are in the house. If they're not in the house we're all going out as a family. As a family. They don't go outside and play and associate with a lot of those kids on that street. If she [referring to her daughter] sees them, they're usually at school. When she comes home, she comes in.

Wanda, an African American nursing assistant, described changes that had occurred in her neighborhood with respect to drug sales, and explained why she and her neighbors were so concerned:

> We been there 7 years and it done changed drastically. . . . My street is a known drug block. . . . Last year it was really, really bad. This

year it got better. But last year it was, oh my goodness, the cops was
there every single day. The guys on the corner got locked up just
about every day. And this year, it got better 'cause a lot of us is getting
involved now. Because my neighbor, they have kids. Then last year
they was shooting and all that stuff and, you know, we got kids on this
block.

Not only did Wanda worry about the exposure her children had to drug
dealers, the illegal substances they sold, and the violence they wrought, but
she soon found herself having to confront drug dealers directly when she
learned they were storing weapons on her front porch. She recalled:

I mean, I wake up in the morning and I got to chase people off my
porch at 7:00 in the morning; 5:00 in the morning when I'm on my
way to work. Or people be like, "Well, did you know so-and-so was
on your porch asleep all night?" I can't watch this porch at night
time. Then I heard people was hiding guns underneath the pillow on
the chair, so I got rid of the chair. They put another one there. [As if
speaking to the drug dealers:] "What is ya'll people doing this for?"
I said, "Well, I'm just gonna tell ya'll if you keep doing it, I'm gonna
call the cops, and it's just as simple as that." [In the voice of a drug
dealer:] "Well you ain't got to go that far." [Wanda in reply:] "Oh
yes I do because I'm tired of saying 'stay off my porch.' I don't have
nothing to do with what ya'll do out here, but in any event the cops
come up on ya'll and ya'll on my porch, then I guess they going to feel
like you all live here and will want to run into my house. No. Stay off
my porch, and we can avoid all of this."

Given shootings in the neighborhood, Wanda felt she had to take matters into her own hands to ensure the safety of her children. She continued:

And I went to the drug dealers myself, and I said, "Well, you know,
I don't say too much to none of ya'll out here. Ya'll speak, I speak
back." . . . And I said, "Well how would you feel if your kids was
outside and somebody came shooting down the block with your
kids on the block?" [In the voice of a drug dealer in reply:] "Well,
you know we wouldn't hurt your kids." "Well it's not the point of
you trying to hurt them, but bullets have no name." And who's to
say that one of those bullets won't hit a tree or something, or a car
or something, and bounce off and hit one of my kids? So, I said, you
know, "I'm just telling ya'll, you know 'cause ya'll parents just like
I am, and I care about my kids just as much as ya'll care about your
kids, and I'd appreciate it if ya'll just don't do that on this block. You
know, because people got kids. Not just my kids, but anybody's kids

is on this block, you know, and it's bad." And I said, "Ya'll don't even live on this block. And ya'll just took over our block."

Although drug selling and consumption remained problems in the neighborhood, Wanda was relieved that drug-related violence had declined. She attributed the improvement, in part, to the efforts that she and her next-door neighbor made to help men who were incarcerated during the previous year obtain legitimate jobs.

Wanda was neither the only working-class parent in our study to be personally touched by drug activity in her neighborhood, nor the only one with personal encounters with guns. Tamara, who had recently worked for the international shipping company mentioned previously, encountered a young man with a gun on a routine walk to the neighborhood store:

> My neighborhood used to be a good neighborhood. Well it used to be an alright neighborhood. . . . [Now] you can't walk a certain part of [a nearby] street. . . . You go down there, they don't know you, they beat you up, OK? And they sellin' drugs. You got one bar that you can buy "coke," then you got another bar that you can buy guns, OK? So, I'm walkin' down [another nearby] street . . . [and a] young boy, like he was no more than 12, 14 years old, he waits 'til he get right in front of me, and he sticks a gun down in his pants, and wiggle his butt like this in front of me. And I'm like, "Oh my goodness." I said, "OK." I looked at him; I looked at him dead in his face and I said, "Is it like that?" Right? He went on and shrugged off. I picked up my phone and told them [the police], I said, "Look . . . this young boy just walked in front of me and wiggled his behind and showed me that he had a gun." I said, "So if you come down here . . . right now, you will catch him [by the] time he get up to [the next] street." So I went on in a store and I asked him (the clerk), "You didn't just see that boy leave out of here with a gun?" He said, "Yeah, I saw him. They gets it [from] across the street." I said, "Oh my god." That's the night I found out they buying guns [for] $40, $50 across the street in the bar.

The availability of guns in her neighborhood materialized in a much more frightening incident for Tamara and her daughter, Vanessa. Tamara explained:

> [Vanessa] had come from her game, and she said she had a headache. So, she laid on the chair, and said when she looked up, she seen her sister. . . . When my [other] daughter went back out the house, she didn't lock the door. So, [Vanessa] laid back down on the sleeper, and she said when she looked up again there was this man standing over

her. She said [describing the events to Tamara], "Mommy I jumped up. He grabbed me around my neck and put the gun to my head, and said if I tell anybody he would come back and kill me. [Then he asked:] Where's the money?" She said, "I told him we ain't got no money," so he let her go. He ran up there on the second floor and she ran out the front door.

Tamara described how this incident affected her daughter:

> So that put her back a little bit where she didn't want to go to school. She was [an] "A," "B" student, [but] she ain't wanna go. She ain't wanna go [to] baseball [or] softball no more. She just had shut down on me. She wouldn't talk to me.

Prior to this incident, Tamara's then-fiancé, Derrick, was assaulted in her neighborhood during a routine trip to the store and was in a coma for 4 days. With such experiences, it is no surprise that Tamara felt that her neighborhood had become increasingly dangerous. Indeed, some streets were to be avoided altogether. Violence wrought on innocent bystanders, whether on the street or in their homes, along with the ready availability of guns and drugs, elevated and foregrounded parents' fears about the safety and well-being of their children.

To be sure, not all working-class parents described their neighborhoods as dangerous places. However, even working-class parents who felt safe where they lived found themselves in close proximity to crime. It is worth noting that in describing their neighborhoods as safe, such parents defined their neighborhood in rather restricted terms, referring to their particular street or block. Comments from Harriet, a Black mother who works as a drug counselor, are illustrative:

> Well, where I'm at it's a nice neighborhood. . . . You barely see the cops. In this street that I live on, there's not a lot of violence. There's no drug dealers on the corners. The kids can play freely. . . . Now, around the corner might be somethin' different, but in my street and the couple streets that are around my street, it's been peaceful.

Likewise, Polly, the sales clerk previously mentioned, kept her kids on her own block because she felt it was safer than other streets in the neighborhood:

> I don't live in the best of neighborhoods, so I keep up on that a lot so I don't have to worry about them being on the corner. . . . I wind up with half the corner in the front of my house, which most of the parents love cause then they know the kids are not getting into

trouble. . . . And a lot of my household is full of kids from all [age] ranges, from 20-year-olds on down to . . . a little 5-year-old that goes flying through my house; I think he knows my house more than he knows his own. . . . So needless to say, "Come on over here. . . . Be outside my house. You're safer."

Although Polly felt that her block offered a relatively safe environment, her description of the scene near her home depicts a hazardous place for children:

> You go two blocks down, you have a street that almost everything on it, every house on there, there's drugs going on. A couple of the corner stores, drugs being sold. So, you have to watch.

As Table 1.3 makes clear, the neighborhoods in which middle-class parents lived also were affected by crime. However, criminal activity was not prevalent enough to undermine their sense of safety in and appreciation for their neighborhoods. Erica, the African American middle-class mother who valued so much the cultural diversity of her neighborhood, also appreciated that she and her daughter had easy access to public transportation and the city's downtown:

> I like where we live because . . . it exposes [my daughter] to so much. She loves the city so much and being right here in the middle of everything is pretty cool for her. . . . We're within walking distance [to downtown], so in the summer time, we spend a lot of time down there.

Similarly, Kira, the White middle-class mother and part-time entrepreneur mentioned earlier, appreciated the walkability and kid-friendliness of her neighborhood:

> It's a very nice neighborhood. It has a main little street where you can walk to everywhere. So, the kids can walk out and go to [the bookstore], Starbucks, whatever. They've been able to do that [since they were] pretty young, like 5th or 6th grade. There's a playground near there. It's great. . . . [And] they have access to [public transportation].

Jayna is a computer programmer who immigrated from India. Her daughter, Kami, often played at her friends' houses or with them at her own house. But now that those friends have moved, Kami plays mainly on the neighborhood playground, a place Jayna and her husband permit Kami to go by herself. Jayna described the situation:

When Kami was in this [neighborhood elementary] school, she
had a couple of friends from the behind streets and everything. On
weekends, they might call and she might go to their home. Then, the
kids from there came here. But now those people moved away for
some reason, so Kami doesn't have any friends in this neighborhood.
But she goes out to the playground for bicycling or she goes with my
husband.

The sense of safety that some middle-class parents felt in their neighborhoods withstood personal experiences with crime. For example, Gwen,
the psychologist, described her neighborhood as safe even as she recounted
being a victim of crime:

It's pretty safe. We have had some sort of little break-ins. We've had
our car glass broken on a couple of occasions. Before we got our
security system, one time somebody climbed in one of our windows
and stole our car keys and stole our car. But if we're sensible about
locking everything, it feels pretty safe. I feel safe walking around when
it's dark.

Several middle-class parents associated criminal activity in their neighborhood and a need to be cautious with living in the city. Still, they assessed
their neighborhoods as safe spaces. When asked about her neighborhood,
Wendy said, simply, "I think it's pretty safe, but it's the city. I mean, you
are still in the city, you know?" Petra, a White social worker, went further:

It's pretty safe. It all depends on who you ask. If you ask somebody
from the suburbs, they wouldn't say so. Well, anywhere in the city, I
wouldn't leave a younger child out front by themselves, but it's safe
enough. I feel comfortable enough with [my daughter] walking three
blocks from where she catches the bus on her own. At night? No. But
even sometimes she'll walk if she's with the dog. I'm fine with that. But
it's the city, so you still have to be alert. . . . But I feel it's safe. Am I
afraid that she's gonna get shot in front of our house? No.

Part of the reason Petra does not fear her daughter being shot in
front of her house is because her financial resources, like those of other
middle-class parents, allowed her to purchase a home in a relatively safe
neighborhood. To be sure, the neighborhoods of our middle-class respondents are not without their problems. Their rates of violent crime exceeded
national averages, although that is largely a function of being located in
a major northeastern city. Many of our middle-class respondents told us
that living in the city, rather than the suburbs, was a deliberate decision

and an expression of their values—they valued the city's vibrancy, its diversity, and its public transportation.

SUMMARY

In this chapter, we situated working- and middle-class parents in two of three social contexts that shape parenting practices and that we argue are central for understanding social class differences in educationally relevant parenting practices. It should come as no surprise that working- and middle-class families in our study reside in qualitatively different neighborhoods and their children attend qualitatively different schools, given that America's public schools and neighborhoods are segregated by class, a condition that rarely benefits disadvantaged groups. That our statistical description of their schools and neighborhoods yields entirely expected portraits of contextual disadvantage to working-class parents relative to their middle-class counterparts is a feature rather than a bug of our research endeavor. It is precisely *because* working- and middle-class families live and learn in such different places that their social contexts must be not merely acknowledged but attended to when seeking to understand why working- and middle-class parents utilize divergent approaches to parenting. And this *attending to*—the incorporation of contextual differences into one's analysis—must be informed by the descriptions, interpretations, and perspectives of parents themselves.

Parents' descriptions, interpretations, and perspectives regarding their social contexts—schools and neighborhoods in this chapter, social networks in the next—paired with statistical portraits, make plain why attempts to achieve the shared goal of raising children into healthy, happy, and independent beings demand from working-class parents something altogether different than that required of middle-class parents. As we will see in subsequent chapters, social contexts expand or constrain the range of parenting practices that can be reasonably employed. Having decided to reside in the city, middle-class parents, due to their financial resources, were able to choose neighborhoods where crime is far less prevalent than in the places working-class parents reside. Relatively safe residential environments facilitate certain kinds of parenting practices, such as developing children's independence and sense of freedom, that are part of strategic parenting. Conversely, neighborhoods that are unsafe or feel unsafe encourage, if not require, defensive parenting—the pursuit of social mobility paired with the constant, active management of threats to children's well-being and prospects for the future.

CHAPTER 2

Networks to Get Ahead and Networks to Get By

This chapter continues our analysis of parents' social contexts to under-stand how they facilitate and constrain educationally relevant parenting practices. Studies of the relationship between social networks and par-enting are often concerned with how networks affect parents' abilities to effectively aid the development of their children (Bronfenbrenner 1979; Cochran and Brassard 1979; Cochran et al. 1990). Yet, most such stud-ies do not have at their core an explicit focus on social class dynamics. Therefore, we pair the conceptualization of networks as a social context that influences parenting with social resources theory, given that the latter explicates how and why social networks and the resources they contain vary by social class.

A basic premise of social resources theory is the existence of a positive relationship between social class and the amount and quality of network resources, known as the "strength of position proposition" (Lin and Dumin 1986). What is more, social networks tend to comprise similar individuals, and the resources embedded within them tend to be of the same quality as one's own personal resources (Lin 1982, 2001; McPherson, Smith-Lovin, and Brashears 2001) because of a positive relationship between sentiment and interaction, such that the more sentiment there is between people, the more those people will interact with one another, and vice versa. Nan Lin (2001) argues that "social interactions tend to take place among individuals with similar lifestyles and socioeconomic characteristics" (39), thereby gen-erating a three-way relationship between sentiment, interaction, and social resources. This three-way relationship implies that "individuals whose po-sitions are situated closer to each other in social structures are more likely to interact" (39). As a consequence, it is relatively easy to exchange class-based resources among people in the same class location, but more difficult to exchange resources between people who occupy different class locations (Bourdieu 1986). The ease of within-class exchanges of network resources benefits those who possess valued resources, such as members of the middle class, but it works to the detriment of those who possess fewer resources, such as members of the working class (Lin 2001). Therefore, as a departure from studies that locate the sources of class differences in parenting practices in norms and values, we employ social resources theory and the tools of network analysis to investigate an alternative possibility—that class differences in parenting are shaped by class differences in resources tied to social contexts, in this case, parents' social networks.

The analysis presented in this chapter, like that on neighborhoods and schools, is used to contextualize the parenting practices of working- and middle-class parents in this study rather than to make generalizations about all working- and middle-class parents. The analysis proceeds in two parts. First, we analyze the structure of and resources within the social networks of working- and middle-class parents. The results inform as to whether and to what degree working- and middle-class parents in our study have access to different resources that may be brought to bear on the tasks and challenges involved with parenting and supporting their adolescents' schooling. Second, we analyze parents' utilization of their social networks. From qualitative analysis of narrative data, we identify the goals and objectives for which parents put the social resources in their networks to use. We interpret the utilization of networks as reflective of parents' concerns. Therefore, this part of the investigation indicates whether and how working- and middle-class parents differ in the priorities they bring to parenting and schooling during their adolescents' transition from 8th grade to high school.

MEASURING SOCIAL NETWORKS

From members of our interview sample, we collected information on parents' social networks using the tools and procedures of social network analysis. We collected egocentric network data for each parent. Name generators and position generators are used to define the areas of ego's life about which data are collected. Name generators are questions that produce a list of individuals a respondent knows or interacts with in particular domains of life or circumstances. Information on the characteristics and nature of the relationship with each named individual is collected and used to calculate indices that describe ego's network (Marsden 1987; Scott and Carrington 2011). The position generator describes the social positions within an occupational hierarchy to which respondents have social ties. Lin and Dumin (1986) developed the position generator, arguing that connections to social positions in an occupational hierarchy reveal much about the social resources to which individuals have access. Research suggests that name and position generators yield distinct measures of social networks (van der Gaag, Snijders, and Flap 2008).

Position Networks

We use the position generator to analyze class differences in parents' access to network resources, broadly defined—that is, resources not tied to a specific domain of their lives (van der Gaag, Snijders, and Flap 2008). To collect data on "position networks," we showed parents a list of 16 occupations from the low, middle, and high strata of the U.S. occupational hierarchy, and asked them to tell us whether they knew anyone with an occupation on the list (see Appendix B). Because the purpose of the position generator is to determine whether respondents know anyone in an occupation, respondents could name only a single person per occupation.[1] We collected information on each named person, including whether they knew others the respondent named for other occupations. To use respondents' social ties to occupations as a measure of their access to social resources as Lin and Dumin (1986) propose, each occupation was assigned a Duncan SEI score, which is a measure of the occupation's socioeconomic status.[2] From this information, we calculated summary measures that describe the structure and diversity of parents' position networks.

Discussion Networks

To assess class differences in access to resources within the networks that parents specifically use to discuss parenting and schooling issues, we used the following name generator: "Who are the people with whom you discuss either parenting or issues regarding your child's schooling?" We then collected information on each network alter. Unlike many studies of social networks, we allowed parents to name as many network alters as they wished.[3] As before, we asked respondents whether each alter knew other alters, which allows us to discern how dense or interconnected each parent's "discussion network" is. Denser networks are expected to bring less innovative information to parents because that information is expected to come from socially similar alters, given their connection to one another (Campbell, Marsden, and Hurlbert 1986).

Utilization of Social Networks

We turn from mere access to social resources to their utilization, to understand class differences in how and why parents mobilized their social networks. We analyze parents' descriptions of when they utilized their social networks to achieve some parenting aim or when their networks provided assistance of any kind that helped parents achieve their goals. Each time a parent mentioned someone to whom they turned for assistance, or who provided assistance without a specific request for it, we coded that portion of the narrative to identify the kinds of social resources parents used, as well as the goals for which those resources were employed.

CLASS DIFFERENCES IN SOCIAL NETWORK RESOURCES

Resources in Parents' Position Networks

Table 2.1 displays the share of middle- and working-class parents who have social ties to occupations that constitute our position generator. Occupations are ordered by the size of class gaps that exist in social connections. As expected, middle-class parents in this study have more and better social resources in their position networks than do working-class parents. For example, middle-class parents' connections to a professional occupation exceed those of their working-class counterparts by 12.8%, and by 62.5% if the profession requires an advanced degree. That working-class parents are disadvantaged with respect to ties to occupations that require a bachelor's degree (e.g., teachers), but have greater ties to occupations that require only vocational training (e.g., operatives) or no formal training at all (e.g., laborers), indicates that working-class parents have less access than their middle-class peers to persons who have direct experience with navigating their way to and through college.

Regarding structure and composition, the position networks of middle-class parents are more extensive, less dense, and more resourced, and provide access to positions higher in the occupational hierarchy than do the networks of working-class parents. Middle-class parents' position networks are slightly larger than those of working-class parents in that the former have, on average, access to approximately one more occupational position (11.6 compared with 10.8). Middle-class networks are also less dense. That is, among all the possible connections that could exist among alters identified in various occupations, only 27.8% of them actually exist, on average, in the networks of middle-class parents, whereas 49.9% of potential ties actually exist in the networks of working-class parents.[4] The networks of middle-class parents reach slightly higher into the occupational hierarchy than do those of working-class parents, with SEI scores of 70.2 and 68.1, respectively. Yet, the higher upper reachability of middle-class networks does not come at substantial expense of lower reachability; middle-class networks reach almost as low into the occupational hierarchy as do the networks of working-class parents, with SEI scores of 11.5 and 9.8, respectively.

Although social class disparities are in the direction expected, their magnitude is smaller than anticipated. Working-class parents have access to almost as many occupational positions; their contacts reach almost as high into the occupational hierarchy; and the range of positions accessed is just as wide as those of their middle-class counterparts. Expressed in percentage

Table 2.1. Range and Composition of Parents' Position Networks by Social Class[1]

	Middle Class	Working Class	Middle Class Relative to Working Class (% Difference)[2]
	Mean/Pct.	Mean/Pct.	
Occupations (% Accessed)			
Professional (advanced deg. required)	100.0	61.5	62.5
Small business owner or contractor	86.4	53.8	60.4
Farmer/Farm manager	27.3	19.2	41.8
Schoolteacher	100.0	73.1	36.8
Craftsperson	95.5	73.1	30.6
Technical	68.2	53.8	26.6
Manager/Administrator	90.9	76.9	18.2
Professional	95.5	84.6	12.8
Clerical	90.9	80.8	12.6
Service	86.4	80.8	6.9
Sales	63.6	65.4	-2.7
Full-time homemaker	77.3	84.6	-8.7
Laborer	63.6	73.1	-12.9
Military	45.5	57.7	-21.2
Operative	40.9	69.2	-40.9
Protective service	27.3	73.1	-62.7
Network Range and Composition			
Extensity (# of positions accessed)	11.6	10.8	7.3
Density	27.8	49.9	-44.4
Diversity (race)	24.9	25.6	-2.9
Range occupational status	58.7	58.4	0.6
Total occupational status	510.3	431.8	18.2
Mean occupational status	50.0	45.1	10.9
Highest occupational status	70.2	68.1	3.1
Lowest occupational status	11.5	9.8	17.7

1. N = 49 because one parent has missing values on all quantitative network measures.
2. Calculated as [(middle-class value/working-class value) x 100] − 100.

terms, the position networks of working- and middle-class parents differed, on average, by only 7.3% in size (extensity), 3.1% in highest position accessed, and 0.6% in range or breadth. The only substantial difference is in network density; the networks of middle-class parents are, on average, 44.4% less dense than those of working-class parents. Although class differences in social resources exist and all point to advantages to middle-class parents, those advantages are unexpectedly modest.

Resources in Parents' Discussion Networks

Whereas position networks describe the resources to which parents have access and that could be brought to bear on a range of objectives, parents' discussion networks describe the resources contained in relationships that parents actually rely on to discuss parenting and schooling issues. Figure 2.1 displays sociograms of parents' discussion networks. Sociograms are graphical representations of members in a network and the ties that exist among them. The top panel presents the networks of working-class parents, while the bottom panel shows those of their middle-class counterparts. Within each sociogram, the large circle, often centered, represents the parent-respondent; small circles represent their network alters; and lines between circles denote the existence of a "knowing" relationship between network members. Of course, the parent-respondent knows all the members of their discussion network, but not all members know one another. Note that the length of lines indicates whether an alter is a weak tie (long line) or strong tie (short line). Lines should be interpreted within each sociogram rather than across them, as line lengths vary from sociogram to sociogram due to the shape of the network.

Figure 2.1 makes clear that parents' discussion networks vary in size and shape. Some parents speak with many people about parenting and their child's schooling, with discussion networks so large that circles representing parent-respondents are surrounded in every direction by representations of their network alters, such as sociograms at locations 2E and 6G in the figure. Other parents speak to no one about parenting or their child's schooling. Such parents are represented by large circles without any lines connecting them to others (sociograms at locations 1J and 5G). Some parents have very dense discussion networks, with most if not all network alters knowing one another, which gives the sociogram a look akin to a spider's web (sociogram at 5E, for example). The networks of still other parents have few lines that connect them, even when there are multiple network members (sociograms at 5C and 6D, for example).

Table 2.2 summarizes in numerical form what Figure 2.1 displays graphically. The table describes numerous and substantial advantages to middle-class relative to working-class parents. Middle-class parents have larger discussion networks than their working-class counterparts: 5.2 members compared with 2.6. Although some parents of both social classes reported having no more than a single person with whom they discussed parenting and schooling issues, only three middle-class parents (13.6%) but 10 working-class parents (35.7%) reported such small discussion networks (not shown in Table 2.2 but see Figure 2.1).

Figure 2.1. Discussion Networks of Working-Class and Middle-Class Parents

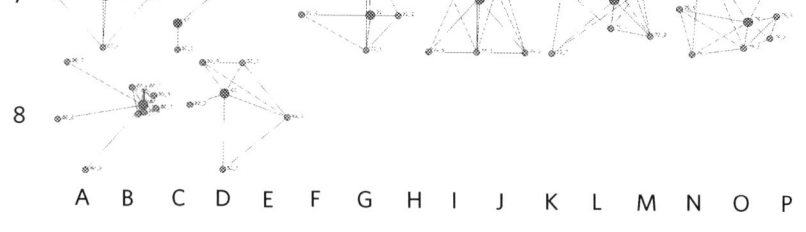

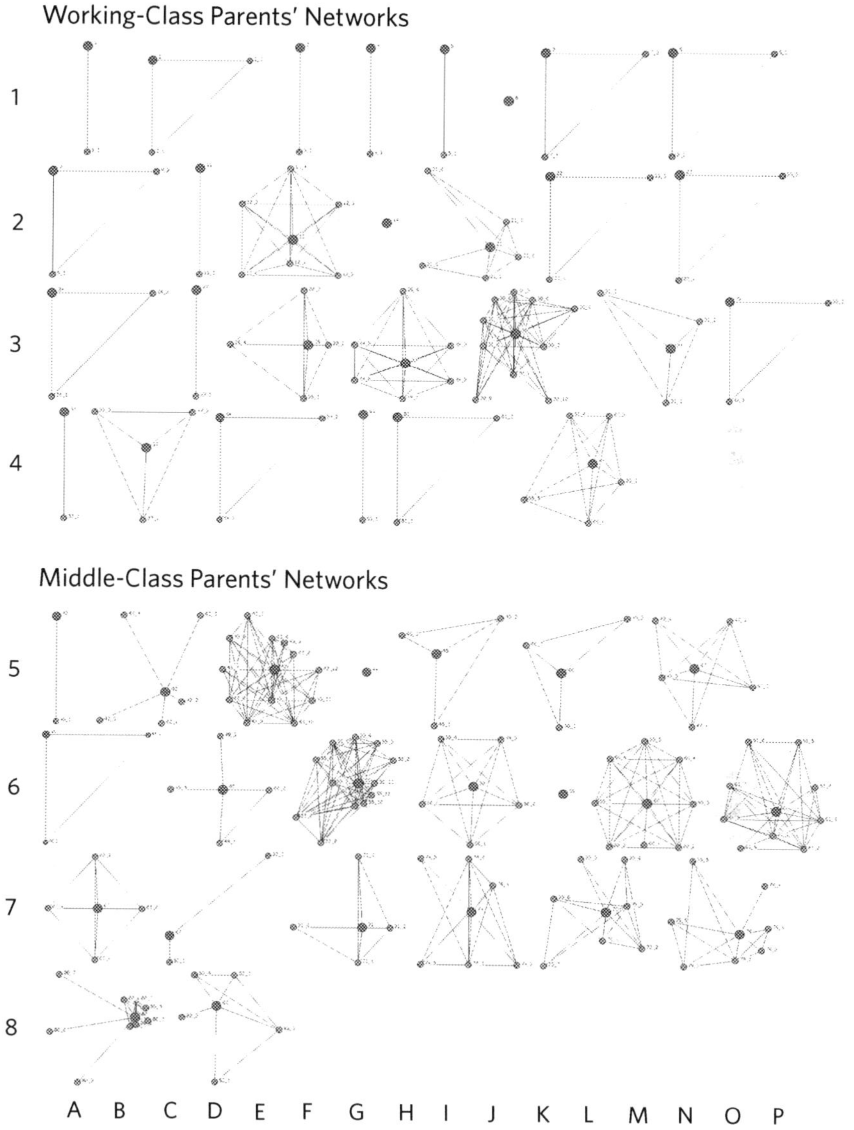

Working-Class Parents' Networks

Middle-Class Parents' Networks

A B C D E F G H I J K L M N O P

Table 2.2. Structure and Composition of Parents' Discussion Networks by Social Class[1]

	Middle Class	Working Class	Middle Class Relative to Working Class (% Diff.)[2]
	Mean/Pct.	*Mean/Pct.*	
Network size	5.2	2.6	99.9
Density	59.4	95.4	-37.7
Diversity (race)	18.2	14.6	24.6
Percent weak ties	13.9	7.1	95.6
Percent strong ties	86.1	92.9	-7.3
. . . Percent family	30.3	80.6	-62.4
. . . Percent friends	55.7	12.2	356.1
Percent who reside elsewhere	25.2	19.1	31.9
Percent frequently in touch	63.0	79.4	-20.7
Percent White	81.2	9.7	735.7
Percent middle class	87.0	19.9	337.3
Mean occupational status	62.3	37.8	64.8
Highest occupational status	69.6	49.7	40.1
Lowest occupational status	43.7	23.0	89.5

1. N = 49 for network size, because one respondent has missing values on all quantitative network measures. N = 37 for all other measures, because we exclude from the calculation parents with fewer than two network alters (see Marsden 1987).
2. Calculated as [(middle-class value/working-class value) x 100] – 100.

Excluded from analyses of the structure and composition of discussion networks are parents who have fewer than two network alters. For such small networks, measures of range and diversity either are incalculable or have little meaning (Marsden 1987). Therefore, indices in Table 2.2 (other than network size) reflect the networks of 37 parents, of whom 19 are middle class and 18 are working class.[5] Among this group, middle-class parents have, on average, less dense, more racially diverse, and more socioeconomically advantaged discussion networks than their working-class counterparts. Fewer than two thirds (59.4%) of alters in the networks of middle-class parents know one another, on average, but the vast majority (95.4%) of alters in the networks of working-class parents do. Thus, middle-class discussion networks are, on average, 37.7% less dense than working-class networks. As measured by the index of qualitative variation (IQV), neither group has much racial diversity in their discussion networks. Among middle-class parents, there is only an 18.2% chance that two randomly drawn alters are members of different racial or ethnic groups, although that is 24.6% higher than the amount of diversity observed in the networks of working-class parents, for whom there is only a 14.6% chance of the same.[6]

Perhaps as expected given the domain of interest, neither group has many weak ties, although middle-class parents have almost twice as many as working-class parents. Nor do parents report having many members in their discussion networks who live outside the city in which they themselves live, although middle-class parents reported about 32% more of such ties. Weak ties are theorized to connect dissimilar social networks, thereby providing a bridge to sources of information to which one otherwise might not have access via one's close personal ties, that is to say, strong ties (Granovetter 1973). Geographically distant ties are expected to operate similarly. Thus, weak ties and geographically distant ties are thought to increase the diversity of network alters and therefore the uniqueness of the information they can provide. Based on these measures, working-class parents are at an informational disadvantage.[7]

The complement to weak ties is strong ones, representing connections to individuals who are expected to be similar to respondents and who may offer them support. Although the majority of ties in the discussion networks of both groups are strong, there are important class differences in their composition. Friends make up the majority (55.7%) of all ties among middle-class parents, whereas family members constitute the vast majority (80.6%) of ties among working-class parents. Thus, the tendency for strong ties to link respondents to socially similar individuals is especially strong in the case of the working-class parents in this study, as most of those strong ties are to family members (see also Stack 1974; Horvat, Weininger, and Lareau 2003; McPherson, Smith-Lovin, and Brashears 2006). As noted, this particular composition of strong ties is expected to reduce the amount of unique information that flows in the networks of working-class parents relative to that of their middle-class counterparts. However, it may, conversely, indicate that working-class respondents have access to higher levels of support (Wellman and Wortley 1989, 1990), which is suggested also by the higher frequency of contact with network alters among working-class compared with middle-class parents.

In addition to being larger and less dense, the discussion networks of middle-class parents are more socioeconomically advantaged than those of their working-class counterparts. We measure socioeconomic advantage as access to members who occupy advantaged positions in racial/ethnic, class, and occupational hierarchies. The discussion networks of middle-class parents are majority White (81.2%), while Whites represent a clear minority (9.7%) in the discussion networks of working-class parents. Moreover, 87.0% of middle-class parents' network alters are themselves middle class, while only a fifth (19.9%) of the network alters of working-class parents are middle class. Middle-class parents also have greater occupational resources in their discussion networks compared with working-class parents.

Whereas the mean occupational status for the alters of middle-class parents is 62.3, which correlates with technical occupations (SEI score of 61.4), the mean occupational status for the network alters of working-class parents is only 37.8, corresponding to the occupational category of protective services (SEI score of 38.0). Further, the discussion networks of middle-class parents reach higher into the occupational hierarchy than do the discussion networks of their working-class counterparts—69.6 compared with 49.7. These values correspond to professionals (SEI score of 70.2) and small business owners (SEI score of 49.7), respectively.

In contrast to position networks, class disparities in parents' discussion networks point to clear advantages to middle-class compared with working-class parents. Those with whom middle-class parents tend to discuss parenting and schooling issues can be described as predominantly White, middle class, with occupational status on par with technical workers, and more likely to be friends or acquaintances than family members. This contrasts sharply with the portrait our data paint of the networks of working-class parents; their discussion networks are predominantly non-White, working class, with an occupational status similar to that of protective service workers, and composed of individuals who are most likely family members. Therefore, we can expect that while working-class parents may receive greater support from their discussion networks, middle-class parents have better access to information that can help them achieve their parenting objectives, and greater access to individuals who can wield influence on their behalf.

Are Class Differences in Network Resources Explained by Racial Composition?

Given that the majority of middle-class parents in this study are White, whereas the majority of working-class parents are not, we check the possibility that the observed class disparities in measured network resources reflect merely differences between those that Whites possess compared with those of other racial and ethnic groups. We observe the same patterns among non-Whites as we do in the full sample. The class gap in the percent of network alters who are White reported for the full sample is 71.5 percentage points (see Table 2.2), and is a sizeable 36.4 percentage points among non-White parents. The class gap in the percent of alters who are middle class is 67.1 percentage points in the full sample and 46.4 points among non-Whites. Finally, the class gap in mean occupational status of alters in the full sample is nearly identical to that for non-White parents—24.5 and 24.9 points, respectively. Thus, class differences in network resources are not reducible to the representation of Whites among middle-class versus working-class parents.

CLASS DIFFERENCES IN THE UTILIZATION
OF SOCIAL NETWORK RESOURCES

Most parents reported utilizing their social networks to achieve parenting and other objectives.[8] The rate of network utilization varied little by social class, with 95.5% of middle-class parents and 96.4% of working-class parents having reported drawing on social network resources. Parents described a total of 153 instances of network utilization. Middle-class parents account for 55.6% of those instances, even though they make up only 44.7% of parents who reported utilizing their network. Thus, middle-class parents in our sample evinced greater network utilization than did their working-class counterparts.

Social Resources Utilized by Parents

From the narrative data, we identified the kinds of network resources parents used. Nine categories of resources emerged: (1) generalized financial resources (e.g., money for a transit pass), (2) contributed or pledged financial resources for adolescents' college education, (3) influence alone (e.g., ability and willingness to intervene on parents' behalf), (4) influence paired with information, (5) information and advice, (6) material resources (e.g., a computer), (7) opportunities, (8) skills and knowledge (e.g., math skills), and (9) general support (e.g., listening to parents). The top panel of Table 2.3 displays the share of parents who used these resources arranged by rates of utilization.[9] Note that four of the five resources with the highest rates of use are the same for middle-class and working-class parents: information and advice, support, opportunities, and the skills and knowledge of network members. The bottom panel of the table shows that the same set of four resources are among those most intensely used by parents. Perhaps this is because parenting involves a set of challenges and responsibilities common to both social class locations; these particular social resources may be universally helpful in meeting them.

Despite similarities in mobilized resources, middle- and working-class parents differed in how they put network resources to use. Indeed, the sole divergence among the top five resources used by parents highlights class differences in both their material conditions as well as how their networks contribute to their children's social mobility. Whereas more than a third of middle-class parents (38.1%) received financial contributions to their children's college funds from network members, only 15.4% of working-class parents received financial support for their children's college education. By contrast, 42.3% of working-class parents received generalized financial assistance from their social network compared with 14.3% of middle-class parents.

Table 2.3. Social Network Resources Ranked by Rate of Utilization by Social Class[1]

Parents (N = 47)			
Middle Class (N = 21)	*Pct.[2]*	*Working Class (N = 26)*	*Pct.[3]*
Information/Advice	81.0	Generalized financial resources	42.3
Financial resources for college	38.1	Information/Advice	42.3
Support	33.3	Opportunities	30.8
Skills/Knowledge	28.6	Skills/Knowledge	26.9
Opportunities	23.8	Support	23.1
Influence/Information	19.0	Financial resources for college	15.4
Generalized financial resources	14.3	Material resources	15.4
Influence	14.3	Influence/Information	3.8
Material resources	4.8	Influence	0.0
Instances of Network Utilization (N = 153)			
Middle Class (N = 85)	*Pct.[4]*	*Working Class (N = 68)*	*Pct.[5]*
Information/Advice	41.2	Generalized financial resources	23.5
Financial resources for college	11.8	Information/Advice	20.6
Opportunities	11.8	Skills/Knowledge	13.2
Skills/Knowledge	10.6	Support	13.2
Support	10.6	Opportunities	11.8
Influence	4.7	Financial resources for college	8.8
Influence/Information	4.7	Material resources	5.9
Generalized financial resources	3.5	Influence/Information	2.9
Material resources	1.2	Influence	0.0

1. N = 47. One parent has missing data on utilization and two parents report no utilization. Describes parents' utilization of social network resources during children's middle school years; 2. Share of middle-class respondents who utilized resource; 3. Share of working-class respondents who utilized resource; 4. Share of instances reported by middle-class respondents; 5. Share of instances reported by working-class respondents.

Take Bette, for example, a White middle-class attorney who worked part-time in her own law practice while raising two children with her husband. Her family earned between $75,000 and $100,000 a year. When we asked whether she and her husband had saved money for their 8th-grade daughter's education, she explained, "My husband's mother actually put some money away . . . I think we have $80,000 for Chloe and $20,000 for [our son]." Similarly, Gwen, a White middle-class psychologist who was raising her son, Harris, with her long-term partner, Andrea, described receiving contributions from a family member. Although both women held college degrees, were professionals, and owned their home, their annual household income was less than $50,000, perhaps because Andrea, an artist, worked part-time. Nevertheless, they had substantial resources to put toward Harris's college education thanks to Gwen's father. Gwen explained: "My father has an educational trust for his grandchildren. . . . This year, it's $29,000 per child per year."

Jerome, an African American father in a long-term interracial relationship with the mother of his 13-year-old son, Karl, had at the time a daughter enrolled at Duke University. Jerome attended college but did not earn a degree, although his partner did. Both parents worked full-time and together earned between $75,000 and $100,000 a year. However, their long-term income was less assured than it had been previously because of uncertainties related to Jerome's work as a consultant and his partner's health. As with Bette and Gwen, Jerome's family had contributed to his children's college education, but in a more modest way. Jerome's mother used some of the money she obtained from his father's life insurance policy to cover some of his daughter's living expenses during her freshman year in college. She promised to do the same for Karl.

Although Jerome was concerned about how he and his partner would pay for Karl's college education, they had received substantial assistance with their daughter's tuition. A long-time friend, whom Jerome described as "extremely wealthy," thought very highly of his daughter and was motivated to support her education. Jerome explained:

So, we were agonizing over college financial aid and what-not [and my friend] said, "Listen. I'm 45. I don't have kids. I always wanted kids, but it looks like I'm not gonna have them. Why should your kid . . . have to worry about going to college when, if I had a kid, they wouldn't? It was not because I did anything [but rather] just 'cause I inherited money." So, she offered to pay part of [the] college tuition for Lena and has done so part of that time, which made our lives much easier. I mean, it was just a fluke.

That his good friend decided to use her wealth for the education of another person's child may appear to be a fluke to Jerome, but this and other studies indicate that it is no coincidence that someone like Jerome, with his family's class status, is socially connected to someone with enough resources to help his family pay college tuition at an institution like Duke.

Certainly, not all middle-class parents received contributions toward their children's college education in such large amounts. For example, Monica, a White special education teacher who lived with her husband and two sons, reported a family income of more than $100,000 annually. Monica noted that her "husband's family has offered [money] for books and everything" for both of her children. Another teacher, Mallory, indicated that she and her husband, a craftsman with a high school diploma, earned between $35,000 and $49,999 a year and own their home. Mallory worked part-time although her husband worked full-time. Mallory explained that her parents "put aside some money" for her son Nicolas, but made clear that "it's not a lot."

Even though the majority (76.9%) of working-class parents wished to see their children attend college, only one reported having access to resources for college through social networks on par with those reported by middle-class parents. Anne, an African American mother who worked as a caseworker, shared that she and her husband collectively earned between $50,000 and $75,000 annually and own their home. Anne's father and sister saved money for her daughter's college education. She explained:

> My father has a pretty good fund set up. . . . I think that's about $30,000. . . . And then I have [a] sister who's single, and she's this big DJ in Cleveland. So, she's got about $10, $15,000 for Brandy saved.

More typical for working-class parents was support that helped them meet daily living expenses. For example, because Patricia, an African American woman, was unemployed, a friend gave her financial support in the form of funds for transportation. Patricia explained: "[My friend] knows I'm not really making any money. He's buying me a monthly [transit] pass today, so I could go looking [for work]." Tamara, also African American, worked as a clerk at an international shipping company, but was on disability temporarily due to an injury she suffered in a car accident. She was thankful for financial assistance that her oldest daughter provided: "The good thing was my daughter workin', and she didn't mind breakin' me off some and addin' to it." Wanda, like most working-class parents in the study, was employed. Although she worked full-time providing inpatient care at the time of our interview, she earned less than $20,000 a year. Therefore, she relied on financial assistance from her boyfriend given that her job provided insufficient income. She explained:

> If it wasn't for my boyfriend a lot of times, I be like, "Well, what would I be doing? How would I deal with it?". . . I'm just looking for another job right now, 'cause that one that I have, it's paying the bills, but it's just not enough for me right now.

That this pattern of greater financial resources possessed by middle-class compared with working-class parents is matched with greater financial resources within their social networks is a manifestation of the relationship among sentiment, interaction, and resources previously described (Lin 1982, 2001).

Looking beyond the resources with the highest rates of use reveals further differences between middle- and working-class parents in terms of three centrally important kinds of network resources: information, influence, and what we call "socioeconomic substitutes"—socioeconomic resources in a parent's social network that serve as stand-ins for a parent's own resources, such as cash for immediate expenses, savings for college, needed material goods, or the knowledge and skills to help children with homework. Information and influence are two basic resources expected to flow through social networks (Granovetter 1973; Campbell, Marsden, and Hurlbert 1986; Coleman 1988; Burt 1992). Indeed, these resources are the primary means through which social networks are expected to facilitate social action. But given our interest in how class differences in parenting practices may be structured by inequality, it is also important to take notice of how network resources can operate in place of parents' own socioeconomic resources or lack thereof.

Table 2.4 displays the number and percentage of parents who reported using information, influence, and socioeconomic substitutes, as well as the percentage of all instances of utilization that involved those resources. The majority of middle-class parents (85.7%) reported using their networks as information channels, paired with either advice or influence. In contrast, fewer than half of working-class parents (42.3%) received educationally relevant information from their networks. Moreover, in almost half (45.9%) of all instances in which they drew on their networks, middle-class parents received information, whereas working-class parents received information in fewer than a quarter (23.5%) of instances.

Whether parents received information from their network members had meaningful consequences for the education of their children, as the following examples demonstrate. Barbara, an African American working-class mother described how she came to decide on a high school for her daughter, Chrystal, who had attended Augusta Middle School. Barbara was prepared to send Chrystal to a technical high school that had what Barbara felt was a good reputation, although she admitted to knowing little about the schools in her district. An acquaintance had, at one time, lived near the high school and passed along some important information, which altered Barbara's plans. As she recounted it: ". . . one of the girls was tellin' me that I should take [Chrystal] out of [the school] because the environment over there has changed. . . . There's a lot of shootings and stuff over there and the environment is bad." Barbara explained that a member of her church suggested a different school: "So, the First Lady at our church [the pastor's wife] was saying, 'Why don't you try and transfer her over to Chisholm High School?'" Armed with information about the bad environment around the technical school and with a specific recommendation for an alternative, Barbara changed her plans: "I'm gonna try and get her into Chisholm High," thereby avoiding sending her daughter daily into an area that reportedly struggled with violence.

Table 2.4. Parents Who Used Information, Influence, and Socioeconomic Substitutes by Social Class[1]

	MIDDLE CLASS		WORKING CLASS		MIDDLE CLASS		WORKING CLASS	
	Num.	Pct.[2]	Num.	Pct.[3]	Num.	Pct.[4]	Num.	Pct.[5]
	Parents Who Used Information				*All Instances of Information*			
Information/Advice	17	81.0	11	42.3	35	41.2	14	20.6
Influence/Information	4	19.0	1	3.8	4	4.7	2	2.9
Total number and percent	18	85.7	11	42.3	39	45.9	16	23.5
	Parents Who Used Influence				*All Instances of Influence*			
Influence	3	14.3	0	0	4	4.7	0	0.0
Influence/Information	4	19.0	1	3.8	4	4.7	2	2.9
Total number and percent	5	23.8	1.0	3.8	8	9.4	2	2.9
	Parents Who Used Socioeconomic Substitutes				*All Instances of Socioeconomic Substitutes*			
Generalized financial resources	3	14.3	11	42.3	3	3.5	16	23.5
Financial resources for college	8	38.1	4	15.4	10	11.8	6	8.8
Material resources	1	4.8	4	15.4	1	1.2	4	5.9
Skills/Knowledge	6	28.6	7	26.9	9	10.6	9	13.2
Total number and percent	12	57.1	20	76.9	23	27.1	35	51.5

1. N = 47. One parent has missing data on utilization and two parents report no utilization. Describes parents' utilization of social network resources during children's middle school years; 2. Share of middle-class parents who used resource; 3. Share of working-class parents who used resource; 4. Share of instances reported by middle-class parents; 5. Share of instances reported by working-class parents.

Information provided by network members also had important consequences for the education of Harris, the son of Gwen and Andrea described above. Although Harris attended McKinley Middle School, he initially was not accepted into several of his preferred (and academically selective) high schools. The information Gwen obtained from network members changed that. After Gwen learned that many students from McKinley had been denied admission into Bell High School because of poor grades in English, one of her contacts confirmed for her that Harris's English grade had, indeed, kept him out of Bell. This information would prove critical to Gwen's efforts to get Harris admitted, because there was an agreement between McKinley and Bell that English grades assigned by a problematic teacher would not be held against that teacher's students. Clearly, something had broken down in the admissions process for Harris. However, with information from her contact inside Bell, Gwen approached the principal at McKinley, who helped her resolve the matter. Harris was subsequently admitted.

Despite this victory, Harris did not attend Bell High School. Rather, he opted to enroll at Mendel Science Academy, a school that initially had waitlisted him. Here again, information from a contact was instrumental to getting Harris admitted. Gwen described how it happened:

> One of our friends called up and commiserated [with us] that Harris didn't get in anywhere, or he got in someplace that he didn't wanna go at all. And our friend said, "Well, you know, everybody from McKinley got waitlisted at Mendel because they didn't want to compete, so you should call them." So, even though I work for the district, I didn't think of that. And then I called them. I just called them right away and the principal answered the phone and I was quite struck by the impact that I had. [The principal said] he was actually sitting by the phone waiting for parents to call.

A bit of information from a friend, along with the simple action of a phone call, transformed Harris's position at Mendel Science Academy from waitlisted to admitted. As these examples make clear, information can help parents make critically important decisions that shape their children's educational experiences. Yet, working- and middle-class parents differ sharply in the extent to which their networks provide this particular resource (see Table 2.4).

Table 2.4 shows the percent of parents who recounted drawing on the socioeconomic resources of their network members. We have already observed class disparities in the extent to which parents received financial assistance to meet the challenges of paying for college and routine living expenses. Here, we also see a class gap in the use of social networks for material assistance. Although relatively few parents of either social class location utilized their networks for material resources, such as clothing and furniture, for example, a larger share of working-class (15.4%) than middle-class (4.8%) parents did so.

Unexpectedly, a similar share of middle- and working-class parents drew on the skills and knowledge that exist in their networks (28.6% and 26.9%, respectively), and both groups often used this network resource for the same objective—to obtain help for adolescents with homework when parents themselves could not provide it. Sal, a White middle-class graphic designer, described how he obtained help with math for his son from a neighbor:

> One of the neighbor kids who's older, just graduating from high school this year, was good in math. And that's who we'd send him to when he had math questions.

Josephine, a multiracial working-class typist, described how her boyfriend, Shane, helped her son with his math homework, the subject that seemed to give most parents difficulty:

> Math was my worst subject. . . . I try to the best of my abilities. Sometimes, we'll have to put the math on hold and wait 'til Shane comes and helps him. Well, this was before the new job.

Shane had taken a second job working at the airport and had much less free time than before his new position. Still, Josephine relied on him:

> But we will wait for him to come because he's a whiz with math and he would map [guide] him through it. . . . So, yeah, whatever I can't really help him on, I always look to Shane for the backup.

Combined, there are important class differences in the share of parents who used socioeconomic substitutes, with 57.1% of middle-class parents doing so compared with 76.9% of working-class parents. Even larger differences exist in the frequency with which the two groups drew on those kinds of resources. Working-class parents used socioeconomic substitutes almost twice as often as middle-class parents (51.5% of all network utilization compared with 27.1%).

In sum, then, not only do middle-class parents possess more and better personal resources than their working-class peers, but their networks provide access to more and better social resources. Although the majority of both groups of parents hoped or expected their children would attend college, more than a third (38.1%) of middle-class parents could count on their social networks to help make that aspiration or expectation a reality via financial contributions to college funds compared with proportionally half

(15.4%) as many working-class parents. And while middle-class parents displayed clear advantages in their ability to obtain information, advice, and influence from their social ties, working-class parents' only advantage was in drawing on their social connections as stand-ins for their own modest socioeconomic resources.

Parenting Objectives for Which Network Resources Were Used

Although there was no network resource used by middle-class parents that went unused by their working-class counterparts, social networks served very different functions for these two groups. We identified seven categories of objectives for which parents utilized their networks: (1) academic objectives, (2) receipt of financial or material assistance, (3) monitoring adolescents, (4) preparing adolescents for college, (5) selecting a high school, (6) adolescents' participation in structured activities, and (7) a collection of objectives that mirror components of Lareau's ([2003] 2011) concept of concerted cultivation—intervention in school decisions, customization of adolescents' experiences, and development of their talents and skills.[10] Academic objectives include, for example, obtaining assistance with homework and making decisions regarding course selection. Monitoring objectives include, for example, keeping informed about youths' whereabouts and their behavior in school, and confirming with school personnel adolescents' reports about goings-on at school. Preparing adolescents for college includes, for example, gathering financial resources to pay for college, talking with individuals who have ties to and prior experiences with particular colleges, and visiting colleges. Finally, receipt of financial or material support includes the receipt of such support when it is not tied to other parenting objectives. For instance, it includes the receipt of clothing for adolescents and money to help pay bills, but it does not include the receipt of money to help pay for college or organized activities. The seven objectives identified account for the vast majority of the instances of network utilization reported by middle- and working-class parents. Other objectives, such as child care, family entertainment, or finding an adolescent a job, were too infrequent to constitute their own category and therefore are grouped together in the category "other."

The top panel of Table 2.5 displays these objectives arranged by the rate of utilization by middle- and working-class parents. Almost half (47.6%) of middle-class parents drew on their networks to further academic objectives. For example, Nancy, a White middle-class consultant, described how she and her husband help their son, Miles, with his struggles regarding "time allocation and paper management." Nancy shared that:

> [Miles will] be in a frantic state because he'll realize something is due and he can't find the assignment. So, first, we give him a lecture; we

yell at him. Then he cries. And then, I will sometimes call someone who I know is a more responsible person and ask if they know what the assignment is. I do that less; but, that way, I will save him and then he does the assignment.

Table 2.5. Percentage Distribution of Parents Who Used Social Networks by Parenting Objective and Social Class[1]

PARENTS (N = 47)			
Middle Class (n = 21)	Pct.[2]	Working Class (n = 26)	Pct.[3]
Academic	47.6	Receive financial, material assistance	46.2
Structured activity participation	47.6	Structured activity participation	42.3
Preparation for college	38.1	Academic	30.8
Intervening, customization, cultivation	23.8	Monitoring	23.1
Selecting a high school	23.8	Preparation for college	15.4
Other	23.8	Selecting a high school	15.4
Monitoring	19.0	Other	15.4
Receive financial, material assistance	14.3	Intervening, customization, cultivation	7.7
INSTANCES OF NETWORK UTILIZATION			
Middle Class (n = 85)	Pct.[4]	Working Class (n = 69)	Pct.[5]
Structured activity participation	24.7	Receive financial, material assistance	25.0
Academic	18.8	Structured activity participation	22.1
Preparation for college	15.3	Academic	16.2
Selecting a high school	11.8	Preparation for college	10.3
Monitoring	8.2	Monitoring	8.8
Intervening, customization, cultivation	7.1	Other	8.8
Receive financial, material assistance	7.1	Selecting a high school	7.4
Other	7.1	Intervening, customization, cultivation	2.9

1. N = 47. One parent has missing data on utilization and two parents report no utilization. Describes parents' utilization of social network resources during children's middle school years; 2. Share of middle-class parents who utilized resource; 3. Share of working-class parents who utilized resource; 4. Share of instances reported by middle-class parents; 5. Share of instances reported by working-class parents.

The same percentage of middle-class parents used their networks to enroll their teens in organized activities or support their participation in those activities, which has been shown to impact whether and where adolescents attend college (Kaufman and Gabler 2004; Gabler and Kaufman 2006; Soares 2007; Stevens 2007). More than one third (38.1%) of middle-class parents also used their networks to expose their teens to information about college or to help pay for college. Sal, the White middle-class graphic designer who asked his neighbor to help his son with homework, was able to give his son direct exposure to an elite college through a friend. In response to our question about whether he thinks his son will go to college, Sal responded:

> I have no doubt he'll go to college. He's already talked about college. I think he's even been kind of sizing them [up] on his own, because we have a friend who works at Yale, and we visited her up there. He was looking around [asking], "This is a college? It looks like a bunch of churches." And, you know, he's talked about it with us a little bit.

Although working-class parents also drew on their networks for academic objectives, almost half (46%) of them used their networks to receive financial and material assistance. For example, Josephine, a multiracial working-class mother who earned less than $10,000 annually as a typist, and whose boyfriend Shane helped her son with math homework, described her conflicted feelings about receiving financial help from him. His financial support was needed, although she found it difficult to accept. She noted:

> I pay $750 to rent here and that's not including the utilities, the gas, electric, etcetera. I'm paying for all of that. My boyfriend helps me out, but there's only so much that I allow him to do. We had that conversation today. Because I've been so used to taking care of [myself], I don't know how to accept the help. That's what I had to explain to him. It's hard for me to say, "Can you help me?" So, I told him it's something I have to work on.

Polly, the White working-class sales clerk, received material support from a coworker, which met a need that more than one working-class parent articulated—a need for a computer at home. She noted: "We just were given a computer. I just gotta get it running. It's in Italian." In response to our inquiries about why the computer was in Italian, Polly explained: "One of my managers . . . bought a new computer and gave us his old [one]. Well, it ain't even really that old. . . . He's from Italy . . . and it's all in his native language." Polly's receipt of the computer is notable because she directly linked it to her daughter's ability to do homework at home. In response to our question about whether Robin had at home what she needed to do homework, Polly said:

> Not yet. Once I get that computer up and running [she will] because a lot of the stuff [homework] is projects that she needs to use the computer [for]. Once I get that computer going . . . I'm hoping to get the computer going, then she'll be a little more set up.

Prior to this, Polly's daughter used a friend's computer, which Polly found to be problematic because it meant that her daughter was away from home too frequently.

Like middle-class parents, a substantial share of working-class parents (42.3%) drew on their networks for their children's participation in organized activities. Additionally, both middle-class and working-class parents used their networks to engage in elements of concerted cultivation. Middle-class parents did so at three times the rate of their working-class counterparts (23.8% compared with 7.7%). The size of this class difference is notable and consistent with direct observations of parents' behavior (Lareau [2003] 2011), although this particular parenting objective accounts for only a small percentage of either group's instances of network utilization: 7.1% among middle-class parents and 2.9% among their working-class counterparts.

FROM GETTING BY TO GETTING AHEAD

Collectively, our quantitative and qualitative data reveal how the networks of middle-class parents served to help their families get ahead while those of working-class parents helped their families to get by. Not only did middle-class parents in our study have larger and more-advantaged social networks relative to working-class parents, but they used those networks primarily in ways that helped transmit middle-class status to their children. To see this more clearly, let us combine all objectives that have implications for adolescents' chances of attending college: academic achievement, structured activity participation, preparation for college, and high school selection or destination. Collectively, these objectives represent 70.6% of the reported instances for which middle-class parents utilized their networks, whereas they constitute only 56.0% of network utilization by working-class parents (see bottom panel of Table 2.5). What's more, that substantially more middle-class than working-class parents received from their networks contributions to their teens' college fund (38.1% compared with 15.4%); used their networks as information channels (85.7% compared with 42.3%); and used their networks as sources of influence for parenting and schooling issues (23.8% compared with 3.8%) reflects how the networks of middle-class parents were prepared to help them achieve the long-term goal of college attendance, even before their adolescents had transitioned to high school.

Although the majority of working-class parents shared with their middle-class counterparts the aspiration of sending their children to college, working-class parents' use of network resources was more varied. They, too, used their networks to help their teens pursue college attendance, but at a substantially lower rate. To some, this difference might suggest that working-class parents place less emphasis on objectives that could affect their adolescent's social mobility. However, this difference must be placed in the context of another class difference evident in our data—the relative importance of the receipt of financial and material assistance. Middle-class parents reported using their networks to obtain financial or material support a small fraction as often as they used their networks to support the college-going prospects of their adolescents (7.1% compared with 70.6%). In contrast, working-class parents reported doing so almost half as often (25.0% compared with 56.0%).

These patterns are clearly related to class disparities in the personal resources middle- and working-class families possess: 60% of middle-class families in our sample reported annual household incomes greater than $75,000 (or $99,408 in 2020 dollars), while the same share of working-class parents reported household incomes of less than $25,000 per year (or $33,136 in 2020 dollars). Middle-class parents' personal resources free them from having to routinely rely on their social networks for financial and material assistance. In contrast, network resources are so important to the budgets of a segment of working-class families that Kathryn Edin and her colleague deem them part of low-income single mothers' "economic strategies for survival" (Edin 1991; Edin and Lein 1997). Our findings further suggest that this economic strategy may have unanticipated consequences for working-class families. Financial concerns appear to restrict working-class parents' use of networks to support the education of their children by requiring parents to direct network resources toward meeting more pressing demands (e.g., money for a transit pass to look for a job)—that is, to helping their families get by.

Getting by is good, but can working-class parents' social networks also help them to get ahead? That we used a position generator along with a name generator allows us to speak to this question, as the two generators reveal that stark class differences do not characterize *all* types of social networks. For example, the advantage to middle-class parents in mean occupational status in position networks is only 10.9%, whereas it is 64.8% in discussion networks. Similarly, the advantage to middle-class parents in how high into the occupational structure their position networks reach (i.e., upper reachability) is only 3.1%, but it is 40.1% for discussion networks. And middle-class parents have a slight disadvantage relative to their working-class counterparts with respect to the racial diversity of their position networks, but they have a 24.6% advantage in discussion networks. Thus, working-class parents appear to have resources in their position networks that are more comparable to those of their middle-class counterparts than can be found in their discussion networks. The position networks of working-class parents were almost as large, almost as wide, and almost as resourced as those of their middle-class counterparts. This means that when working-class parents in our study move from a pool of individuals in various social positions with whom they have ties (their position network) to a pool of people they utilize to help them navigate parenting and schooling issues (their discussion network), they move from a wider to a narrower network and from a more-advantaged to a less-advantaged one.

If working-class parents were able to draw on the resources in their position networks for parenting and schooling concerns, the impact of stark class inequalities in discussion networks could be reduced. Such a possibility raises the question of how parents choose among members in their larger social network to discuss parenting and schooling issues. Research tells us that we tend to discuss personal matters with those we are close to, such as family members and friends, in contrast to more-distant associates, which is why members of parents' discussion networks tend to possess resources similar to those that parents themselves already have. However, this tendency can be altered, allowing the possibility to engage network alters who are knowledgeable and skillful with respect to issues for which we need help—what Mario Small (2013) calls "targeted mobilization."

To be sure, there may be complications with mobilizing the network member who is best able to help. Why individuals make use of only some of their network resources is a complex question. Parents, for example, may be uncertain about whether a network alter is willing to help (Smith 2007) or whether they themselves could reciprocate if assistance was forthcoming (Stack 1974). Notwithstanding those challenges, targeted mobilization may allow working-class parents to benefit more from their social networks than they currently do, by bringing more of the resources that inhere in their position networks into their discussion networks and, at the same time, putting into service resources that are more comparable to those of their middle-class counterparts.

In the process of triangulating our findings through member checking, we became aware of the following example that illustrates the potential benefits that can flow to working-class parents who tactically utilize members of their position networks. During her 20s, Mariah was an unmarried, working-class mother of two who worked as a custodian in a Catholic hospital. She had applied for a seat in the hospital's internal training program for clerical medical positions, which paid more, came with more responsibilities, and provided more opportunities for promotion via an internal job ladder. Mariah was certain that she qualified for the program and suspected that her application had been dismissed because she was then a member of the janitorial staff. Rather than accept the rejection, Mariah tried again to access the program by utilizing her relationship with one of the nuns she had come to know. Mariah and Sister Lillian were not close, but they chatted from time to time while at work. Mariah told Sister Lillian about her application and asked for her help. Sister Lillian intervened. Mariah was admitted to the training program, completed it, and was promoted, thereby improving her occupational status and, most important for our consideration, the resources she provided to her family, which included not only more income and health insurance, but a regularized work schedule that allowed her to be more involved in her children's schooling. Use of her position network allowed Mariah to get ahead rather than merely get by.

SUMMARY

In this chapter, we have situated parents in the third social context that we consider—their social networks—to investigate how it informs class differences in parenting practices. The findings we present raise questions about whether class differences in parenting practices can be well understood apart from the very different social contexts in which working- and middle-class parents are embedded. Not only do middle- and working-class parents have access to different social network resources, but those resources operate differently by class in parents' lives. Middle-class parents, already advantaged, are further advantaged as soon as they activate their social networks, for social networks magnify the advantages conferred to privileged race, gender, and class positions (Loury 1977). Middle-class parents' greater access to information and influence helps to transfer advantages to their children to an extent not possible for working-class parents. Investigating the relationship between social networks and parenting illustrates the ways parents' priorities, decisions, and practices are shaped by more than their cultural orientations, but also by their social contexts—in this case, by the individuals to whom parents are socially connected and the resources those people make available.

CHAPTER 3

Navigating Adolescence in Unequal Contexts

In this chapter, we explore the major approaches parents used during a critical transition in adolescents' educational trajectories: the movement from middle school to high school. We find that working- and middle-class parents engaged in different approaches indicative of defensive and strategic parenting, respectively. Those differences were intimately connected to variation in the social contexts in which families were embedded. Because working-class parents' neighborhoods and schools were fraught with threats to successful transitions to adulthood (see Chapter 1), working-class parents emphasized vigilance in monitoring their children's peers, romantic relationships, and clothing choices (see also Jarrett 1999; Burton and Jarrett 2000; Kling, Liebman, and Katz 2005). The goal, reflective of defensive parenting, was to ensure the physical safety and potential social mobility of adolescents. However, given that most working-class parents worked—often multiple jobs—vigilance was difficult to maintain. In contrast, middle-class parents, unencumbered by the perilous environments within which working-class families lived, viewed the transition to high school as a time to strategically grant adolescents greater autonomy. Middle-class parents' expectation that their children would go to college motivated a focus on fostering their children's independence and making sure they had the best credentials to get into college.

VIGILANCE AMONG THE WORKING CLASS

Prior research shows that parents in disadvantaged neighborhoods spend a great deal of effort monitoring their children to protect them from harm (Furstenberg et al. 1999). Harding (2010), for example, finds that "safety and supervision absorb tremendous energy when violence and crime are ubiquitous" (61). Kling, Liebman, and Katz (2005) find that mothers in high-poverty neighborhoods structure their days around keeping their children out of harm's way. In contrast, Lareau ([2003] 2011) observes that working-class parents are content to let their children spend relatively unstructured days playing in the neighborhood. Her concept of the accomplishment of natural growth entails a relatively unmonitored existence for working-class youth. Below, we show that, consistent with prior work, the working-class families in this study engaged in vigilant monitoring, not only as a way to keep young people safe, but also to fend off threats to their prospects for social mobility, some of which centered on sexual activity and the risk of pregnancy. In this way, working-class parents engaged in defensive parenting.

Vigilance in the Neighborhood

Working-class parents were preoccupied with protecting their children from harm. Documented rates of crime in their neighborhoods, along with descriptions of their own experiences with crime, as presented in Chapter 1, make clear the reasons why. To mitigate perils in their neighborhoods, some working-class parents maintained a vigilance over their children not described by middle-class parents.

Working-class parents sought to protect their children whenever they moved about their residential environments. Several parents, for example, worried about getting their children safely to and from school.[1] Gabriela is an immigrant mother from El Salvador. She took her son, Hugo, to and from his middle school because she was concerned about his safety, even though the school was nearby. When Hugo entered 9th grade, his new high school would be only six blocks from their home; but Gabriela planned to drive him because, she said: "He has to pass by where they sell drugs." She was concerned about how he would get home, though: "It's going to be difficult to go and pick him up, but I'm going to achieve everything with God's strength. I'm going to try to find a way to be able to. . . . It's my responsibility." Although Gabriela wanted to protect her son while on his way to and from school, she was not sure she could do so:

> I'm going to take him. But I don't know if he's going to walk home, which is what I don't want. . . . But since I have so many responsibilities right now, I think that he's gonna have to walk home this year.

Gabriela had a good reason to be concerned. The drug dealers that she mentioned were not an amorphous threat—she had seen them sell drugs to kids. Other working-class parents likewise mentioned the need to take their children to and from school. Paige, a White working-class mother, walked her son Quentin to school "up until last year" when her son begged her to stop, saying, "Mom, please." Prior to that, Paige had persisted: "Snow, rain, I walked him to school." Similarly, Adrienne, an African American working-class mother, worried about the route to school for her kids. She said:

They don't catch no busses. Mommy got two vehicles. I'll be there, and I'll drive up [to] the door to pick my children up. That's how I am.

Several working-class parents, but no middle-class parents, described efforts to make sure that their kids stayed in school for the duration of the school day. Adrienne continued:

When I drop him off, I know [he goes into] the building 'cause Mama [referring to herself] sit there for 10 minutes. [When school lets out], I'm now standing at the first, second stair when he come out that door. . . . I think he'd be fearful to leave the building knowing he got to deal with me. He going to have to hear my voice [scolding him]. . . . I'm not goin' to beat him. It's just in my voice. I'll be plain with him: "When I come to pick you up, you better be there."

Juliette, a Haitian immigrant mother, checked up on her daughter at school to make sure she was there during the day or at her after-school program. Juliette noted: "I make sure that she's in the school. . . . Sometimes, I go to the school. She don't even know that I'm coming [to the] after-school program. . . . I just pass by [and say to her] 'I just pass by to say hi to you,' and I see she is busy doing some work." Barbara, an African American working-class mother, shared that her daughter signed up for an organized activity at school, but stopped going to it to hang out with her friends instead. Because she could not be sure of her daughter's whereabouts, Barbara required her daughter to come home immediately after school, having told her: "You come home after school because after school is where a lot of things go wrong in school, because all the teachers aren't there. . . . I know you get out [of school] at 3:09; I'll be there to pick you up and you ought to come home."

While working-class parents generally viewed school as a place where their children were safe from the surrounding neighborhood, they sometimes worried about whether school personnel were reliable partners in monitoring children's whereabouts during the school day. For example, Josephine, a multiracial working-class mother, described an incident in which her son was suspended from school and told to go home. She learned about it, not from the school, but from her son's friend the next day when she overheard him asking her son why he had been suspended. She described what happened:

There was an incident where my son apparently was suspended. . . . His teacher let him out at 12:00 and no one called me and made me aware of it, whatsoever. But here the child is free, walking the streets. . . . So that was a very big issue for me.

Josephine called the teacher and then talked to her again in person, along with the guidance counselor. During the conversation, Josephine communicated her expectation for how the school should handle issues with her son going forward:

> I just explained to her for future reference, if ever there is an issue with my child, always contact me. Never, never allow him to just walk off the school grounds and I not know about it because I need to know his whereabouts every day, all day, as much as possible. . . . There's too much that these kids are doing that I didn't even think to do at that age, so it's very easy for him to be misled. . . . To lead him is more important, and that's a harder task than it is for him to get drawn into drugs and . . . anything else.

Josephine's concern about the out-of-school suspension had a lot to do with her concerns about the safety of the neighborhood and the risks that she believes it poses for an 8th-grader alone at home or on the streets.

Working-class parents worried that their children would lose their way under the influence of peers and older adolescents in the neighborhood, particularly those who hung around outside. Unsupervised teens are more likely to engage in juvenile delinquency (Galambos and Maggs 1991), and working-class parents' descriptions of violence and drug issues in their neighborhoods often involved teenagers. Consequently, some working-class parents attempted to mostly keep their kids inside their homes, away from negative elements on the street. For example, Juliette, a Haitian working-class mother, did not let her daughter, Katrina, play with kids in the neighborhood. Katrina was mainly restricted to playing inside her home, or she could go to a friend's house whose parents Juliette felt were similarly strict. Of her daughters, Juliette said, "They not too much friendly with kids out there; talking too much and go to friends' house, door by door. I don't like that." She continued:

> I don't leave my kids . . . [to] run around with the other kids. . . . I got everything for my kids at home. That's why I don't let the kids go out too much. I have the video games. They have so many games.

Vigilance in monitoring children's whereabouts was difficult to maintain for parents who worked. This was especially true for single parents who did not have others to help them. Carina, a working-class Puerto Rican mother, shared that growing up on the island is "healthier" for children than growing up on the mainland. She felt that in Puerto Rico, parents have a greater sense of community and watch out more for one another's children:

The neighbors keep an eye on your kids, too. . . . Not here. Here everyone take[s] care of their own kids and if they see that someone else's [kid] is doing something wrong, they don't say anything. I mean, it's different.

What Carina described is collective efficacy, or the "linkage of trust and cohesion with shared expectations for control" (Morenoff, Sampson, and Raudenbush 2001, 520). Collective efficacy is said to be lower in disadvantaged neighborhoods (Sampson, Raudenbush, and Earls 1997), but there is evidence of it in the narratives of some working-class parents in our study. Layla, a Puerto Rican mother, had a good relationship with her neighbors, who are also Puerto Rican. Layla used these members of her social network to help monitor her children—twin daughters and a son—while she was at work. She described an incident in which her son tried to cut school without her knowledge, only to have the neighbors call her and foil his plans:

They can't cut classes and stay home 'cause my neighbors will call me. My son tried that one time and it didn't work. So, they know it's not goin' to work. My neighbor called me and said, "Layla, the music in your house is on." I'm like, "What? What you mean my music in my house is on? [The neighbor asked:] Did anybody stay home?" I'm like, "No. I sent 'em all to school." I said, "Don't worry about it. I'll be there in 5 minutes." I open the door [and] my son is like, "What are you doing here?" That was his worst nightmare. "How did you know I was home?" . . . How stupid can you be [to] not know that I'm gonna come home? But my neighbor called me.

Layla relied on her neighbors because she and her husband worked, leaving their kids home alone some part of each day. She said:

I can't really tell you exactly what my kids are doing 'cause I'm working. But I talk to my neighbors. They help me out. They have my cell phone number. [I tell them:] "If you see anything, call me." I work in the field so I can drive home. . . . I get [to] my house in 10 minutes if I have to. So that's the good thing about my job. The bad thing about the job is that I work 3 to 9; 3 to 10, which is the time they have to stay home alone. My husband works. He don't get home 'til late too. So basically, they're on their own. I got the help from the neighbors that they can call me if anything happens or they see anything wrong at my house.

As Layla's comments illustrate, even though parents may have wanted to watch their kids all the time or be kept abreast of their whereabouts, it was virtually impossible, especially for parents who worked. Thus, some parents allowed their children to be at home unsupervised while they were at work and therefore may have lacked knowledge about the children's whereabouts (Byrnes et al. 2011). Wanda, an African American working-class mother, highlighted the conundrum in comments about her son:

> You can try the best you can with your kids and it's still never enough. I can't watch his every move because I have other kids, and I have to work. . . . Every time you turn around, it's something different with him.

Because they could not always be with their children, some working-class parents talked to their children about ways to stay safe and on track. Parents hoped that adolescents would keep their guidance in mind when they were physically apart. Rosalinda described her strategy of using real events, as well as those depicted on TV, to talk about important issues with her daughter:

> The other day, we were at a [teenage] event and when we came out, there was a big fight. [There is] this one girl who we all know [is] very attitudy and thinks she's big stuff. This girl's really tough or she's really mouthy. As we were comin' out some other girls from behind took her and they beat her up. . . . That was an opportunity right there. [To her daughter:] "Serena, you got a mouth on you sometimes and you get people riled up. They're not gonna fight [you] one-on-one and they're not gonna fight you when you're lookin'. This is what can happen to you if you act that way. This is [what can happen] in [our] neighborhood." It was a learning lesson. The girl's face [was] all swollen. So, I take opportunities when stuff happens.

In sum, escorting children to and from school, limiting their exposure to peers in the neighborhood, and keeping them in the confines of the home were ways parents sought to keep them away from danger, as was keeping them involved in organized activities, as shown in Chapter 4. When those options were unavailable, working-class parents hoped their prior guidance would see their children through.

Vigilance Regarding Sex and Pregnancy

Among the concerns that motivated working-class parents to engage in vigilant monitoring was a specific worry, due to threats they perceived in their neighborhoods, that their daughters might be sexually objectified, might experience sexual violence, or might have an early sexual debut. Working-class mothers, many of whom described their own past sexual and domestic abuse, responded by monitoring their daughters' clothing in an effort to reduce their risk of receiving inappropriate attention from men. Parents limited their daughters' fashion options to ones that were not overtly sexual, prohibiting short skirts and tight clothing. This was a point of disagreement between mothers and daughters. Joella, a working-class African American mother, had to approve her daughter's outfits before she could leave the house:

> I kind of monitor where she goes or what she does. Everything. The clothes she wears. Well, of course, she ends up having to wear what I tell her. But she's a girl. Of course, she likes tight things, and I don't approve of them.

Joella and her daughter had different fashion tastes in general; Joella liked sporty styles while her daughter, Kendra, was a "girly girl" in her fashion. To deal with their differences, Joella let Kendra shop for clothes with one of Joella's friends whose fashion sense was closer to Kendra's. This way, Kendra could choose clothes she liked, with input from an adult to ensure that the items were not too sexy. Joella explained:

> [My friend] doesn't buy her or allow her to wear the short shorts and tight things because it isn't appropriate. We're trying to teach her the correct way to dress and messages it sends guys and things like that.

Polly, a White working-class mother, worked to maintain an open dialogue with her daughter, Robin, and wanted to trust that she would make good decisions, including good clothing choices:

> That gets really hard, because my daughter is built like a brick shit-house. My daughter is built like me. OK? At 15 years old, she's almost as big-chested as me [with] hips, butt. I walk down in the street with her and there's guys close to my age looking at this girl. It's hard when she goes out and [she's] not always dressed exactly how I like to see her dressed—in something that doesn't show her figure at all. But she's 15. She wears stuff that sometimes is not totally what I want her to be in. . . . When we went to go clothes shopping, when it was a skirt, [I said,] "Touch your toes. I better not see no cheeks."

Polly was beginning to let Robin shop for some of her own clothes. However, she wanted to make sure that Robin would not, as Polly put it, "bring anything home that I'm not going to let [her] wear out the door."

Working-class parents also worked to minimize the chances that their daughters would get pregnant—a development that would alter the trajectory of their daughters' lives. Some parents sought to reduce the risk of pregnancy by sharing information through open communication; others employed birth control; still others banned their daughters from having boyfriends. Latina mothers that we interviewed, for example, were very appreciative of the sex education courses offered at school, noting that their daughters had more information about sex than they did when they were young. Rosalinda, a working-class mother, worried about her daughter's transition to high school because, she said: "There are a lot of dropouts when kids go in the 9th grade," and she worried that her daughter was getting "boy crazy." Rosalinda described conversations she has had with her daughters, having told them:

> "If . . . you feel like you want to be sexually active, I may holler and scream at first, but let me know 'cause I will take you [for birth control], 'cause I don't want you to have babies young like I did." I preach to them more: "Live your life. Have fun. Go to school. Marriage and babies can wait until you're in your 30s." Don't do like we do. It's so many kids having babies.

Harriet, an African American working-class mother, went further. She has two daughters and a son. She required her daughters to use Depo-Provera, an injectable form of birth control, something that she could not use for her son. She was glad, however, that her son was not yet showing an interest in girls. About her daughters' use of birth control, she said:

> When they [became] teenagers, [I gave them] protection from havin' a baby. One of my coworkers was like, "I don't think you should do that." . . . Well, I did anyway 'cause I believe that if I didn't, she would end up like anybody else with a bunch of babies and no life. And I remember one of my coworkers saying, "The middle one [isn't sexually] active." She's not active, but the bottom line is I don't know when she'll become active. Because when I became active, my mother wasn't there. And, matter of fact, my first encounter was bein' raped. So, you know, you never know what can happen. The only way to prevent [pregnancy] is prevention. And that's what they teach you now, which most people don't even heed to. That's why you got all these teenagers with all these babies 'cause the parents don't understand that you have to instill somethin' to prevent that. Most people would say, "No. You makin' them think that it's OK to have sex." Well, my middle daughter didn't start havin' sex 'til she was 17. But still, she [was] protected. You know, I still feel bad about what I did. But I feel good I'm not a grandmother.

Harriet explicitly linked controlling her daughters' fertility with social mobility. She said:

I was raised in the projects. You get to a certain age you start rebellin.' Most people end up pregnant, and you get a [public assistance] check and that's all you know. Well, I taught my daughters differently. Maybe you haven't gathered, but I'm in recovery. So, I was one of them ones who strayed for whatever reasons and found my way back 13 years ago. And I had to look at how I ended up that way. I tend to teach my daughters differently, you know—precaution. [There's] always a way to prevent some things. So, my kids don't have babies, which is a difference from the way we came up.

Harriet wanted her daughters to have a better life than she did, and she felt that controlling their fertility was important for providing that better life.

Although Wanda, an African American working-class mother, was relieved to not yet have to discuss pregnancy with her son, some mothers did. Polly, a White working-class mother, noted that it was easier to have those conversations with her son than with her daughter. She said:

When [my son] came to me and asked me questions about sex and stuff like that, I didn't have as much trouble talking with him . . . 'cause, here goes the thing, he can't come home with a baby in his belly, and I have to deal with it. You know?

With her daughters, Polly sought to maintain an open dialogue about sex. She wanted her daughter, Robin, to talk to her about birth control when the time came. She said:

I've seen so many of her other girlfriends sneaking around and stuff like that, and getting themselves in more trouble. . . . Like one of our neighbors, at 15 years old, pregnant, because she was sneaking around behind her mom's back. . . . When her mom would go to work she would sneak out the door because she wasn't allowed out when mom wasn't home. If you don't want that kind of stuff, you better be open with your kids and you better teach them about safe sex and about being responsible for yourself and how to carry yourself. And you better be able to say the blunt stuff.

As Polly's comment illustrates, despite their efforts to prevent their own children from becoming pregnant, working-class parents could not prevent their children's friends from doing so. Rosalinda, the Latina mother who so valued the access her daughter had to sex education in school, explained that her daughter's classmate had become pregnant. She described the severe consequences it might have:

Serena has a friend in class that is pregnant or just had a baby, and it's so sad 'cause they don't realize how they ruining their lives. I think that's one of the [challenges with] having girls. [I'm] just trying to help them stay on the right track. . . . I would take them to get the contraceptives in a heartbeat. Not that I'm allowing it; not that it's OK with me, but I rather do this and rather that [she] be protected than there being a possibility of [her] having a baby. They don't need that burden. Life is hard enough.

Barbara, an African American working-class mother, handled the pregnancy of her daughter's classmate and neighbor in a different way:

We have a young lady on our street, Sarah, that was in her class last year. Sarah has a 2-year-old boy. And I said, "I'm not saying Sarah is bad . . ." 'cause supposedly Sarah got raped by her mom's boyfriend or something like that. . . . So, I'm like, "Number one, you're not to be down there [at Sarah's house]. I don't have a problem with Sarah per se. I [just] don't want this for you. Therefore, if you want better, you have to hang around people who want better. Your standards have to be a little higher. That's not saying you can't speak or conversate with Sarah. That's saying Sarah is not goin' to be the focus of your life . . . because when you hang out with people like that, whether your standards is up here [motioning], eventually they come right on back to theirs. I want your standards to be up here and I want them to remain up here. Therefore, you hang around with people whose standards are up there."

Although Barbara was empathetic toward her daughter's friend, she wanted her daughter, Chrystal, to take a different path. Barbara attempted to help Chrystal along that different path by restricting her from having boyfriends. She stated her position bluntly: "Boyfriends? We don't do boyfriends." Mona, a Latina working-class mother, had a similar view. She said, "I mean, just going out with boys and that—no!" In contrast, Tamara, an African American working-class mother, emphasized self-control to her daughter, on the one hand, and "watchin' every move she make," on the other. She explained:

I just have to keep an eye on her. I'm just, so far, lucky that I am not no grandmama. . . . [Vanessa is] still a virgin, cause I took her to the doctor to make sure of that. . . . I'm just tryin' to keep Vanessa on that level where she's still a virgin and keep her in school 'cause she keeps sayin', "Mommy, I want to go to college." [I] said if you want to go to college, you can't be taggin' a baby along with you. . . . I know she got grown men lookin' at her. It's gonna be the same way with boys. I just want her to have control of that; have control of the flesh and she doesn't have to worry about nothin' else.

Working-class parents wanted their daughters to get through their teenage years without having to endure a pregnancy or sexual assault. Avoiding pregnancy, in particular, was key to maintaining working-class parents' hopes for their children's successful transition into adulthood.[2] For many working-class parents, this meant attempts at delaying their daughters' sexual debut—by limiting boyfriends, openly discussing sexual matters, and monitoring their clothing choices—and providing access to birth control.

In short, working-class parents saw their children's transition to high school as a key moment in negotiating a successful transition to adulthood. For them, it was a transition fraught with potential peril. Given the criminal behavior, drug use, and teenage pregnancy they encountered in their neighborhoods and their children's schools, working-class parents saw how easily adolescents could lose their way. Barbara's description of what she thought was important to parenting her daughter through this stage of life reflects well those of her counterparts:

Bein' more hard on her and keepin' her closer to me and knowin' exactly where she is. Not sayin', "Yeah, go ahead, you can go," but takin' her there and knowin' that she's goin' to be there. Knowin' that there is another parent there if there's supposed to be, and if they're not she gets back in the car and comes home with me. Just bein' more aware of her whereabouts, where she's goin', what's she doin', who's she being involved with, you know, socializing with, and like everything.

As a group, working-class parents underscored the importance of vigilance in their parenting. Watchful vigilance was almost impossible to maintain when parents had to work and adolescents spent time in places beyond their parents' gaze. It is also part of a parenting strategy that contrasts sharply with that of their middle-class counterparts.

FOSTERING AUTONOMY AMONG THE MIDDLE CLASS

Autonomy in the Neighborhood and Larger Urban Context

Middle-class parents described early adolescence as a time to develop their children's autonomy. Middle-class parents did so by developing in their children the skills and competencies needed to live away from home during college, as well as by granting them increasing freedom to move about their neighborhoods and city on their own, as well as to stay at home alone. Jacky, a White middle-class mother of twin boys, felt that it was time for them to take more responsibility for themselves. She said, "You really want them to take the responsibility . . . you wanna shift all that stuff." Continuing, she explained:

> You got 4 years to practice [for] when they are on their own. They gotta be able to do their laundry, they gotta be able to go grocery shopping. . . . I mean, there's a lot. Those are really key things—to know how to cook for yourself. You know, if I had to ask my kids how to get to our house by public transportation, I think their main way is to go to the school and get the bus that they know home, even though there are other routes that go to our house. But they know little pieces. My goal, before they leave, is they can go to a city they don't know, get the transits thing and figure out how to get where they needed to go. . . . It's all a matter of preparing them to go off into the world and be able to take care of themselves.

Preparing their children to be "in the world" made fostering independence an important parenting goal for middle-class parents. Their sense of safety in their neighborhoods helped them to pursue it. Kira, a White middle-class mother of 8th-graders at different schools, increasingly gave her children freedom to roam their neighborhood, even while keeping in mind their residence in a major city. She said:

> I respect that it's city life, but, in general, I don't worry that they're out and about. Just recently, we've let Ruby walk around without a friend. They've got cell phones, [and] we're always more careful with just a single girl than my son. So, [the neighborhood is] fairly safe, but I think they both know that they live in the city.

Like several other middle-class parents, Wendy, a White middle-class mother, began to let her son come home alone after school. She said:

> I think it's pretty safe, but it's the city. I mean, you are still in the city. He comes home and he has a key. Up until 2 years ago, I had a woman in after school [who] would come in.

However, allowing children to travel home alone was not without worry for middle-class parents. Erica, an African American middle-class mother, told us about her daughter's transition to taking public transportation home from school alone. To verify that she arrived safely, Erica called her daughter every afternoon on her cell phone, demonstrating what Nelson (2010) observes to be a growing practice for middle-class parents—using cell phones to be "aware of and intimate with their children" without crossing the line toward excessive monitoring (10). Yet, Erica worried about Faith forgetting to turn on her cell phone because, she said, Faith "would get so tired [that] she would fall asleep on the bus. She would end up at the end of the line, wake up, and be panicking." Erica worked with a family therapist on a technique to help Faith remember to turn on her phone. She described the technique:

> When I started Faith on public transportation, I had a hard time getting her to remember the things that she was supposed to do. . . . So [the therapist] would say, "Tell Faith, and this is exactly how you want to tell her, Faith, when you get out of class, go to your locker, open your book bag, turn on your cell phone." So, we did this every day until Faith would say it. She taught me how to do that, so that I'd get [Faith] to remember things that were really crucial as far as I was concerned, because when she first started [using public transportation], I would panic so bad.

Erica allowed Faith the freedom to travel home after school alone, but she taught her strategies to be safe. Erica said:

> It's more teaching her [how] to protect herself: don't put yourself in certain situations; when you get on a bus, look around the bus, [note] who's on the bus, and make a conscious decision [about] where you're gonna sit. Same thing when she gets to the [train]. . . . I tell her all the time, "If you see a bunch of boys all the way in the back of the bus, you don't want to go way in the back to sit." She had something stolen from her when she got on the bus, and she said, "Mom, I can't remember it being taken out of my bag." I said, "Probably you didn't feel it, because the busses are so crowded at school time." I said, "What are you gonna do the next time you get on a bus?" She said, "Well, maybe I should take my bag off my back and put it in front of me." So, now it's more of teaching her how to be aware of her body, her surroundings, where she's going, what she's doing. Before, I was the one that would protect her. Now, it's: "You gotta pay attention."

Erica even allowed for the possibility that her daughter might like to do something after school instead of coming straight home. She had no problem with that, so long as Faith informed her:

I take for granted that she is only 14 years old, and instead of coming right home from school, they might go to the bookstore or stop at the pizza shop or things like that. I don't see anything wrong with that, because it's right down from the school. But I just need her to be aware of the need to phone [me in case] anything happens, I know where you are.

Grace, a middle-class mother who identifies as African American and Asian, worried about her daughter, Haley, traveling alone, but felt that it was time to give her daughter "more wings." She explained: "I don't really like her catching the bus to many places, where[as] her girlfriends catch the bus all over the place. I can't do it . . . but I noticed I have to 'cause it's holdin' her back. So, I have to give her more wings and let her go a little bit more." Like Grace, Theresa, a White middle-class mother, began to rethink her former limits on her children's freedom of movement:

It seems like it's the beginning of that figuring out what they can do. With Violet, [we've asked ourselves,] "OK, so, are we gonna let them take the bus to the movies with a group of friends?" So, thinking about boundaries, what the rules are, and then talking with the kid about them.

Sal, a White middle-class father, described the process of extending more freedom to his sons so that they eventually could feel like the "city's theirs." He said:

And now that he and his brother are older, every month their territory gets a little bigger and now they're riding public transit on their own and walking to their friend's house that's six blocks away. So, we're hopefully gradually building up to where they can feel safe and know what's going on, know what to watch out for, and get out there on their own.

For middle-class parents, in contrast to their working-class counterparts for whom adolescence meant a continuation of or recommitment to vigilance, entry into high school marked a time of extending greater freedom and expanding opportunities for children to move outside parents' purviews and to navigate larger swaths of the city on their own (see also Harding 2010). Middle-class parents' expectation that their children would leave home for college and be "in the world" motivated their focus on developing their children's independence. Thus, developing children's facility with public transportation and their competence in being home alone and doing more for themselves constituted a kind of training for when they would leave home for college.[3]

Securing the *Best* Academic Experiences

Middle-class parents had fewer concerns about their children's peers and emerging sexuality than working-class parents had. For example, not a single middle-class parent brought up the issue of teen pregnancy. What middle-class parents did worry about was providing their children with the *best* academic experiences. Middle-class parents strategically sought to provide not just good academic experiences for their children, but the *best* ones to prepare them for elite high schools and colleges. For some, this meant hiring a tutor to help with academics. For others, it meant getting their kids into the most advanced courses offered at school, in particular, starting the algebra sequence in middle school (Gamoran and Hannigan 2000). Jerome, mentioned above, told us about the advantages of enrolling his children in the advanced math track at McKinley:

> The way McKinley structure[s] it, in terms of its math curriculum, it's a year ahead of the rest of the district. If you're in the advanced math track . . . you are 2 years ahead of the rest of the district. So, [my son is] taking Algebra II now as part of a group of 35 kids. [For] my daughter, for example, what it meant for her is that she had 2 years of calculus before she went to college; 2 full years of calculus . . . which really helped her. She's [got] like near perfect scores in math.

The advanced math sequence, which began in 7th grade, prepared the way to college for Jerome's daughter. His son is on the same path.

Getting into advanced math was not a given for all students who wanted to take the course. Performance on an exam at the end of 6th grade (that was administered without notice to students and parents), along with some other criteria that was not freely shared, governed placement into the one available section of the Algebra I course in 7th grade. Those who were not selected, the majority of students at McKinley, would take pre-algebra in 7th grade and then proceed to Algebra I in 8th grade. At the time there were two 6th-grade math teachers and, according to parents, one of them specifically prepared students for the placement exam while the other did not. Jacky, a White middle-class mother, explained: "They create an elite at this point (end of 6th grade), and this one teacher determines it mostly because he preps the kids for the test. . . . They don't tell the parents. It's all secretive." About the other 6th-grade math teacher, Jacky shared: "We had a horrible math teacher last year. He didn't teach things properly . . . a lot of kids flunked math and a lot of kids got really derailed." Wendy, a White middle-class mother also expressed concern: "Nothing was sent home to the parents as far as how the determination was made. Nothing was sent home about your kid even." The lack of transparency about the testing procedures alongside the disparate math education received in 6th grade raised questions for these parents. They felt that if the test had been announced in time to prepare and that all students received the same test preparation at school, their children would have been successful in placing into advanced math. But perhaps most upsetting to them was their own children's reactions. Jackie said that her son "was really traumatized by not being in there" as he "gets hundreds on all his math tests this year. He certainly should have been in." And Wendy recalled, "Victor came home and he was upset. He had a 98 percentile nationally, and it just didn't make any sense to me."

Given these concerns, Jackie, Wendy, and other McKinley parents individually emailed the principal to find out more about the placement process. The school was transitioning from one principal to another. Wendy felt the outgoing principal "brushed her off" with the response, "Well, you know, Algebra I is for kids who love math and have math-related interests." Wendy, whose son plays on the schools' highly ranked chess team, wrote back: "What is chess?" And when Jacky requested her child's test results, the principal simply refused.

These parents persisted in their efforts, expressing their concerns about the placement process to the new principal and chair of the math department. They demanded that their children have access to the double-accelerated curriculum. Jacky explained: "They have a school full of gifted kids and they select 32 for a special math tracking. That was my point. Well, the [new principal] actually agreed with me." In other words, Jacky and other parents objected to stratification of the accelerated math curriculum at their elite middle school.

It was too late, however, to add an additional section of Algebra I. As an alternative, the principal provided supplemental math education for students who desired it. Jacky narrated: "So he gave us a teacher two mornings a week [at 7 a.m. before school] to do Algebra I. But then they ran out of money, so the program got cancelled [after four months]." Nevertheless, the parents felt this approach was successful. Students' supplemental math education, along with their pre-Algebra course, and test review by Jacky, prepared them to take Algebra II in the 8th grade. As Jacky explained: "We got two days, but that was enough time for me. I got all the kids at my house, and I prepped them [for the next placement test]." Jacky reported that the students did well on the placement exam and advanced to Algebra II in 8th grade. Wendy added that after this experience, the principal decided to put all 7th-graders at McKinley into Algebra I.

The efforts of McKinley parents to secure the best math education possible for their children is rooted in their understanding of the importance of higher-level math for STEM majors in college. For example, Jacky ran a science-based business with her husband and had something very specific in mind when she thought about her children's education. She said: "We want them to be able to take physics with calculus. We want them to have calc in the 11th grade, so they can take the good physics in 12th grade. That's our goal." Middle-class parents had knowledge about math curriculum and prerequisites for a variety of educational pathways. They also had the skills to negotiate with school administration as well as the ability to remain firm, persistent, and organized in their objectives, and supplement the school's efforts with their own tutoring. They strategized to obtain an additional acceleration at a school that already enrolled all students in an accelerated curriculum. Their efforts paid off, and their children received not only the best math instruction that McKinley offered, but the most elite math education available in the school district.

SUMMARY

All parents were concerned with their children's safety and well-being and wanted them to make successful transitions to adulthood. Parental approaches for helping their children accomplish that goal varied by social class, however. The approach we take to understanding class differences in parenting highlights how social contexts relate to parenting practices. The class differences documented in this chapter, we suggest, are rooted in the contexts and conditions in which parents found themselves.

Working-class parents in our study engaged in defensive parenting. They described their children's proximity to physical danger and to temptations to engage in behavior that could thwart their social mobility. Working-class parents attempted to protect their children from harm and negative influences by intensely monitoring them and restricting their behavior and privileges. For girls, parents tried to prevent early childbearing by various means, from educating them to requiring the use of birth control to prohibiting boyfriends and sexy clothing. Working-class parents vigilantly monitored their children's lives through what was, for them, a precarious transition to adulthood within the context of a perilous environment.

Middle-class parents, who did not live in areas where crime, drug dealing, and pregnant teens were commonplace, while not casual about their children's safety and well-being, viewed their role as parents as one of developing autonomy in adolescents as they entered the high school years. In general, a key strategic goal for middle-class parents was to foster their children's autonomy, creating the confidence and skills they would need in order to safely and competently move about the city. These are skills that middle-class youth will need as they encounter new cities and contexts outside of their parents' purview when they go off to college in 4 years. Rather than threats to their children's well-being or social mobility, middle-class parents were concerned with providing their children the best academic credentials they could in order to successfully navigate the college track.

CHAPTER 4

Opportunities to Participate

Unequal Contexts and Social Class Differences in Structured Activity Participation[1]

Participation in organized activities has important implications for adolescents. In addition to shaping how young people spend their free time, involvement in organized activities is associated with emotional and cognitive development (Hofferth and Sandberg 2001), attachment and commitment to school (Finn 1989; Marsh 1992), and academic performance (Marsh and Kleitman 2009). Structured activity participation also provides adolescents with opportunities to develop interests and skills that may alter the trajectory of their lives. Working on the school newspaper may spur some teens to become journalists; taking private piano lessons may set some on the path to becoming professional musicians; while playing in the city soccer league may reveal to others that they are destined for something other than professional sports. Moreover, organized activities can influence adolescents' educational trajectories, given their effects on youths' chances of attending college as well as on their odds of enrolling in selective institutions (Kaufman and Gabler 2004; Karabel 2005; Gabler and Kaufman 2006; Soares 2007; Stevens 2007; Marsh and Kleitman 2009).

The benefits of organized activities flow disproportionately to children in middle-class families because they evidence higher participation rates than their working-class counterparts. In this way, participation in organized activities has become a mechanism through which social inequality is maintained and reproduced. Our objective in this chapter is to engage with the debate about the causes of class differences in activity participation. Some scholars offer cultural explanations for class differences, while others offer more structural ones (Furstenberg et al. 1999; Lareau 2002, [2003] 2011; Hofferth 2008; Hughes 2008; Lareau and Weininger 2008a). For example, Annette Lareau, based on extensive observations of middle- and working-class families, argues that middle-class parents use enrollment in extracurricular activities as a means to cultivate children's talents and skills, while working-class parents are comfortable giving their children comparatively greater autonomy in how they spend free time, and therefore emphasize enrollment in activities less (Lareau [2003] 2011; Lareau and Weininger

2008a). Thus, for Lareau, class differences in activity participation stem from divergent class cultures. Chin and Phillips (2004), in contrast, investigate the ways cultural, social, and "child" capital shape children's participation in organized activities during the summer. Their research suggests that class differences in activity participation arise from differences in financial resources, knowledge of ways to develop children's interests, and information about how to connect children to activities. Consistent with Chin and Phillips (2004), we observed in Chapter 2 large class gaps in the utilization of social networks as information channels regarding matters in the domains of parenting and schooling, with middle-class parents using their network resources for this purpose more than working-class parents.

Our focus on how social contexts matter for parenting practices calls for situating the class gap in activity participation not only within families (e.g., Lareau [2003] 2011; Chin and Phillips 2004), but also in the various contexts in which the family is embedded—schools, neighborhoods, and the wider community (Bronfenbrenner 1979; Luster and Okagati 2005; Kotchick and Forehand 2002).

Class differences in activity participation may reflect differences in the school contexts of working- and middle-class children; however, processes of social reproduction and leveling by schools have yet to be fully explored with respect to class gaps in structured activity participation. School systems in the United States are characterized by both racial and class segregation, which creates the conditions under which working- and middle-class children attend separate and, often, qualitatively different schools (Kozol 1992, 2005; Orfield and Eaton 1996). Bourdieu and Passeron (2000) most famously theorized the ways in which schools reproduce social inequalities. McNeal (1999) finds that school size and climate significantly affect participation, such that students in large schools and schools with difficult climates display lower levels of activity involvement.

Conversely, schools may serve to narrow or "level" class differences in activity participation by equalizing opportunities to participate. Several researchers have revealed how schools ameliorate social class differences in a variety of educational outcomes (Holloway and Fuller 1992; Entwisle and Alexander 1992; Downey, von Hippel, and Broh 2004; Condron 2009). Because myriad structured activities are offered for little or no cost in public schools, schools may provide low-income students more opportunities to participate in activities than are available to them outside of school. To the extent that public schools that serve working-class youth offer a variety of organized activities, schools may have a leveling effect on class differences in participation much the same way they do with respect to other educational outcomes (Entwisle and Alexander 1992). Neighborhood institutions may play a similar role by offering low-cost activity options that are easily accessible, both financially and geographically, to working-class families. The leveling effect that schools and neighborhood institutions may have on organized activity participation has been little explored by social scientists, thus far.

By analyzing activity participation in schools, neighborhoods, and the wider community, as well as investigating parents' cultural logics regarding participation, this chapter shows that class differences in social contexts provide a better explanation for the class gap in participation than do cultural differences. First, we show that the size of the gap varies dramatically by social context, in this case, between activities at school and activities away from school. Because of financial constraints, working-class families rely on social institutions for affordable participation opportunities but have access to few such institutions beyond schools and churches, which are the ones prevalent in their neighborhoods. This explanation is consistent with beliefs expressed by working-class parents regarding the value of activity participation for their children, the concentration of their children's participation in school and religious activities, as well as the virtual lack of participation outside of school in the kinds of elite activities that colleges and universities value. Thus, we find that working-class parents in this study are quite supportive of organized activities, but their children participate in fewer and different activities than their middle-class counterparts due to limited financial and institutional resources.

Second, we show that working-class parents in our study use organized activities as part of their parenting strategies just as middle-class parents do, and they articulate many of the same reasons for doing so as their middle-class counterparts. Third, the reasons for participation that are specific to each group illustrate our concepts of defensive and strategic parenting. That is, working-class parents, but not middle-class parents, indicate that they support their children's involvement in organized activities for safety reasons and to open doors to future opportunities. These reasons reflect the dual objectives of defensive parenting, which are to shield children from harm *and* to facilitate their social mobility. The sole reason uniquely articulated by middle-class parents—customization—reflects strategic parenting. Middle-class parents, by virtue of their financial resources, have a great deal of choice regarding their children's activities; that freedom allows middle-class parents to be strategic about their children's experiences, choosing only those that mesh with their children's capacities and that will further their development.

STUDYING PARENTS' ENGAGEMENT WITH STRUCTURED ACTIVITIES

In our interviews with parents, we asked about programs in which their 8th-grade children participated at school and outside of school, extracurricular and after-school programs, as well as activity participation related to community, religious, and ethnic organizations. In other parts of the interviews, we asked parents to describe their typical weekdays and weekends, which often revolved around their children's schedules. Answers provided to those questions create a natural way to triangulate narratives about structured activity participation.

We leverage the strengths of interview methodology by employing two approaches to assess parents' cultural logics regarding youth activity participation. First, we utilize a structured activity participation scenario for discerning parents' beliefs and values regarding structured activity participation. The scenario is a description of the organized activities and schedule of participation for a fictional child. As such, it is a hybrid instrument that sits between reliance on observations of parents' behavior to reflect their beliefs about activity participation and soliciting their thoughts on this particular aspect of parenting. Here, we ask parents to comment on the fictional child's activity participation schedule, which makes the inquiry into their beliefs more concrete than if we had asked parents to comment on activity participation generally. Moreover, by constructing the scenario around a fictional child, we implicitly invite parents to step outside of their own reality in an effort to free them from resource considerations as they evaluate the activity level depicted in our scenario.[2] Thus, their responses should be expressions of their "conceptions of the desirable" (Kohn [1969] 1977, 7) rather than expressions of what they think is possible given their present circumstances. Separately, we asked parents to share with us their thoughts regarding their own children's participation (or nonparticipation) in activities.

We define a structured or organized activity as one that (1) is adult led, (2) occurs on a regular basis, and/or (3) has an organizational or institutional affiliation. Structured activities do not include time spent alone or activities in which children merely hang out with friends or relatives (e.g., watching TV, playing games, going to the mall). With activities identified, we then grouped them into seven types: (1) sports, (2) cultural, (3) academic, (4) school service, (5) hobby, (6) youth development, and (7) religious. Activities that qualify as sports and hobby are well known, but those we classify as cultural, academic, school service, and youth development may not be. Cultural activities include those that involve the arts (e.g., music, theater, and dance). Academic activities include ones that focus on academic pursuits (e.g., tutoring, science club). School-service activities are those that assist the school with its functioning (e.g., student government, yearbook, library assistance, student diplomat). Youth-development activities are ones designed to help children with life skills (e.g., scouting, secular teen groups). Finally, religious activities include church/synagogue/temple/mosque going and other activities offered by places of worship, such as youth groups.[3]

We incorporate social structure into our analysis by paying attention to the ways in which opportunities to adopt particular parenting practices are socially distributed, in this case, how they vary by social context. We do so by distinguishing between school-based and out-of-school activities. This distinction reveals the role that schools play in structuring opportunities for participation, particularly for working-class children. In addition, we use information gathered from the websites of schools to form what we call *structured activity choice-sets* that each school offers its students. We supplement this material with information obtained during interviews with parents. That is, we add to a school's activity choice-set any school activity in which a respondent's child participates but that is not listed on the school's website. We believe this approach permits us to come close to forming a comprehensive picture of the opportunities for participation in activities that each school offers its students.

SOCIAL CLASS DIFFERENCES IN STRUCTURED ACTIVITY PARTICIPATION

Parents reported a total of 186 nonunique activities in which their children participated during their 8th-grade year, ranging from as few as none to as many as 10 per child. Consistent with prior studies (Lareau [2003] 2011; Chin and Phillips 2004; Dumais 2006; Lareau and Weininger 2008a), we observe class differences in participation, with the middle class having participated in the most activities (5.0 per child) and the working class having participated in the fewest (2.4 per child), on average (see Table 4.1).[4] Examining the frequency distribution for working- and middle-class families reveals further differences between them. Middle-class families are much more evenly distributed across the entire range of activity participation than are working-class families (see Figure 4.1). The majority of working-class families are concentrated at the lowest levels of participation, with three of them reporting no activities. Nevertheless, participation among working-class adolescents is not trivial. Collectively, working-class parents reported 71 nonunique activities. Additionally, involvement in activities is widespread among working-class families; 26 of 28 families reported activities in which their child(ren) participated.

Table 4.1. Level of Participation in Structured Activities by Middle-Class and Working-Class Adolescents

Social Class	No. Activities	Means		
		All	In School	Outside School
Middle Class	115	5.0	2.0	3.0
Working Class	71	2.4	1.5	0.9

Note: Sample contains 23 middle-class and 30 working-class adolescents.

Figure 4.1. Distribution of Middle-Class and Working-Class Parents Across Number of Reported Structured Activities

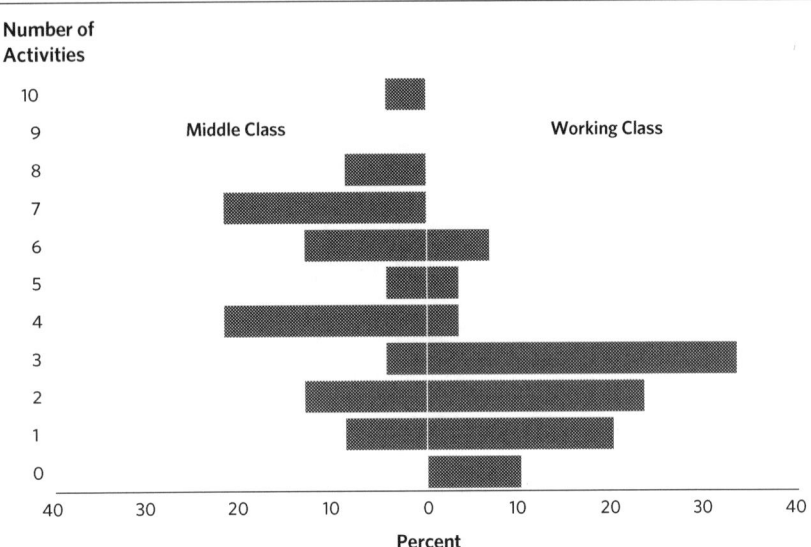

Figure 4.2 presents the percentage distribution of activities across activity types for working- and middle-class families and paints an overall portrait of the kinds of activities in which adolescents and parents became involved. Working-class adolescents participated in a variety of activities. Among the seven types that we identify, religious, sports, academic, and cultural activities were the most prevalent reported by working-class families, accounting for 79% of their activities. These types of activities were also popular among middle-class families, but to a somewhat different degree.

There are, however, differences in the kinds of activities in which working- and middle-class families invested their time, money, and energy. Three are worth noting. First, religious activities—often church attendance—account for a sizeable percentage of the activities of working-class adolescents but only a small percentage of those of middle-class teens (22.5% compared with 8.7%). Second, hobby activities, such as chess club, were relatively popular among middle-class youth but account for a much smaller percentage of the activities of their working-class peers (11.3% vs. 4.2%). And third, participation in youth-development activities is almost absent among middle-class adolescents, although it accounts for 9.9% of the activities of working-class teens.

Together, these findings reveal that while activity participation among working-class families was not as high as it was among their middle-class counterparts, participation was routine for them. Adolescents from both

Figure 4.2. Distribution of Middle-Class and Working-Class Involvement in Structured Activities by Type of Activity

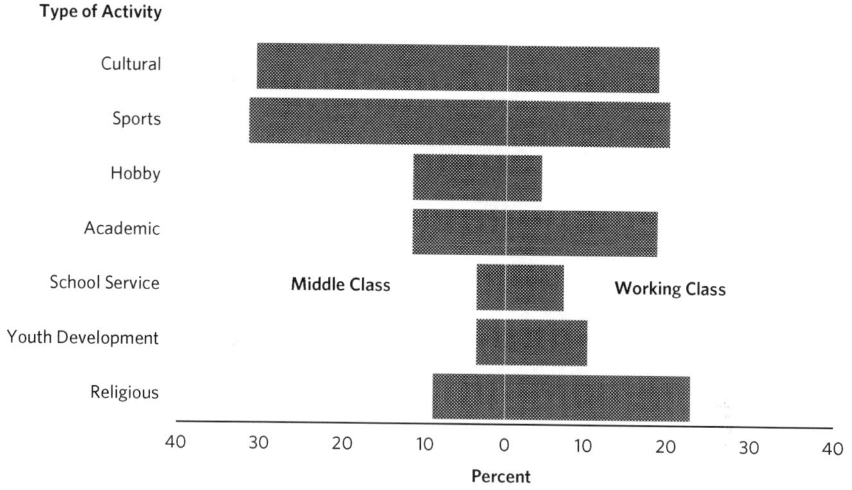

Type of Activity: C = cultural; S = sports; H = hobby; A = academic; SS = school service; YD = youth development; R = religious.

social classes participated heavily in sports and cultural activities, which are precisely the kinds of activities that are expected to have implications for later educational outcomes. Kaufman and Gabler (2004), for example, find that participation in interscholastic sports is associated with increased likelihood of attending college. Such activities are expected to facilitate students' academic achievement by helping them to increase their commitment to school (Marsh 1992) and to create identities that are tied to their school and its mission. Likewise, cultural activities are associated with increased odds of attending elite colleges, as participation in such activities may signal to teachers and admissions officers that students are familiar with and appreciate middle-class norms and culture (Soares 2007). That working- and middle-class youth participated heavily in such activities suggests that both groups of parents have positioned their children in activities that may pay educational dividends. These commonalities exist in the presence of an important difference, however. Despite meaningful participation in cultural activities by working-class adolescents, youth from middle-class families had even greater involvement in such activities, in addition to higher participation in hobby clubs, both of which are associated with enrollment in elite colleges and universities (Kaufman and Gabler 2004; Gabler and Kaufman 2006), whereas working-class children made greater investments in religious activities.

PARENTS' EXPRESSED CULTURAL LOGIC

Parents' Responses to the Structured Activity Participation Scenario

For our first approach to assessing parents' beliefs about involving children in organized activities, we analyze their responses to our structured activity participation scenario. Recall that the scenario is designed to free parents from the particular constraints in their personal lives so that they may express their "conceptions of the desirable" (Kohn [1969] 1977, 7), unencumbered by what they feel is merely possible. In it, we describe the activities and schedule of a fictional child. The scenario reads:

> Some children participate in many school and out-of-school activities. For example, let's take an 8th-grader who plays in the school band, which means he/she has band practice for an hour and a half three times a week after school. He/She also plays on a neighborhood sports team and has practice every Saturday afternoon and has a game once a week. Sometimes the games are away and so he/she travels with the team.

After we read this scenario to parents, we invited their responses with the question: "What do you think of this child's level of participation in extracurricular activities?" Table 4.2 displays the results of this exercise.

There are several points to take away from this table. First, a similar percentage of working- and middle-class parents responded positively to the fictional child's level of activity participation—57.2% and 45.5%, respectively, indicated it was "good" or "great." Second, parents of both classes indicated caveats to their positive disposition toward the schedule of activities. Yet, those caveats reveal possible differences in concerns between the two groups. Working-class parents were concerned with whether the child's activities interfered with their ability to do well in school (14.3%), while

Table 4.2. Percentage Distribution of Middle-Class and Working-Class Responses to Structured Activity Participation Scenario

Social Class	Depends on Child	Too Much	Too Little	Good or Great Amount	QUALIFIERS TO GOOD AMOUNT			Missing	Total
					None	If School Work Is Ok	If Family Is OK		
Middle Class	18.2	27.3	4.5	45.5	31.8	9.1	4.5	4.5	100.0
Working Class	0.0	32.1	0.0	57.2	42.9	14.3	0.0	10.7	100.0

proportionally fewer middle-class parents expressed that concern (9.1%). Rosalinda, a Puerto Rican working-class mother who worked as an office administrator, commented: "I think it's good for a kid to stay active; to do other things as long as it's not interfering with the homework and that kind of stuff." Similarly, Carla, an African American working-class mother who worked as an assistant preschool teacher, noted:

> It seemed like a lot, but if it's something that works out for the child, and his grades are still where they should be, then I would say that it is still a good outlet because it's time that they're not gettin' in trouble or finding [out] about things that they shouldn't be into. So, it is a busy, busy schedule but, I don't know, our schedule might be the same. [Laughing]

Third, working- and middle-class parents were somewhat similar in their assessment that the amount of participation in our scenario was unequivocally too much for our fictional child (32.1% and 27.3%, respectively). Moreover, they arrived at that assessment for similar reasons. Both groups expressed concerns about (1) the lack of rest or down time such a schedule would afford the child, (2) the complicated logistics and stress placed on parents inherent in such a schedule, and (3) the amount of time such a schedule requires. Working-class parents in this "too much" group differed from their middle-class peers only in their concern that a busy activity schedule might reduce the amount of time the fictional child had available to do homework.

Perhaps working- and middle-class parents were similar in their assessment of the scenario in part because some middle-class parents, but no working-class parents, made their responses contingent on the child in question. Almost a fifth (18.2%) of middle-class parents indicated that they could evaluate the level of participation of our fictional child only in light of what the child wanted or was capable of managing successfully. For example, Bette, a White middle-class attorney, stated: "I think it depends on the kid. There are some kids that thrive on that and there are some kids who stress on that. So, it just really depends on the kid."

Thus, working-class parents in our study were as likely as their middle-class peers to view active participation in the scenario positively. This finding is bolstered by class similarities in parents' use of social networks to support their children's activity participation: 47.6% of middle-class parents did so as did 42.3% of working-class parents (see Table 2.5). Only when working-class parents saw participation as a threat to children's academic performance did they waiver on whether an active schedule was positive for children. Among those who expressed concerns regarding our fictional activity schedule, worries about time for schoolwork was a prominent theme, but one not mentioned by middle-class parents. For their part, middle-class parents were distinctly concerned that the schedule fit with a child's interests, capacity, and desired level of involvement; these concerns were not expressed by working-class parents.

Parents' Support for Their Children's Activity Participation

To further understand parents' cultural logics, we analyze their thoughts about and reasons for supporting their own children's participation (or nonparticipation) in structured activities.[5] Although a variety of reasons for activity participation emerged within and across social classes, the majority of reasons fall into a relatively small set of categories. Research contributing to cultural explanations for class gaps in activity participation indicates that working-class parents support a parenting philosophy that does not emphasize enrollment in organized activities (Lareau [2003] 2011), but we find much support for children's participation among working-class parents in this study. Moreover, those parents offered many of the same reasons for supporting activity participation as their middle-class counterparts. Yet, we also find that working-class parents gave two reasons that are scarcely mentioned by middle-class parents: safety and pathways to future opportunities. Both groups of reasons—common ones and those unique to working-class parents—are explored below.

Shared Reasons for Supporting Participation in Structured Activities

Working- and middle-class parents provided similar reasons for their children's participation, such as supporting their child's interest in an activity, keeping active, personal development, increasing the academic skills of their adolescents, and providing a venue for teens to socialize with peers.

Child's interest. For many parents in both social classes, their child's interest in an activity was a primary reason for supporting it. In many cases, children independently chose activities based on their interests, with little to no initial input from their parents, but with their parents' support.

Carina's daughter is a fan of sports. Carina, a Latina working-class mother, enrolled her daughter in sports based on that interest and her daughter's athletic talent: "She likes anything related to sports, [especially] track. She always got first place. I like it [too]. I support her in everything she wants to do."

In another example, Marie, an African American middle-class mother, discussed her son's enthusiasm for acting in plays, noting that "Jeff wants to sing. Jeff wants to act. So, that play allows him to do it. He's so excited, and this is what he loves. I'm hoping that next year he'll get a lead part. He takes it seriously. He just gets all into it." There is little doubt that Jeff's participation in plays during middle school allowed him to hone his skills, and it may have been instrumental in his admission to a performing arts high school.

Personal development. Both middle- and working-class parents cited personal development as a primary reason for their children's participation in activities. Personal development through organized activities can include the learning of values of the larger society or social group (e.g., cooperating with others), the development of adolescents' personal qualities (e.g., overcoming shyness or gaining emotional well-being and maturity), or the learning of personal skills or lessons that may be useful or advantageous to have as adolescents grow and transition into adulthood (e.g., how to persevere or handle rejection). Bette is a White middle-class mother whose daughter participated in Girl Scouts, acting classes, school book club, school guitar ensemble, and a writing program at a local university, among several others. She also participated in two summer camps during the year of the interview: a Buddhist family camp and film camp. Bette indicated that her daughter's many activities are important in terms of self-exploration:

> I think it opens doors and allows you to try new things, explore
> who you are, meet new people, find out what kind of people you're
> comfortable being around, and how to be comfortable with different
> kinds of people.

Rosalinda, a Puerto Rican working-class single mother of three who worked as an administrative assistant, described how her daughter's participation in a salsa dance troupe helped her to develop persistence:

> It helps them. There are certain moves that are difficult and they have
> to figure it out and practice it. It gives them that drive, that goal, like
> "I want to do this." So, it teaches them to kinda fight to get where
> they want, where they need to be, and to get better. It shows them that
> practicing gets better.

Harriet, an African American working-class mother, felt that her son's position on the school football team was positive because "he gets to see both sides of the coin—the good and the bad of life." Holly, a White middle-class mother, felt her son's participation in sports taught him similar lessons. She especially appreciated that her son was "learning how to handle rejection if you don't play, and take defeats and wins, and be a good sportsman."

Parents in both social classes observed how sports participation helped their children learn to handle winning and losing, as well as how to cope in a competitive environment in which they may not always be the best. Some

parents also stressed that team sports helped their teens appreciate cooperation and unity, while others noted that sports contributed to their children's
self-esteem.

In comparison to the domains of family and school, parents saw structured activities as an alternative environment where children might feel
more comfortable trying new things, meeting different people, and, along
the way, overcoming shyness. In this way, parents described structured activity participation as a positive opportunity for personal development.

Academic knowledge. Working- and middle-class parents cited the acquisition of academic knowledge as an important reason for participation
in extracurricular activities. This reason was offered primarily by parents
whose children participated in tutoring programs or academic teams. Sarah
is an African American working-class mother whose daughter received tutoring after school. Sarah worked as a housekeeper at a hotel and liked her
daughter's participation in tutoring. She considered after-school programs
as indicators of a good school, particularly because she did not feel that she
had the knowledge to help her daughter with homework:

> I look for after-school homework programs because the work that
> they teach the children now, I don't know how to do it, and my
> children come to me and say, "Mom, how do you do this? I'm lost!"
> I'm lost. I can't—the math is new math and the way they, the teachers,
> teach them is different from what I was taught. And I'll show them my
> way and they say, "No; this is how we do it."

Likewise, Grace, a middle-class paralegal of African American and
Asian descent whose daughter participated in math tutoring, offered academic knowledge as a primary reason for her daughter's participation in
this activity: "She chose to go on her own because she was having problems
with math. I'm good at math, but [her school's] math is kinda like college
math, so we kind of worked together. So, yeah, she picked that herself and
I'm glad for it."

Keeping active. Another reason for activity participation given by both
working- and middle-class parents was that it keeps their children busy and
active. For example, Grace, mentioned above, said, "I don't see any drawbacks [to participation in activities]. The benefits—that it keeps her busy."
Juliette, a Haitian working-class mother who worked as a nurse's aide, said,
"You know, that's me. Keep her busy, you know."

Olivia is a White middle-class parent with a multiracial child. Her
son participated in basketball and track at school as well as ice hockey
and keyboard lessons. Olivia, a teacher, said, "I really encourage him to,
because like I said, I don't like him to sit at home all the time. And I don't

want him hanging out, that kind of thing. So, yeah, I'm really happy that he does it."

Socializing. Both middle-class and working-class parents indicated that they appreciated extracurricular activities because they give children an opportunity to get to know and socialize with other kids. For example, Holly, a White middle-class social worker whose son participated in basketball at school and basketball, baseball, and football outside of school, said, "The benefits are, you know, definitely socializing."

Anne is an African American working-class caseworker whose daughter participated in two church youth groups and tennis camp in the summer. Of her daughter's participation in the church youth groups, she shared: "I think it's great. She's really well-rounded. She's not just focusing on the religious aspect. It's very social for her, too. They have movie night; they go bowling; they ride bikes." She went on to say: "It's keeping her faith-based, but it's also expanding the group that she's in. Primarily since [her school] is such a small school, she's able to meet other kids who don't go to that school. So, she has other outside interests, which is good."

Jerome is an African American middle-class father who has his own consulting business and works from home. His son participated in a variety of cultural and academic activities both in and outside of school, which gave his son an opportunity to "meet girls" and socialize with other kids. Jerome said: "I think sometimes he just kind of . . . hangs out at school with other kids, or hangs out in the library or hangs out and just chats with other kids, and gets to know some of the kids that are in the choir and all that. So, it's like a social function."

Variation Across Social Class in Support for Participation in Structured Activities

In addition to sharing with middle-class parents some reasons for supporting involvement in extracurricular activities or viewing them as beneficial, working-class parents offered reasons that were distinct to their experiences.

Safety. Ten working-class parents but no middle-class parents cited keeping children safe and away from trouble as an important reason for their children's participation in structured activities. These parents described their neighborhoods as dangerous places and preferred to see their children stay in the environment of their school or other location where organized activities take place. Among those who gave safety as a primary reason for their adolescents' activity participation, 80% also articulated concerns about the level of danger in their residential environment. This is consistent with differences in the amount of crime in the neighborhoods of working-class and middle-class parents in this study, as documented in Chapter 1.

Gabriela is a single working-class mother of three from Central America who worked as a hotel housekeeper to support her family. She was very concerned about dangerous elements in her neighborhood. When asked to describe her neighborhood, she replied: "I think it's the worst. [Chuckling] It's the worst, but the economic situation forces me to live where I live, unfortunately. But I ask God, that I can get out of there one day." Gabriela did not want her children to spend time outside for their own safety. She stated: "It worries me. The thing is, I want to know what it is that they're doing. I don't know; I don't trust the surroundings." Her 8th-grade son participated in a youth-development activity at school. As part of the program, he tutored younger children after school. Gabriela felt her son's involvement kept him away from danger:

> There are too many drugs. There, in [this city], that school, it's very dangerous. Too many people selling it [drugs] on every corner, and definitely, we have to see all of it. The kids can see, and I thank God and this program. Really, that's what has helped keep him occupied, that after school he helps kids around the age of my youngest girl. It's a program with parents that work like me. We don't pay. It's a great help. And that's how my son hasn't gotten involved with those people, guns, drugs, with bad people.

When asked about how satisfied she is with her son's participation in the after-school program, she said:

> Yes, I'm satisfied, because it's helped those kids a lot, that they not be on the street. Definitely. I don't know who invented that, but [it is] the nicest thing. Kids that could be on the street with drugs, they're entertained there.

Gabriela liked her son's participation in the youth-development program because it reduced his exposure to the neighborhood. She said, "I try for them to stay occupied." Sarah, an African American working-class mother, voiced similar sentiments about the potential for her son to be exposed to what she characterized as "negative" behaviors in the neighborhood. She shared:

> I like homework programs and I like football for the children. So many children get caught up in the street and they have nothing to do, so they sell drugs and rob people. They do more negative things than positive things. So, the longer they stay in school the better. For me, being in the neighborhood that I grew up in, I think doing stuff away from the neighborhood is better than being in the neighborhood, standing on corners, getting involved in the wrong crowd. I'd rather

for my child to be involved in something. Like they say, "If you don't stand for something, you'll fall for anything." So, I'd rather for them to be involved in something.

Sarah hoped her son's involvement in football and in a program that provides homework assistance would both afford him a safe environment during after-school hours and give him opportunities to "stand for something" one day.

Overall, the working-class parents in our study articulated both the danger they perceived in their immediate surroundings as well as how they addressed threats to their children's well-being. Structured activities were a primary component of their efforts to keep their children safe.

Future opportunities. Another reason for supporting children's involvement in structured activities given by five working-class parents but no middle-class parents is that structured activities are linked to future opportunities. In this sense, working-class parents saw their children's activity participation as part of their mobility strategy. Some parents saw a link between activities and educational success, while others viewed the activities themselves as pathways to future opportunities. Polly, a White working-class mother, described how her 8th-grade daughter participated in a variety of extracurricular activities, such as church youth group, Civil Air Patrol, summer prep for military school, and a modeling program. Polly saw participation in these activities as part of a pathway to college:

All of it's geared to getting them into a good college, which I like. The Civil Air does a lot of the college type thing. If they finish the whole entire program in Civil Air, there's grants available to go to college through that program, which is one of the reasons why I put my son in it [and] also part of the reason why I like [my daughter] being in it. Between the school and the grants that are gonna be available because of the school, and then Civil Air's grants, she's got a very good chance of getting into an extremely good college.

Juliette, the nurse's aide from Haiti, viewed her daughter's extracurricular activities as part of a strategy to help her academically as well as to give her ideas for future careers. Her daughter participated in the youth-development program at school and in church band. As part of the youth-development program, her daughter received help with homework, which is something Juliette valued:

For me, the benefit is that I see it's helping the kids to do something after school. Helping the kids to do homework is very good. You pushing the kids to do something for tomorrow; so, it's very good.

Juliette felt that the youth-development program helped her daughter to move toward a positive future, both by providing her daughter with homework assistance and by teaching her particular skills that could make available future opportunities. Juliette noted:

> If she focus on so many things that [she] learn at the [youth-development program], it could [set] her for tomorrow. She says she wants to be nurse, pediatrician nurse, but she could change her mind; she say, "OK, I learned art at the [youth-development program], I think I'm gonna do art. I'm gonna open art school," whatever. So, if she do that, that will be good, because she's gonna show somebody else what she learned.

Entertainment and recreation are insufficient reasons to participate in structured activities, according to Juliette. She wants her daughter to participate only in activities that provide something valuable for her future:

> Some parents be happy to send the kids all over the place; let the kids [be] involved with so many different things, see so many friends, they don't care. But for me, it's a little bit different. I want my kids involved with something that I know is gonna [be] good for your life. I don't see any basketball, I don't see a lot of these activities [as] good. I really want to see my kids doing something, you know, make me happy about.

For some of the working-class parents in this study, not only were structured activities desirable for their intrinsic value; they were important for their utility in securing future opportunities.[6]

Making Sense of Parents' Support for Youth Participation in Structured Activities

Overall, both working- and middle-class parents were overwhelmingly supportive of their children's participation in organized activities. Among those who viewed participation positively, 19 parents expressed some drawbacks to it, which for most (16) included concerns about time, rushing, transportation, and potential overscheduling that could reduce time for family, homework, and relaxation. These concerns were raised primarily by middle-class parents (12). In only one case was a parent mostly unsupportive of activity participation; in this instance, a working-class father was unsupportive of his daughter's involvement in activities (sports, in particular) because of concerns about outside influences on her. However, even this father expressed that he wanted his daughter to take voice lessons but could not afford them.

Together, our findings raise questions about the extent to which cultural logics explain class gaps in involvement in structured activities. Working-class parents in our study showed a great deal of support for participation in organized activities in general, and for their children's participation in particular, as did middle-class parents. To the extent that working-class families voiced concerns about active participation schedules, they did so with concerns for children's academic performance in mind. They also worried about coping with the logistics of getting children back and forth to activities, given school and work schedules, along with the stress that heavy participation places on parents themselves. These concerns similarly were voiced by middle-class parents.

Consistent with prior work, however, is evidence that middle-class parents are interested in customizing their children's experiences (Lareau [2003] 2011). Recall that almost a fifth (18.2%) of middle-class parents, but no working-class parents, attempted to evaluate the activity schedule of our fictional child only from the perspective of the child's wishes, talents, and ability to handle the commitments that such a schedule entails. This group of middle-class parents placed no universal value on a highly active versus a somewhat inactive participation schedule apart from the child's specific abilities.

Some of the reasons for supporting participation among the working-class parents were similar to those of the middle-class parents (such as the child's interest, personal development, and the acquisition of academic knowledge). However, some working-class parents, but no middle-class parents, cited primarily a desire to keep their children safe and, to a lesser extent, shape future outcomes. In this way, working-class parents' use of structured activities illustrated their use of defensive parenting—the combined pursuit of safety and social mobility for their children. The responses of working- and middle-class parents to our structured activity scenario and their articulated reasons for their own children's activity participation are summarized in Figure 4.3.[7]

Our findings on parents' practices (i.e., enrollment of children in activities) combine with our findings on their expressed logic to reveal a puzzle—differences in the behavior of working- and middle-class parents but substantial overlap in their perspectives on activity participation. That is, class differences in behavior do not appear to reflect class differences in parenting logics regarding organized activities. In the next section, we attempt to shed light on the question that has emerged from our data: Why do working-class youth demonstrate less participation in structured activities than their middle-class counterparts, given similarities in their parents' perspectives on the value and desirability of participation? The answer, we argue, lies in what our data reveal to be the role that social structure plays in the lives of working-class families.

Figure 4.3. Parents' Concerns About and Reasons for Children's Participation in Structured Activities by Social Class Location

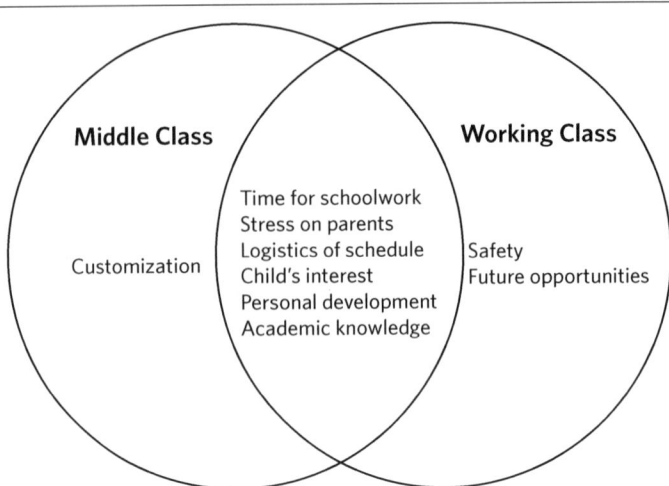

SCHOOLS AS EQUALIZING INSTITUTIONS

We distinguish between school and out-of-school activities to investigate structural influences on activity participation. We find that a clear majority of the activities in which working-class children participated were school-based activities; more than half (62%) of their activities were organizationally tied to their school compared with only 40% of the activities of middle-class youth. Moreover, the class gap in activity participation is smaller for school activities than for out-of-school activities. Working-class youth participated in an average of 1.5 school activities, which compares favorably with the 2.0 school activities in which middle-class adolescents participated (see Table 4.1). Where working-class children fell short, and much shorter than their middle-class counterparts, is in participation in out-of-school activities. For these, they participated in fewer than one activity (0.9), on average, compared with 3.0 activities among the middle class.

These findings have at least three implications. First, schools serve as a critical avenue through which the children of working-class families become involved in organized activities. Second, where opportunities for participation are readily available, working-class parents demonstrate an interest in and commitment to supplementing the lives of their children by investing time, energy, and money in their children's involvement in activities. Finally, without the opportunities for participation that schools provide, the social class gap in activity involvement likely would be much larger than that previously documented.

That working- and middle-class children in our study differentially be-came involved in school versus non-school activities has implications not just for their *level* of participation but for the *kinds* of activities in which they participate. Figure 4.4 presents percentage distributions of school and out-of-school activities for working- and middle-class children across activity type. This figure underscores the role schools play in class differences in structured activity participation in this study. The working-class and middle-class distri-butions for school-based activities are somewhat similar. Both groups display high levels of participation in sports and cultural activities and, to a lesser ex-tent, academic and school-service activities. Middle-class children had greater participation, however, in hobby activities while having no involvement in youth-development activities, although these class differences are rather small compared with those found in out-of-school activities.

Figure 4.4. Percentage Distribution of School and Non-School Activities Across Activity Types by Social Class Location

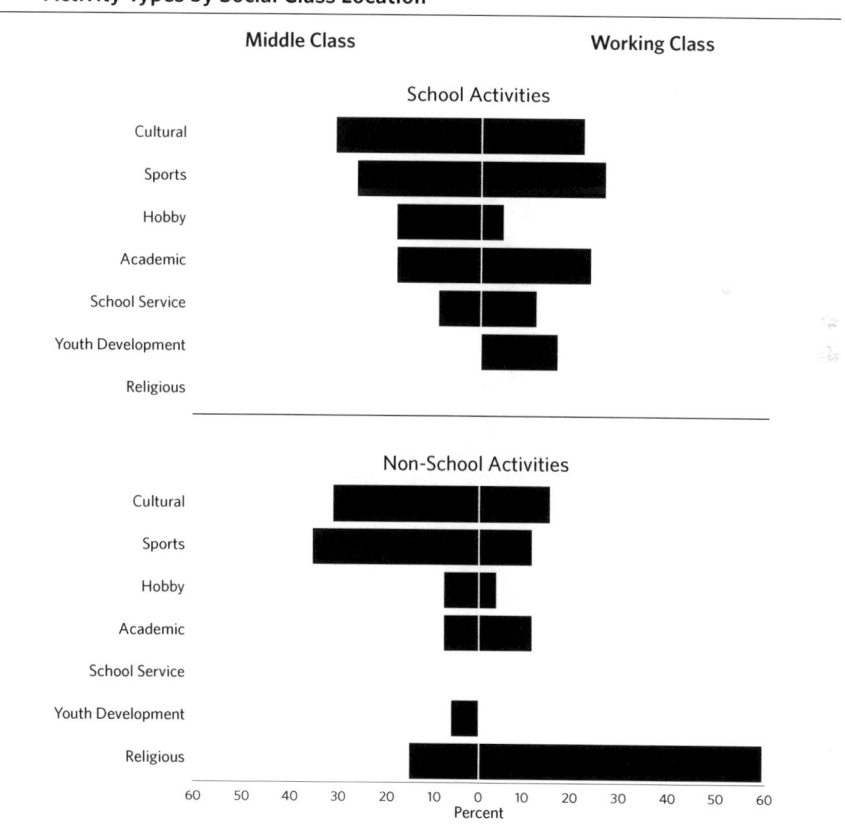

Activity Type: C = cultural; S = sports; H = hobby; A = academic; SS = school service; YD = youth development; R = religious.

Working- and middle-class families in this study differ strikingly in their non-school activities. Middle-class children display heavy participation in cultural and sports activities, with less participation in academic and hobby activities. Thus, their investments in activities outside of school mirror, to some extent, those they made in school. In contrast, working-class children invested heavily in religious activities, often regular church attendance, church choir, or church youth group. Although these children also participated in cultural, sports, and academic activities outside of school, they did so to a much lesser degree than in school. Thus, it appears that the decisions that the working-class parents and children in our sample made about where to invest time, energy, and resources outside of school are rather different than the choices they made about which activities to pursue in school.

The seven categories of activities reflected in Figure 4.4 necessarily mask the variety that exists within them. But it is the diversity within cultural, academic, and school-service activities across schools, for example, that also may shape class differences in the kinds of activities in which working- and middle-class children participated. Indeed, the activities offered to children through schools are surely structured by the financial and human resources that schools possess. Consequently, the range of activities available to children—their *activity choice-set*—is structured by the schools they attend. The extent to which working-class children attend schools that offer a limited choice-set of activities, particularly compared with the range of activities available at schools attended by middle-class children, may serve as an underlying source of class differences in extracurricular activity participation. It also may have implications for the ways in which organized activities pay off, or fail to pay off, given connections between activity participation and educational outcomes (Kaufman and Gabler 2004).

Research on the academic consequences of participation in organized activities suggests that certain school-based activities may increase the odds that students will be admitted to college, while other activities may raise their chances of enrolling in selective colleges (Eccles and Barber 1999). Gabler and Kaufman (2006) find, for example, that participation in music, student government, and interscholastic sports is associated with an increased likelihood of attending college, while participation in hobby clubs, school yearbook, and school newspaper increases the chances of attending an elite university. Using these findings as an evaluative lens on the activity choice-set offered at our two schools, we find that the middle-class school offered its students somewhat greater opportunities to participate in activities that may pay educational dividends in terms of college attendance and selectivity.

Before reporting on the differences between the two schools, however, we describe their similarities. First, the two schools offered a similar number of structured activities (see Table 4.3). Second, there is overlap in the choice-set of activities at the two schools, particularly with regard

Table 4.3. Structured Activities Offered by Working-Class and Middle-Class Schools

Type of Activity	Augusta Middle School	McKinley Middle School
Sports	Golf Cheerleading* Indoor Soccer Softball Basketball* Track* Volleyball* Flag Football Net Sports Drill Team*	Flag Football* Gymnastics* Basketball* Track* Volleyball*
Cultural	Dance Club* Drama Club* Combined Chorus	Jazz Band Orchestra Choir Concert Band Guitar Ensemble* Drum Lessons* String Orchestra French Heritage French Club Ink Drinkers Literature Club Musical Stage Crew
Academic	Science Club* Book Club/Books Without Borders* Oratorical Competition 1 Oratorical Competition 2 Words Shook World Odyssey of the Mind Math Club Math Power Hour Reading Tutoring Reading Prep for State Exam Math Homework Club Open Library	National Academic League* National Honor Society Spanish National Honor Society Book Club/Books Without Borders* Biology Tutoring Physical Science Tutoring Math Tutorial English Tutoring Science Tutoring Ecology General Science/Biology Homework Club Math "Twenty-Four" Game Science Fair Activities Science Fair Computer Open Lab Library Extended Day

(continued)

Table 4.3. Structured Activities Offered by Working-Class and Middle-Class Schools (continued)

Type of Activity	Augusta Middle School	McKinley Middle School
School Service	Literary Magazine Yearbook Fundraising Committee* Tutoring (as tutor)* Volunteering* Library Assistance* Student Computer Technicians Morning Announcement	Literary Magazine Student Council Eighth-Grade Council/ Graduation Student Diplomat Yearbook Coordinators Library Assistance*
Hobby Club	Model Program* Computer Club* Sports Club Sewing	Chess Club Chess Team Run Club
Youth Development	Girl Talk Youth Development*	Girl's Circle Project Teens
Other, Unclassified	Fast Forward 24 Club IRAP (Internet Research & Publishing) Eighth-Grade Sponsor Amigos de Clemente Day Generation Next	Allies SADD

*Reported by parent, but not by the school.

to sports and school-service activities. Both schools provided students the opportunity to participate in team sports (e.g., flag football, basketball, softball, and volleyball), serve on yearbook committees, publish literary magazines, and work in libraries alongside school librarians. Both schools also offered an array of academic activities. In sum, both schools gave students opportunities to participate in activities that have the potential to pay educational dividends.

There are meaningful differences, however, in the range of activities available at the two schools. In particular, the schools offered markedly different hobby and cultural activities. Although the working-class school presented a greater variety of hobby activities, the qualitative differences between them and those offered by the middle-class school are substantial. In one hobby activity, chess, the middle-class school is rather unique in that it provides its students expert-level instruction such that its team is able to compete nationally. There were no expert-level hobby activities at the working-class school. Moreover, the middle-class school offered a number of cultural activities that research suggests may serve as credentials that boost students' chances of attending college by signaling to teachers and college admissions officers that students either come from middle-class backgrounds or have elite cultural tastes. Activities such as jazz band, orchestra, choir, and concert band are just such activities, yet they were available only at the middle-class school. According to data obtained from the list of activities on the website of the working-class school, students there could participate in only one cultural activity—the school chorus—although parents indicated that drama club and dance club were options. If students were interested in participating in other kinds of cultural activities in order to acquire cultural capital, they would have to do so outside of school and with, no doubt, greater financial and time investments than would be required if these activities were offered at their school.

These findings illustrate that schools can serve as both levelers of class differences in structured activity participation as well as contributors to such differences.[8] With respect to the types of activities in which children become involved, schools may contribute to class differences by offering to students qualitatively different activities even when they offer the same number of activities. Regarding level of participation, however, the schools in our study clearly serve to reduce class gaps in participation. Consequently, we are left with the question of what undergirds class differences in out-of-school activities.

FINANCIAL AND INSTITUTIONAL CONSTRAINTS ON NON-SCHOOL ACTIVITIES AMONG THE WORKING CLASS

At least two possible explanations for social class gaps in non-school activities emerge from our interview data: (1) fewer financial resources in working- versus middle-class families and (2) weaker institutional capacity in working- versus middle-class neighborhoods. A classification of activities that emerged from the data (in contrast to the literature) suggests three groups of non-school activities: elite activities, (non-elite) religious activities, and (non-elite) secular activities. Elite activities are ones often discussed in the literature as those that provide cultural capital to youth, as well as provide them with educational benefits like increased odds of attending college. They include activities such as chess, music and dance lessons, and summer programs at selective universities and other institutions. Religious activities are, as we previously defined them, those that are offered by religious institutions, such as church youth groups. Secular activities are non-elite activities that are unaffiliated with religious institutions or organizations, such as sports in community leagues. This categorization makes strikingly clear just how different working- and middle-class children are in their out-of-school activities. Figure 4.5 shows the percentage distribution of elite, non-elite secular, and non-elite religious activities for the two groups. Although the class gap in non-elite secular activities is 17.6 percentage points, it is substantially larger for elite activities—31.7 percentage points.[9] We suggest that class differences in financial resources undergird gaps in participation in elite activities, while the scarcity of secular institutions devoted to youth programs in working-class neighborhoods may undergird class gaps in secular activities.

Participation in elite activities often requires sizeable financial investments. Middle-class parents reported spending $400 a year on foreign language classes, $300 to $1,080 a year on music lessons, $90 to $3,337 a year on dance lessons, and $2,600 to $12,500 per year on chess lessons and competitions per child. Such financial commitments are possible for parents who command substantial financial resources. The relevance of financial capital to participation is further illustrated by examining differences between upper-middle-class and lower-middle-class families.[10] Just over 40% of the out-of-school activities of adolescents in families that earned more than $75,000 annually were elite activities, whereas only 26.3% of the activities of middle-class families that earned less were such activities, which corresponds to a gap of 14.1 percentage points. In contrast, the gap in participation in non-elite secular activities for these groups is only 4.7 percentage points. No doubt, then, that participation in elite activities was more difficult for working-class families who command more modest incomes.

Certainly, there were cases in which working-class youth were able to gain access to elite activities, such as when students obtained scholarships.

Figure 4.5. Percentage Distribution of Non-School Activities Across Elite, (Non-Elite) Secular, and (Non-Elite) Religious Activities by Social Class Location

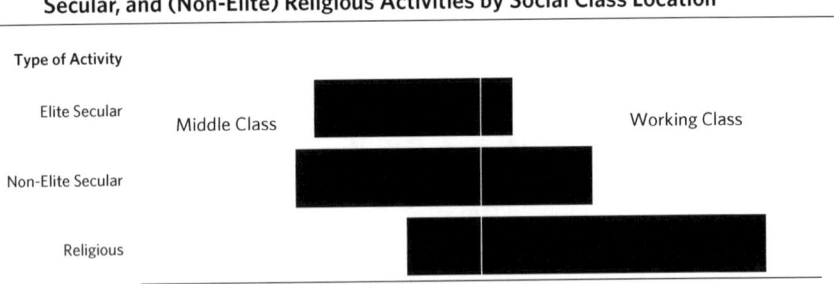

Activity Type: E = elite; S = (non-elite) secular; R = (non-elite) religious.

Kenneth, for example, was a talented emerging artist whose mother in the past had been able to secure scholarships to a local art college where the instructors are professional artists. Other working-class children were able to attend private and university-based summer programs through scholarships. However, these represent exceptional experiences among the working class.

Indeed, the financial realities of working-class families are made clear by their responses to our question as to whether they had ever been prevented from doing something for their child because of financial limitations. Some parents explicitly identified limits on their adolescents' participation in activities. For example, Anne, a Black working-class caseworker, indicated that she was unable to send her daughter to a summer program at an elite university because of financial limitations. She stated:

> A lot of kids are going to summer programs. I know [an out-of-state elite university] had asked, and there's a camp for gifted youth. I didn't have the money. I would have liked her to go, but it was just outrageous. There was a science camp that I wanted to send her to, [but] I just couldn't do it. So, in that regard, I would say, yeah, there's a lot of things I wish I could have been able to do.

The cost of the summer camp would have been approximately $3,500 or more, depending on programming and book fees.

Although Anne made a connection between financial constraints and her daughter's participation in activities, relatively few working-class parents did when asked whether and how financial limitations had prevented them from doing something for their child. Perhaps the reason is that they often mentioned more basic elements in the hierarchy of human needs, like food, bills, and basic school supplies, without addressing the less "prepotent" needs of belonging, self-esteem, and self-actualization that one associates with structured activities (Maslow 1943, 394). For example, Gabriela, a Latina working-class mother who worked as a hotel housekeeper, described why her son had to get by with only two sets of school uniforms instead of the five she wanted to buy for him:

> I'm not gonna go to buy the two changes of clothes until the first [of the month], with what I earned Saturday and Monday. I've left it 'til the last minute, because it's too much. Since I pay $1,600 in rent plus electric, gas, [and] phone, we're talking about $2,100. God willing, next year, I'll be able to give him the luxury of buying him the five pants [and] the five shirts, but not this year. They're going to have to deal; wash and wear.

Other parents (as well as Gabriela) further indicated that financial constraints had prevented them from providing their children with educational opportunities they felt were important, such as attendance at private/
Catholic school, home computers, and savings for college.

Middle-class parents also indicated that they had been prevented
from doing something for their children because of financial constraints.
Slightly more than half of them felt that way, some of whom explicitly
mentioned limits on activities (in particular, summer programs abroad and
at elite universities), but also travel to learn a foreign language, private
school attendance, vacations, and savings for college. However, the tone
of conversations on this topic with middle-class parents was substantially different from that with working-class parents in that no middle-class
parent cited a basic need as something their child had foregone because of
financial constraints.

Middle-class children's enrollment patterns in non-elite secular activities, especially in contrast to their working-class counterparts, implicates the community as a second possible source of class differences in
participation in out-of-school activities. If disadvantaged neighborhoods
contain fewer institutions and organizations than middle-class areas,
then the community emerges as a source of stratification with respect to
structured activity enrollment. Recall that working-class parents relied
more heavily than their middle-class counterparts on schools to provide
opportunities for their children's involvement in activities. This finding,
along with that of their heavy participation in religious activities outside
of school, suggests a broader reliance upon public institutions for activity
participation, particularly given their financial constraints on participation in elite activities. Indeed, the majority of non-elite secular activities
that middle-class children were involved in (organized sports) were tied
to community organizations (i.e., sports leagues). Yet, only two working-
class children in our sample were involved in organized sports outside
of school. We suspect the lack of involvement in such activities is not
reflective of the interests of working-class youth, particularly given their
level of involvement in sports at school, but rather is due to the absence
of organizations devoted to the interests of youth in working-class neighborhoods. This means that activities tied to religious institutions may
substitute for some of the non-elite secular activities working-class youth
might opt to participate in if such activities were available in their neighborhoods, as well as for some of the elite activities that working-class
parents found cost prohibitive.

Indeed, the literature on neighborhood social organization and youth
development describes the relative absence of effective social institutions
in disadvantaged neighborhoods (Wilson 1987, 1996; Quane and Rankin
2006). With respect to organizations that provide opportunities for activity
participation, Delbert S. Elliot and colleagues (2006) note that

Institutions that provide recreational and supportive educational services to youth—YMCAs, Big Brothers Big Sisters, Little Leagues and other recreational programs, Boy Scouts and Girl Scouts, Boys and Girls Clubs—are less likely to be found in disadvantaged neighborhoods and those that are located in these neighborhoods typically have fewer resources than those in more affluent neighborhoods. (107)

We investigated whether the incidence and types of institutions in the community in which our working-class respondents lived, fit such a description. We attempted to identify activities in the community through web searches and communication with the following organizations: the city recreation department, a nonprofit organization that organizes volunteer-led activities in the city (which compiles and publishes a list of all structured activities in the city by zip code), and various organizations that offer youth activities in the vicinity of the neighborhood school. We found few secular activities other than those offered through religious organizations or schools. The absence of activity offerings tied to community institutions is consistent with the neighborhood organization literature (Connell, Alber, and Walker 1995).[11] Given that people with meager resources are disadvantaged in their efforts to create high-quality neighborhood institutions and services, as well as in their efforts to attract and retain external support for those that exist (Connell Alber, and Walker 1995), it is unsurprising that our search for secular activities connected to neighborhood organizations bore so little fruit.

SUMMARY

In our investigation of social class differences in structured activity participation, we relied on the strength of qualitative data analysis to identify elements in the lived experiences of individuals that hold potential to reframe the way we view social phenomena. Like other studies, we find greater participation in structured activities among middle-class children than among working-class children. However, the ways in which class differences vary across social contexts point more toward a structural than a cultural explanation. For example, working- and middle-class youth were similar in their participation in school activities, but differed substantially in their out-of-school activities. If cultural logics substantially undergird class differences in activity involvement, we would observe distinct class patterns in participation in school-based activities, not only in out-of-school activities. That we do not poses a challenge to existing theories in which cultural logics take center stage, at least as they are used to interpret class differences in participation in organized activities. Indeed, only a single expressed belief about activity participation emerged as unique to middle-class parents in this study—a desire to customize children's experiences. Such a desire is a component of strategic parenting and a theme consistent with Lareau's ([2003] 2011) "concerted cultivation." Although working-class parents employed a different approach to parenting than their middle-class counterparts (i.e., defensive vs. strategic parenting), they understood the value of, supported, and instrumentally used their children's participation in structured activities.

Working-class parents' support for structured activity participation is consistent with historical work on shifts in parenting practices regarding children's play (see Chudacoff 2007). Additionally, Lareau ([2003] 2011) reminds us that the emphasis on structured activities among the middle class is the result of their shift to a parenting logic that helps transfer class advantage to their children. We can look to studies on admissions to elite colleges for at least one reason why they made this shift. Historically, academic achievement has accounted for only a portion of what college officials considered in assessing "merit" for admission. To admit candidates who could pay full tuition and maintain a college's connection to privileged families, elite colleges placed "character" and "leadership" on par with, and sometimes ahead of, scholastic achievement or ability (Karabel 2005; Soares 2007). As leadership became synonymous with high-level positions in clubs, organizations, and sports, an impressive structured-activity profile became essential for gaining access to elite colleges. The consequence, according to sociologist Mitchell Stevens (2007), is that "the system that the elite colleges and universities developed to evaluate the best and the brightest is now the template for what counts as ideal child rearing in America" (247). We find that working-class families, like middle-class families, have come to understand (at least somewhat) the relationship between activity participation and educational (and occupational) opportunities.

Indeed, the relatively few ways in which the logic of working-class parents varies from that of their middle-class counterparts map less along cultural lines and more along the objective realities of people whose children live and learn in places with little opportunity but too much danger. Because of limited financial resources, working-class families navigate social contexts that are rather different from those of middle-class families; they attend qualitatively different schools and live in qualitatively different neighborhoods, as demonstrated in Chapter 1. Those contexts inform the foremost goals and concerns that parents have for and about their children, thus making the immediate objectives of working-class parents different from those of their middle-class counterparts. The reasons for activity participation uniquely articulated by working-class parents—to ensure safety and promote routes to future opportunities—reveal their anxieties about the current well-being and future prospects of their children. For the children of working-class parents in this study, the mundane achievements of reaching adulthood unscathed (or at all), graduating from high school, attending college, and finding meaningful employment cannot be taken for granted (Burton, Allison, and Obeidallah 1995). Thus, working-class parents use structured activities to achieve both goals of defensive parenting—securing the immediate physical safety of children while ensuring opportunities for their social mobility.

That these themes are absent from the responses of middle-class parents, we believe, is due to the security they feel regarding their children's physical safety and prospects for status maintenance (or social mobility), both of which are informed by the neighborhood and school contexts that their economic resources help to provide. Middle-class parents, then, are free to focus on which college their children will attend, rather than whether they will attend (much less whether they will graduate from high school). They are also free to use structured activities to develop the talents and interests of their children and to help them navigate a path of adolescent development toward success as they define it, rather than use activities to shield their children from harm. Thus, the extent to which parents adopt particular parenting practices and hold a particular logic for doing so, we argue, reflects less their class culture than the class-related conditions in which they find themselves.

The relevance of structural factors to class differences in activity participation is not limited to the impact on how and why parents use organized activities. Social institutions, like public schools, neighborhoods, and community organizations, also shape opportunities for participation. Schools reduce social class gaps in activity involvement by offering free and low-cost activities in which youth from modest socioeconomic family backgrounds can participate. Because of financial constraints, working-class families relied more heavily on activities that were organizationally tied to their children's schools; without them, class gaps in activity participation likely would be larger than those previously documented.

These findings parallel the phenomenon of "summer setbacks" identified by sociologists Doris Entwisle and Karl Alexander (1992), who found that schools played a "leveling role" (83) by constraining class gaps in achievement, which grow larger during the summer months when children are out of school and exposed only to the environments that parents create. In similar fashion, schools in our study narrow class gaps in structured activity participation. To be sure, what it means to be "out of school" in our study differs from that of the Entwisle-Alexander study. Nevertheless, the gap in activity participation between working- and middle-class families is driven mainly by their out-of-school experiences, when children must rely on their parents to give shape and content to their time away from school.

But the role of schools in class gaps in activity participation was not solely one of reducing class inequality, because schools differed in the kinds of structured activities they offered. Although the working-class school provided opportunities to participate in many of the same kinds of activities

in which middle-class children were involved, there are important qualitative differences between them, particularly in the areas of academic and
cultural activities. The presence or absence of opportunities to participate
in high-quality cultural activities at school has greater implications for
working-class youth, whose families are unlikely to have the financial resources to provide such activities on their own. In this way, our findings are
consistent with those of Chin and Phillips (2004) regarding the importance
of financial resources for children's activity participation, and of Downey
and colleagues (2004), who find that schools both reduce and exacerbate
class differences.

Our findings also reveal the importance of local institutions beyond
schools in shaping opportunities to participate in organized activities. This
is especially consequential for working-class youth. Whether due to the lack
of resources of neighborhood residents or to the political and economic motivations of outside actors to undermine and withdraw public institutions
from inner cities (what Wacquant [2008] calls "organizational desertification
of the ghetto" [218]), the relative scarcity of institutions other than religious
ones in the working-class community contributes to restricted opportunities
for non-school-based activities available to working-class youth.[12] Research
indicates that participation in activities during middle school increases the
chances of participation in the same activity in high school by 30% for ath-
letics, 27% for cheerleading, and 29% for fine arts, net of socioeconomic
background and academic factors (McNeal 1998). Activity participation in
high school is predictive of college attendance and destination (Eccles and
Barber 1999; Kaufman and Gabler 2004), with implications for children's
ultimate educational attainment.

The concern here, then, is whether schools and other institutions in
working-class neighborhoods allow adolescents to begin to accumulate
valuable cultural capital in middle school that can be developed more fully
in high school and then presented to colleges as part of their academic and
personal profiles. Although the working-class school in our study offered an
array of extracurricular activities, other schools may find it difficult to do so
in the presence of financial constraints, the "back to basics" movement, and
high-stakes testing climates that have worked to trim the menu of activity
offerings at schools across the country (Kozol 2005; Stevens 2007). Cuts to
organized activities by policymakers are thought to address both financial
and academic problems by allowing school officials to reallocate funds to
more "pressing" concerns while allocating more time to reading, writing,
and arithmetic. The result is that an important public school function becomes privatized.

Middle-class youth are less likely to attend schools affected by calls
to return to the basics of education, but even when they encounter such
pressures, the financial resources of their families protect against loss of

opportunities to participate in activities. Middle-class families can privately finance their children's study of art, music, foreign languages, and sports, whereas working-class families likely have neither the financial nor neighborhood institutional resources to compensate for reductions in school activities. And even when working-class youth are able to access organized activities away from schools, there is reason to anticipate important qualitative differences between their non-school activities and those of their middle-class counterparts. In our study, for example, four working-class families reported participating in a total of four cultural activities outside of school. Two of these activities were offered by churches, a third was offered by a community theater, and the fourth was organized by parents themselves. In contrast, 15 middle-class parents reported 21 cultural activities in which their adolescents were involved away from school. Middle-class youth participated in these activities as private lessons, through art centers, universities, and foreign exchange programs.

In sum, then, the failure of working-class parents to employ a parenting style akin to concerted cultivation very well may have been the reason for the class gap in activity participation at the time of Lareau's ([2003] 2011) influential study. However, adoption of concerted cultivation by working-class parents would leave in place their class-related disadvantages in financial resources and social contexts that powerfully shape children's involvement in organized activities. For the working-class families in this study, threat of neighborhood danger, dependence on (scarce) local public institutions, and modest financial resources worked to maintain low levels of activity involvement among their children, even when parents demonstrated interest in and commitment to extracurricular activities.

The experiences of working-class families manifest the ways in which the actualization of values is contingent upon social structural support. The dependency between values and social structure has been recognized in other studies of educationally relevant parenting practices. In particular, Min Zhou and Susan Kim (2006) investigated what some believe to be a culturally based phenomenon—high levels of academic achievement among the children of Asian immigrants (Stevenson and Stigler [1992]; see Goyette and Xie [1999] and Hsin and Xie [2014] for discussion). Zhou and Kim conclude that high educational aspirations among Korean and Chinese immigrant parents interact with structural elements in ethnic communities, namely, an ethnic system of supplementary education involving ethnic-language schools, which produces high levels of achievement among their children. Thus, both our study of class differences in activity participation among a multiracial, multiethnic sample, and Zhou and Kim's study of educational achievement among the children of Asian immigrants, demonstrate that the actualization of values requires a "culture-structure interaction" (Zhou and Kim 2006, 17). This implies that in order to close the class gap in organized activity participation, the social conditions in which working-class parents are embedded must be amenable to the full expression of their values around activity participation. So long as structural supports that facilitate participation in organized activities are limited in the social contexts of working-class families, namely, financial and neighborhood institutional resources, there will remain a gap between parents' values and their ability to actualize them.

CHAPTER 5

In Search of a Good School

Middle-Class and Working-Class Parents' Navigation of the High School Application Process

Observations of a Parent Meeting

On the night of the parents' meeting about the high school application process, McKinley's auditorium was packed with parents of 8th-grade students. McKinley is unusual in that it has both a middle and a high school, but the high school classes are smaller than the middle school classes and only about half of the current 8th-graders will be accepted into the high school. The rest will have to resort to other options in the citywide high school choice system. The principal spoke about the benefits and opportunities available to those who stay at McKinley for 9th grade, stressing its academic rigor. He also talked about lighter themes such as the high school sports programs and the privilege of eating lunch in the auditorium or outside.

A teacher put the high school application form on the screen onstage and described the sorting process to the parents. Students apply for area high schools in the fall and hear about their acceptances in the spring. They may apply for a handful of schools or programs, but no more than one program per school. Some schools have additional requirements, such as an essay. The teacher warned parents not to try to game the system by listing only a couple of choices and thinking that the schools will have to accept the student. He went on to say that if you don't apply to more than one high school and you have Cs and Ds, McKinley can't take you and you're going to be "stuck in your neighborhood school." He added that if parents are happy with the neighborhood school, then they don't have to apply for a high school. Parents at the meeting asked many questions about the application process. The parents' meeting wrapped up after a current McKinley 12th-grader spoke about her experiences at the school. She stressed the wonderful community at McKinley and stated that it prepares you for life and provides "the kind of education that you value." She emphasized that the small community of McKinley offers good opportunities for strong college recommendations and emphasized that the teachers have connections with professors at local universities.

Given the introduction of school choice policies in urban districts, the transition to high school is increasingly important and competitive. In such places, students do not universally move into particular high schools from their feeder middle schools. Rather, the middle to high school transition is characterized by a selection process akin to that for postsecondary education, whereby selection into high school increasingly takes choice into consideration. In the district where our study took place, parents and students are not obligated to participate in this process and, if they do not, are assigned by the school system to their neighborhood high school. Alternatively, parents and students can submit applications to various high schools in the city. In this process, high school destination is determined by myriad factors, such as grades, test scores, attendance, punctuality, behavior, and, in some cases, a lottery when schools receive more applications from qualified students or students from feeder schools than they can admit. Outcomes of the high school admissions process are consequential, as they affect the quality of the secondary education students receive. Experiences in high school can encourage or discourage persistence to graduation (Pittman and Haughwout 1987; Teachman, Paasch, and Carver 1996; Lee and Burkam 2003; Ream and Rumberger 2008; Staff and Kreager 2008; Crosnoe 2011), which means that high school destination may critically influence whether students earn the minimal educational credential valued in the United States and thus whether they qualify to pursue postsecondary education or military service (Bennett and McDonald 2013).

Those are the stakes of the high school selection process for all students, but the stakes are even higher for those who reside in places where there is enormous variation in school quality and where the quality floor is exceptionally low (Lee, Croninger, and Smith 1996). In places where high school quality is moderate to high and varies little, the consequences of losing in the selection process may mean the inability to take a particular course of study or participate in certain kinds of school-based activities. However, in places where high school quality varies greatly and where multiple high schools are deemed as "failing," the consequences of losing in the selection process are considerably greater (see Deming et al. 2014). It is exactly the latter context in which the adolescents of parents in our study compete for high school placement. Indeed, this is a city with great variation in school quality. In this city, one high school, McKinley, was deemed one of the best in the nation by *Newsweek* and other publications, while another, Thompson, the neighborhood-zoned school for Augusta students, was declared "persistently dangerous" by the school system. In such a context, the consequences of the selection process extend beyond the domain of education to encompass consequences for health and well-being.

In light of the heterogeneity in high school quality present in the city, the consequences that stem from high school placement, and the absence of any requirement to participate in the selection process, the question arises as to whether and how working-class and middle-class parents actively engage in this process in order to shape the high school experiences of their children. Although school choice processes may vary across school districts, it is a process that involves initiative by students and their parents. As Archbald (2004) notes, the exercise of school choice "require[s] parents to be informed about their children's school options, to make choices among a range of options, and to follow school registration procedures and time lines" (284).

Below, we present analysis of parents' narratives around the high school application process to determine whether and how social class shapes parents' approaches to this important step in their children's transition to high school. We find that middle-class parents participated in school choice in a strategic way in order to secure for their children placement in the limited number of highly selective high schools in the city, ones that will facilitate entry into the colleges of their choice. In contrast, working-class parents participated in the process in a defensive way in order to avoid a highly undesirable high school. To achieve this goal, working-class parents pursued placements for their children in a wider array of high school types compared with their middle-class counterparts. Both middle- and working-class parents utilized the help of teachers to achieve their high school destination goals.

UNIVERSAL PARTICIPATION IN THE APPLICATION PROCESS

Parents of both social classes had high participation in the school choice process. Among our respondents, 100% of middle-class parents and over 96% of working-class parents indicated that their child participated in the high school placement process. That is, all middle-class youth and all but one working-class youth submitted applications to high schools rather than default to their neighborhood school. This level of participation is somewhat higher than the citywide participation rate.

Middle- and working-class parents alike engaged in activities to enroll their children in their preferred high schools. They investigated their children's options, helped their children apply to high schools (often to multiple schools), took them to interviews and auditions where required, and helped them make final decisions about where to enroll. For example, Gloria is a White middle-class mother whose daughter applied to two highly competitive schools. Jerome, an African American middle-class father in an interracial family, noted that his son "really looked at other schools and applied to a bunch of schools." Responding to our question about where her son would attend high school, Olivia, a White middle-class mother in an interracial family, was thrilled to report that her son "got accepted at a lot of good schools," having applied to four of the best schools in the city.

Carla, an African American working-class mother, was excited about the outcome of her son Dominic's application process, particularly given the care they exercised in deciding to which schools to apply:

> If it was a school that [Dominic] was interested in, by his dad being from here, he would already know [about the school]. Like one school, [Dominic's father was] like, "Oh no. They just started. They're not really situated yet." And one school he [was] like, "No, that's located in such and such; you're not going [there]. That's not a good area."

With careful decisions made about where to apply to high school, Carla and her husband received good news:

> Dominic was accepted to four out of five of the schools. The school that he didn't get accepted to was the performing arts school, which was kind of funny because I would have never thought he would have wanted to go there.

Ultimately Carla was satisfied with the outcome of the high school selection process, and her son Dominic elected to stay at McKinley for high school.

Carina is a Puerto Rican working-class mother. She and her husband agreed to incur extra expenses to send their daughter, Daniela, to a school other than the neighborhood-zoned school. Once her daughter was admitted to a charter school, after having to "take several exams," Carina and her husband were obligated to buy school uniforms and other items that Carina described as "expensive," saying, "Yes, the uniform is expensive; they ask for expensive things. But if you want what's best for your child, well you have to make an effort." Carina and her husband connected the effort they put into their daughter's high school destination with the academic effort they expected from her:

> Now, I told her and her dad told her, "I'm going to make an effort and spend a great deal of money so you can go to this school, but in that same way, I want you to make an effort that's reflected in your grades, because it's not about us spending and you taking this as a joke."

Carina and her husband were willing to pay the cost to send their daughter to a charter school and expected their daughter to perform well there.

Gail is a White working-class mother whose daughter, Heather, was accepted to two of the best schools in the city and struggled with deciding which one to attend. Gail described the decision-making process as "a little difficult for her," but Heather ultimately chose to attend the school her older brother attended due, in part, to his ringing endorsement of the school. According to

Gail, her son reported having "an absolutely great time at Bell High School, and if he could do it again, he would do it again."

For only one parent in our study was the neighborhood school acceptable. Harriet, an African American working-class mother, was aware of Thompson's reputation but felt it was within her son's ability to get a good education there if he desired it. Moreover, her positive experience at Augusta gave her confidence in her opinion that a school with a troublesome reputation could do well by her son:

> Any place you go can be good depending on the person. They say that Thompson is one of the schools that is characterized as bad or having problems just like Augusta. But if you want to learn, regardless to where you at, you'll learn. If your personality is bad, you're going [to associate] with bad people. If you want to learn, you're going [to associate] with people who want to learn. So, I don't really blame institutions for how a person is taught or how they adapt to the learning environment. Even though they say Augusta was a bad school, to me, it did us justice.

Except for Harriet, who believed one could obtain a good education in any school, all parents, regardless of social class, sought to customize their children's educational experiences. Their actions and decisions alone could not fully determine where their children attended high school, as outcomes also were shaped by where youth were admitted. Nevertheless, within the context of a school choice regime, both middle- and working-class parents exercised that portion of control they had in order to determine their children's high school. The transition to high school involved a coordinated effort of investigation, consultation, and consideration. It was a process that concluded in celebration, relief, and, sometimes, despair. We show in the next section that it is also a process that illuminates social class differences in the concerns that parents bring to the high school selection process, along with class differences in the consequences of failing to gain admission to schools that parents and their adolescents choose.

THE MIDDLE-CLASS PURSUIT OF AN ELITE PUBLIC EDUCATION

Middle-class parents approached the high school selection process strategically with an eye toward the most selective schools in the city. Their acceptance into McKinley's academically selective middle school put their children on a path for high school that was less attainable for many working-class students from Augusta. In talking about the schools to which their children applied, middle-class parents focused on a relatively short list of schools with strong academic programs that would provide a pathway to a selective college or university. In other words, the middle-class parents in our study wanted their children to obtain an *elite public education*. Ultimately, they were able to secure it, as adolescents from all middle-class families were accepted into the most selective schools in the city.

Although all middle-class students enrolled in elite public schools, there was still room for disappointment for some. Many McKinley students did not think of their high school options in terms of the wealth of alternatives available for 9th-graders throughout the city. They were already at a school whose high school was recognized as one of the best in the nation. Staying at McKinley also would allow for an easier transition to high school, with familiar teachers and friends and a small-school experience. For most, staying at McKinley was the most desirable option. Admission at McKinley is highly competitive as the 9th-grade class is much smaller than the 8th-grade class. When McKinley parents described their child's transition to 9th grade, they emphasized whether their child was or was not chosen to stay at McKinley.

Paola's daughter, Rosana, was worried that she would not get into McKinley after she got a C in art class the previous year when she decided not to turn in an assignment following a rift with her art teacher:

> She was so afraid she wasn't getting into McKinley for high school, even though she didn't come right [out] and say, "I love McKinley." . . . But she was really so relieved. I knew she was getting in. She has really high standardized test scores of like in the 98th percentile, but . . . she was afraid now that, that C would not let her go back to McKinley, and she worked really hard. And she was so relieved when she finally got the acceptance letter. She was getting it from all the other schools but not from McKinley.

McKinley was the last school to send Rosana an acceptance letter. Her mother said:

> The last one she got, yes. I don't know if they did it on purpose or not, but it was fun to watch her. And when she finally got it, she called all her friends and she asked me if we could go out to celebrate and we did. And as we were having dinner, all her friends called her and she would say, "Guess what? I got in." So, she likes the school. You know, it meant a lot to her. The other schools were high in academics, too, but I guess not equal to McKinley, although the new one that's opening, that's supposed to be even superior.

Parents wanted their children to remain at McKinley for high school because the school is academically rigorous and is viewed as a pathway to valuable opportunities after graduation.[1] Mara, a White middle-class mother, and her family lived in a neighborhood that has been home to a lot of kids who have gone to McKinley. They let their daughter Nina make the final decision about which high school to attend, and they approved of her choice of staying at McKinley. Mara said:

> We feel like we really looked at the other schools and Nina did make a good decision. . . . She talked with a lot of her friends. There's a couple of kids on our block who graduated from McKinley, and they've really enjoyed the high school. And they've done well and gone to Harvard. And so . . . the education . . . and I mean one of the things that influenced us on this was that they . . . really weed out [students from the middle school]. They cut the class almost two thirds. So sometimes what the kids have said is that problem kids or kids that would be distracting in class aren't there anymore. It's very demanding and it's challenging and there's a lot of good teachers.

For Nina, McKinley offered the possibility of an elite public education potentially leading to a selective university.

Holly, a White middle-class mother, and her ex-husband were sold on their son Ian continuing at McKinley, even before they found out which schools he had been admitted to, because it "has the reputation of being the best school in the area." Ian was starting to think seriously about going to Bell High School, one of McKinley's main competitors for its 8th-graders' applications and among the most selective high schools in the city. It is a much bigger school and offers a more typical high school experience: new friends and a wealth of extracurricular activities, including a greater variety of sports teams. Sports influenced Ian's desire to change high schools. Ian's parents, however, did not feel that Bell could offer the same academic experience as McKinley:

> [McKinley is] smaller and I feel like . . . for my son's personality, it would be better for him. The size of Bell, I think, it's easy to get lost and sort of fall into the mediocre part. . . . Also the academics . . . McKinley just seems to be the number one school. And Bell, I've heard mixed things about it.

After talking it over with his father and the baseball coach, Ian ultimately decided that the sports at Bell weren't enough to lure him away to another school. He decided to stay at McKinley.

The parents of those who get into McKinley feel that the transition to high school will be an easy one. Kira, a White middle-class mother, for example, said, "Well, I think Ruby going to the same school is going to be quite easy. It's the same group of kids. I think the only thing I need to be aware of is, I do hear it's harder. It's just to be aware of her time management—helping her with that." Likewise, Mallory, a White middle-class mother, thinks the transition to high school will be an easy one for her son. She said:

> I know a lot of the staff. . . . We have a friend who teaches them high school math. So, that's nice. There's no real mystery here. And if I go down there, I know who to contact in terms of most things. I know some of the office staff, etc. That's nice. . . . I don't see it as a huge transition. It's the same building, it's a different side. It's the same group of everything. . . . He knows a lot of kids in high school. . . . I'm not concerned about the transition.

Several parents noted that the smallness of the school and the familiarity with the teachers and programs, as well as maintaining the same friends, would make the transition to high school an easy one for those who continued on at McKinley.

The parents of those who did not get into McKinley for high school had a palpable sense of frustration and disappointment. Sophia, a White middle-class mother, said, "Most of his friends got into McKinley. So, I'm sure that's frustrating. McKinley eliminates a percentage . . . like a big percentage." She went on to say, "I think he was really disappointed in himself with McKinley . . . and realizes that he should have been concentratin' on his schoolwork. And I feel responsible, 'cause I wasn't on top of him too."

When their children are not admitted to their chosen high schools, McKinley parents turn to teachers for help and explanation. When Nancy, mentioned in the Introduction, a White middle-class mother, found out that her son Miles was on the waiting list for McKinley, she first contacted one of Miles's teachers, who is also the chess coach and who had been a mentor to her son, to figure out what to do. She was surprised that Miles did not make the cut because she felt he met the criteria for grades, test scores, and behavior. Nancy started talking to Miles's teachers to try to find an explanation. She said:

> And I called . . . and I contacted the principal, the interim principal. I called the teacher, one of his teachers who is also his chess coach . . . who was also quite surprised, and I just said, "Could you look into this? I don't understand why this happened." . . . And then [I] also asked the principal about that and it also came up the next week during teacher conferences, and the teacher says, "So, is Miles staying at the high school?" And I said, "Well, actually . . . " And the teachers were surprised that he was not admitted, and I just said, "If you can find out, you know, why."

After contacting the principal, she found out that the reason he wasn't admitted was due to his absences following the death of two grandparents, which erroneously were not counted as excused. She contacted some of Miles's other 8th-grade teachers to see if anything could be done. She said:

> Several of Miles's teachers have intervened, and also felt like it was not a fair decision. And now . . . without trying to really annoy people, you know, we're just trying to strike that balance with which you are getting an acknowledgment that it kind of was a mistake and then talk to them 'cause they're trying to not overcrowd the school next year.

In that effort, one teacher in particular was very helpful to the family. About this teacher Nancy said, "He's helped me to frame, to write emails. And then I've been the person who's had the face time." Even with the intervention of the teachers, though, Nancy had a hard time getting her son admitted into McKinley because the freshman class had already been selected. The only way her son could get in would be to wait until the beginning of the school year to see whether another student decided to drop out. Officially, then, he was going to Bell.

Middle-class parents approached the school selection process with an eye toward providing their children with an elite public education, the kind of education that they hoped would facilitate entry into selective colleges in the future. Middle-class youth applied and were accepted to a relatively short list of the most selective schools in the city. For some, acceptance into even a highly selective high school is still a disappointment if they are not admitted to McKinley, which many parents and children feel is the best school in the city. For those who got into McKinley, parents felt that the transition to high school would be a smooth one. When youth did not get into McKinley, middle-class parents turned to teachers to help them find an alternative for their children.

WORKING-CLASS PARENTS' AVOIDANCE
OF DANGEROUS SCHOOLS

Unlike students at McKinley, who considered a relatively small number of schools, students at Augusta contemplated the full range of high schools in the city, including selective high schools, charter schools, and neighborhood schools. Some working-class parents valued strict schools and ones with visible security. Their focus on strictness and security aligned with their use of defensive parenting. For example, Pilar, a Puerto Rican working-class mother, talked about the process of choosing a school for her son and noted the need to consider all the schools in the district:

I want to find a school that's good for him. I tell him that at all schools, there's a little bit of everything: bad students, good students, students that like to fight, that don't like to fight. So, there are times that one hears comments about schools and we get scared. . . . Because we always look for the best for him, that it's a school that won't affect him and he'll pick up bad influences, but it's not good to let oneself be influenced by everything one hears about the schools. Instead, we should go see, to check out the schools—how they're doing; what they have; what they teach, for each one. . . . I don't want a school that's too far; that they have to travel far to get to. If something were to happen to them, [I don't want it] to be difficult for me to get to the school. Yes, mostly that's what we talk about, my husband and I.

The couple's consideration of high schools took place in the context of uncertainty about which school their son would attend if he was not accepted into any of the schools to which he applied. That is, they were still not sure which neighborhood high school he was zoned to because their old house burned down in a fire and they only recently had moved to a new house in a new neighborhood. Pilar's cousin has a child who went to Augusta with Pilar's son and had been talking to her about coordinating their high school applications so that the two boys could continue to go to school together. At the time of the interview, Pilar was waiting to see whether her son would get into a charter school.

Adolescents' applications to high schools were of much concern to working-class parents. If Augusta students did not get into their chosen high schools, they were slated to attend their neighborhood-zoned school, Thompson High School, which was deemed to be "persistently dangerous" by the school district.[2] Working-class parents, therefore, sought out schools that would serve their teens academically, but also would provide safe environments in which they could learn. Safety was a priority for working-class parents, in addition to their children's prospects for mobility. As such, the high school selection process became another domain in which working-class parents engaged in defensive parenting.

Many working-class parents with 8th-graders at Augusta had concerns about the dangerous environment at their zoned high school. Tamara recently had visited Thompson and shared this about the experience:

So when I went up there with my daughter, you got guys standing over here, guys standing over there and they all either rolling blunts or trying to sell drugs. And when I went in there and I seen all them police officers . . . I was so happy. And when I came out, I said, "Look." I said, "What you need to do is go down there and arrest some of them drug dealers. They're stopping them kids before they even cross the street trying to sell them that mess." [They said] "Yeah

miss, we got this. We gonna have the [police] down here today." I
said, "Well that's good." You know, cause even if kids don't wanna,
it's peer pressure.

Although Tamara was happy to see the police doing something about
drug dealers at the school, she did not want her own children in an environment where drugs were so rampant. Her daughter was admitted to
another school across town. She also transferred her son to another high
school in the same area because she was concerned about the violence at
Thompson. Tamara did not yet know much about the school that he was
transferred to, other than that it has smaller class sizes than Thompson;
but she had peace of mind knowing he would not be at the neighborhood
school. She said:

> I didn't want my kids to go to Thompson this year because of what
> they was doing last year. So, when this school [year] started they
> started burning trash cans and stuff like that. . . . So my son was
> scared. He didn't want to go in the school, he said, because when you
> go to the door, it's like the boys are standing there provoking you to
> fight them before you can even get inside the door.

Joella's daughter, Kendra, did not apply to any high schools because
they were planning to move out of state. But when their plans fell through,
Kendra was slated to go to Thompson. Joella said:

> I didn't know what I was going to do. I was thinking about a private
> school, and I was going to call my mom and grandmother to get their
> help financially with the schools. I stopped at [what I thought was a
> private school] one day to ask for an application and things. And they
> said it was a charter school; no cost. It was great. And they gave me an
> application. And we ended up going to the orientations and everything
> worked out well.

Like most other working-class parents, Joella took steps to keep her daughter out of the neighborhood-zoned school.

Some working-class parents opted to send their children to Simón
Bolívar High, a charter school close to where many of them live. One
feature of this school that parents appreciated is its level of security: The
school uses metal detectors and cameras, and requires uniforms. When
Gabriela, a Latina mother, was asked how she picked Simón Bolívar High,
she responded, "Because a lady in the program told me that . . . it's a very
perfect school, very good . . . that they helped. That it was very strict."
The academics of the school appealed to Gabriela, because her son was
reading below grade level and the school said it could help with that.

However, the school's dress code and security also appealed to her. She noted that "they enforce the rules there. There they don't let anyone leave, because each grade goes in and they check the bags and stuff [to see] if they have drugs in the bags . . . very strict." She continued:

> I mean, I see just walking in, I see that there are cameras everywhere. They see the students. If somebody pushed them, and if some of them arrive in sneakers, they send them back or call their parents. Very strict. Very strict. And a boy, I think, at that age, that's what they have to see. They have to see a principal, someone that is firm. . . . You know? I agree with that.

Gabriela felt that the strictness of the school aligned with her own parenting. She shared that she, not her son, picked the school:

> He wanted to go to another school, but I said no. This is perfect for him and since I make the decisions, you know? Many kids laugh at him because he's going to use a uniform and in another school they don't. . . . I was the one that made the decision and he has to respect that.

Carina, another Latina mother, also liked the strictness of Simón Bolívar High:

> I like it because there's a lot of security. [My daughter] tells me there are even cameras in the classrooms. They have an entrance time, and if she's not on time, they don't let her in . . . the uniform . . . they even have IDs. I don't know much about the school, because since they just started they haven't called me at all. But I like it because that's a lot of security for the kids. Sometimes the parents see it like, "Oh, why so much?" But that's where your children are, and the security is very good to keep an eye on them.

Josephine's son, Louis, was accepted to Simón Bolívar High and likes the school, although they were still waiting to hear from another charter school. She was not sure about the necessity of the metal detectors, stating:

> I like it. Personally, I like it. We went to their open house, Louis and I did in June, and I found it to be very nice. I really did. I was amazed when I walked into the school and saw how clean it was. It was nice. The only thing that I didn't like about it, but I understand, was the fact that they have the bar code. What do you call it when you're walking in an airport and you're going through?

Although Josephine, a multiracial mother, did not appreciate the metal detectors, she likes that the school requires parental involvement. She said:

So, I was very amazed by the school and the education that they have lined up for the kids. In fact, their first day of school, which is the 6th of September, they ask for the parents to come for the day. They want you to come and spend that whole day there with your child to see what goes on within the school grounds on a daily basis and I thought that was very different. I've never had a school send me a paper to tell me I have to be at school on a specific day all day. So, that I did like and that just made me very comfortable with knowing that if my child attends this school they're gonna take care of him to the best of their ability and they're gonna make sure he's getting his education. So, that's like a big plus for me.

Other working-class parents planned to send their children to a new military-themed charter school, Citadel High School. Polly is a White working-class mother whose daughter, Robin, planned to attend Citadel. She described some of the military-themed practices at the school:

They're in the uniform, and a lot of the structure is a straight disciplinary-type structure and they do ROTC classes . . . you know, they stand in formation outside the classroom . . . they go in in formation, sit at their desk. You know? Their . . . lieutenant at the front of the class, "You may sit down now." You know what I mean? That kind of . . . more . . . you know, strict.

Polly described how they decided on the military-themed charter school. Her daughter, Robin, "begged" her to go to the school. When Robin asked her mother whether she would "mind if [she] went to a military school," Polly responded, "Why would I mind? I think it would be great for you." Polly described what she likes about the strictness of the school:

Some of the parents were not too happy about the fact that the kids might have to do push-ups if they do something wrong. And I'm like, "What is wrong with it?" You know? I'd rather have . . . my daughter have to do 10 push-ups than be suspended and not have any school and not be learning. You know what I mean? Ten push-ups, they're up in what, 5, 10 minutes? . . . So some of the parents have gotten upset that their kids have had to do push-ups. . . . It's not being mean. It's teaching them that there's consequences to everything you turn around and do, you know? When you're disrespectful, you mouth off to . . . somebody . . . there's consequences. . . . You backtalk to a teacher, you're out of the school. You threaten a teacher, you're out of the school; you're in your neighborhood school. You know, you got that nice embarrassment that you got thrown out of that school. . . . So . . . that's one of the reasons why I like it.

One of Polly's concerns about Citadel High School was, given its military atmosphere, whether it was steering students toward the military rather than college. School officials assured her that this was not the case and pointed to the fact that recruiters are not allowed in Citadel High as they are in some other high schools. This reassured Polly because social mobility was important to her and she was targeting college for her daughter rather than entry into the military. About this, Polly said:

> In a regular high school, the recruiters do come into the high school and try to recruit these kids out of high school to go into the service and . . . pay for their college . . . 'cause one of the first things she said . . . when she went in for her uniform, for her interview, was that she wanted to go into the service and he said, "That's not what this place is for. We're teaching you . . . the things you need to go into college. We want to see you go into college. We don't want to see you go into the service." I like that. That . . . eased me up a little bit 'cause there has been reports where people in the neighborhood and parents [saying:] "Oh, you're just trying to recruit our children." Uh-uh [no], there's a strict policy at the school—no recruiters are allowed to come into the school. There is nothing said about joining afterwards. The only thing that's been said is there is a college . . . it's a military college, similar to the school, that the kids can apply for, but it still doesn't have anything to do with going into the service during . . . or after. . . . [T]he Civil Air does the testing, which . . . would give them ranking, if they wanna go into the military. The school doesn't.

Although she liked the strictness of Citadel High for her daughter, Polly also placed value on a college-oriented curriculum.

Several parents emphasized that charter schools have stricter environments than traditional high schools. Layla, a Latina mother, highlighted what she saw as the difference between a charter school and a regular public school—strictness, which she believed was a benefit. She said:

> You know, right now my kids are in the charter school and one of 'em is in the public school. So the difference [with] the charter [is] they really, really strict. You have to wear uniforms. . . . They don't tolerate no fighting. . . . In public school you get away with a lot. . . . They're not strict about their dress codes. They . . . [are] not strict at all.

Working-class parents had mixed feelings about Booker T. Washington Technical High School, a vocational school that was on some students' lists. Some parents saw it as a good alternative to the neighborhood school, with one working-class mother calling it "the bomb." Others had concerns about safety at the school. For example, Barbara is an African American working-class mother who did not grow up in the city and knew little about the reputations of the high schools there. Consequently, she found the high school application process to be overwhelming. Her daughter, Chrystal, selected Booker T. Washington on her own. Barbara said:

> She bring it home and showed me the sheet and the booklet that went along with it. . . . I knew nothing about these schools around here so I couldn't say, "No, Chrystal. Don't apply to that one because this one is better." I didn't go to these schools. I knew nothing about the school system around here. I didn't know what was good. I knew she liked doing hair. So, one was for fashion or whatever. She went to apply for [it] . . . and this is all I knew.

Although Barbara understood that Booker T. Washington was, as she put it, "an excellent school at one time," she sought an alternative placement after learning from a contact about shootings near the school. As discussed in Chapter 2, Barbara decided to pursue enrollment of Chrystal in a different charter school, one that would allow her daughter to avoid the violence at both her neighborhood-zoned school, Thompson, and the area surrounding Booker T. Washington.

Still other working-class parents were concerned about the academic rigor of Booker T. Washington, given that it is a vocational school. Rosalinda wanted to send her daughter Serena to the same school that her older daughter attended. However, Serena was not admitted to that school. Instead, she was going to Booker T. Washington. About the choice Rosalinda said:

> I know that it's not the best. . . . I've always wished I could put them in private schools and have the tutoring and that attention that I wished they could have. But I know that she needs to focus on getting some skills and stuff like that because academically she's not the strongest and I couldn't put her in . . . an academic school like that.

Rosalinda was resigned to selecting Booker T. Washington for her daughter. She felt that a vocational school could not offer Serena the same opportunities as a more academically oriented school. While attending Booker T. Washington allowed students to avoid their persistently dangerous neighborhood high school—a major goal of working-class parents in this study—some parents felt that vocational schools divert students from college goals and thus the social mobility they hope their children will achieve.

All but one working-class parent in this study supported their adolescents' participation in the high school selection process. While middle-class parents focused on the most selective high schools for their children, working-class parents considered the entire array of selective, charter, and neighborhood schools. Working-class parents, most of all, wanted their children to avoid the neighborhood-zoned school, which they saw as dangerous and which had been so classified by the school district.

TEACHER ASSISTANCE IN CHOOSING SCHOOLS

While parents obtained information about the high school selection process from various members of their social networks (see Chapter 2), teachers played an important role in steering parents and children away from their zoned high school. In their study of parental involvement in school choice, Teske, Fitzpatrick, and Kaplan (2006) find that the lowest income groups use teachers as a source of information about which schools to enroll their children in. Working-class parents in our study said that teachers shared their perception that the zoned school was not a good environment for youth because of its reputation for violence and poor academics. Carina is a Puerto Rican working-class mother. Of the neighborhood-zoned school she said, "The 8th-grade teachers themselves told me, 'Don't put her there because she's a good student; a good girl . . . and there they have bad influences. The teachers aren't too responsible."

Teachers from Augusta also helped Polly, a White working-class mother, with the high school application process. Polly has older children who attended Augusta and it was from their middle school teachers that she learned how much the high school selection process is affected by academic performance during 7th, rather than 8th, grade. She tried to push her kids to do well during 7th grade because she knew, based on information from teachers, that was the grade that mattered when it came to high school admission. Unfortunately, her daughter, Robin, did poorly in 7th grade. Polly went to Robin's teacher for help. Polly said:

> We had help with choosing the different types of high schools that she could go to due to her grades in 7th grade. The teachers [gave] a lot of help saying, "This is the one we think you have a chance of getting into. Don't even worry about these, even though this is something you really want, [and] we've put a word in [for you]. These [are the] ones that we thought you could handle." They worked with us [to know] which ones would take someone with [a] bad 7th-grade report but a very good 8th-grade report.

Polly's daughter Robin decided to go to Citadel High, a military-themed high school, after repeating 8th grade, having done better the second time around.

Juliette, a Haitian immigrant working-class mother, hoped her daughter would be admitted to the all-girls high school that was her first choice. When Juliette's daughter did not get into that school, she turned to people at Augusta for advice. She said:

> She's going to Citadel High. . . . This is a very good school that they pick for her, because she get a good grade. For the kids to go there, you have to be very good kids, and [get] good grades and everything. So, she go there. Her school send her to go there.

Juliette pointed in particular to the role played by the principal and counselor, stating, "Her principal and the counselor for her school sent her to that school, because this is a top high school, too, you know, in [the city], so that's why they picked that high school."

Adrienne's son, Bobby, did well at Augusta. He had perfect attendance, made the honor roll, and scored high on his standardized tests. However, he did not make it into any of the schools he applied to. His mother, an African American working-class woman, was on a quest to get him into a better school than Thompson, the neighborhood-zoned school. Adrienne was very familiar with the atmosphere of the school. She has an older son who graduated from Thompson, and another son starting the 12th grade there. Her middle child has had some problems as a result of witnessing violent episodes in the classroom, which caused him to not want to go to school. She wanted a better school for her youngest son, whom she still called "my baby." Referring to the environment at Thompson, Adrienne said:

> I don't want that for little Bobby. And little Bobby got the type of attitude [such that] he will fall into that pattern, that negativity, and I'm not having that. So, I don't know what I'ma do about high school. I really don't know.

Adrienne had real concerns about sending her son to a high school where she had seen boys smoking pot outside. She was afraid that Bobby would lose the momentum he had built at Augusta. Therefore, she had Bobby apply to several charter schools. However, he did not make the lottery for any of them. Adrienne sought help from Bobby's teachers. She said:

> His teachers were so upset. They had me come over there. They was like, "His standardized test was so hot. What is going on?" They was really pissed, you know, that he didn't get accepted."

Teachers intervened on Bobby's behalf by writing letters of recommendation and suggesting other possibilities for him. The principal at Augusta thought he could get Bobby into a trade school and wrote a letter of recommendation. Adrienne was not sure that a trade school was a good idea, because she worried that Bobby would not have access to the academic courses he needed to go to college.

With only 2 weeks until school started, Adrienne started to think creatively. Someone suggested that she use someone else's address. She said:

> I got a girlfriend live up [in a different school catchment area]. . . . [It used to be that] the person [who lives in the catchment area] will go with you and say, "Well, he stay with me." And they [let] him [enroll] there. But now they want you to change your driver's license. They want you to do all this other stuff to get these kids in these schools. I think that's just a little too much to go through that.

Although she considered using a different address to get Bobby into a better school, ultimately she said, "I'm not going through all that and I don't know what to do about him going to high school."

Adrienne also thought about Catholic school, but she did not have the money for tuition. She thought her son's paternal grandmother might be willing to contribute because she put her own son, Adrienne's partner, through Catholic school, but Adrienne does not want to press the issue. Also, a football scout recently saw Bobby play football in the local park and approached him about going to a Catholic high school to play the sport. Bobby told his mother that the scout said he would pay for him to go to the private school. Adrienne observed, "He sees Bobby is real good and the guy supposed to call me one day this week. I haven't heard from him." With 2 weeks before the start of school, Bobby still did not have an option other than the zoned high school.

Adrienne was feeling discouraged but was still looking into options for her son. She was frustrated that Bobby would have to go to Thompson just because of where they live. She said:

> He want[s] a better education, and that's a shame that he gotta go to a school that sucks. I hear so many of his peers [say], "I'm not gonna go to school if I have to go to Thompson." And that's bad for them children to have to feel that way when they graduated, and he one of them. He, constantly, every day, "Mom, where am I going to school at?" I'm like, "Bobby, I'm trying to find out, too." I [would] like to write a letter. I [would] like to do somethin'. I'm their parent and my voice will be heard, you know. I don't want him going to Thompson.

After Bobby had so much success in middle school, Adrienne said, "I wish he could go back to Augusta. I just really do."

Teachers played an important role in advising parents as to which high schools would be beneficial for their 8th-grade children. Teachers supported the idea widely held among parents that the neighborhood-zoned school was unacceptable. For middle-class parents, the neighborhood school was unacceptable because their focus was on admission to the most selective schools. In contrast, for working-class parents, the neighborhood school was unacceptable because it was seen as dangerous and of low educational quality. Although teachers were not always able to help parents achieve the outcomes they sought, parents relied on the support of teachers and used them as allies in navigating the high school selection process.

SOCIAL CLASS DIFFERENCES IN HIGH SCHOOL SELECTIVITY

The proliferation of school choice policies has raised concerns about whether they perpetuate school segregation and educational stratification (Roda and Wells 2013), outcomes that we observed in our study. Adolescent children of middle- and working-class parents enrolled in a variety of high schools. Figure 5.1 shows the selectivity of the types of high schools they would attend in 9th grade. Middle-class students were much more likely to go to highly selective high schools compared with their working-class peers, while working-class students attended high schools with a greater variety of selectivity. All middle-class students in our study attended highly selective high schools. In contrast, 25% of working-class students attended highly selective high schools, 10.7% attended neighborhood schools, and, in the summer prior to enrolling, 17.9% were still unsure where they would go.

SUMMARY

In the context of school choice, finding a high school is a major challenge. Like other studies, we find that both middle-class and working-class parents sought to meet that challenge by supporting their children's participation in the high school selection process (Teske, Fitzpatrick, and Kaplan 2006; Pattillo, Deale-O'Connor, and Butts 2014; Denise and Gross 2016; Weininger 2014; cf. Teske and Schneider 2001). However, reasons for participation varied by social class and illustrate strategic and defensive parenting by middle- and working-class parents, respectively.

Middle-class parents participated in the high school selection process to provide their children with an elite public secondary education, the type

Figure 5.1. Selectivity of Adolescents' High Schools by Social Class Location

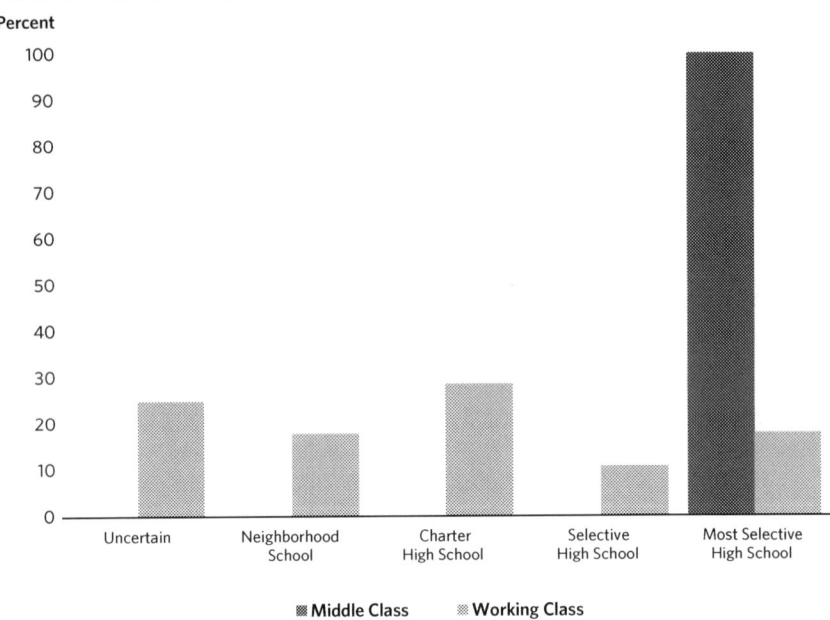

of education that they hoped would enable their children to attend selective colleges (see also Kimelberg 2014; Roda and Wells 2013). To achieve this, they strategically focused on a relatively small pool of the most selective schools in the city. That their children had attended a magnet middle school facilitated this goal, not only for them but for the four working-class parents in our study whose children attended McKinley.

In contrast, working-class parents with children at Augusta, a zoned middle school, participated in the high school selection process to achieve both a good education for their children as well as a safe place for them to be educated; the latter was a concern that middle-class parents in this study did not have to confront. Working-class parents worried about the violence and drug use that their children might encounter at their zoned high school, which had been classified as "persistently dangerous," if they did not se-cure admission to a different school. Therefore, some working-class parents turned to charter schools that offered a strict and secure environment, but one that they hoped also would help their children achieve social mobility.[3]

Demonstrating high levels of engagement in the high school selection process does not, of course, blunt working-class parents' resource and contextual disadvantages. Lauen (2007) finds, for example, that living in a disadvantaged neighborhood is associated with a lower likelihood of at-tending a "selective enrollment school" like the ones that McKinley students targeted, whereas "affluence has the opposite effect, enhancing students' chances of attending a selective school" (196). Among the families in this study, middle- and working-class youth from McKinley went on to highly selective public high schools, while working-class youth from Augusta enrolled in a more diverse array of schools. The different high school destinations of working-class youth compared with their middle-class counterparts likely have implications for their educational and occupational trajectories. We explore their parents' educational and occupational expectations for them in the next chapter.

CHAPTER 6

Unequal Contexts and Parents' Educational and Occupational Expectations

Parental expectations are a strong social–psychological predictor of children's educational and occupational attainment and have been shown to mediate the effects of social background (Sewell, Haller, and Portes 1969; Alexander, Entwisle, & Bedinger 1994). In this chapter, we analyze parents' expectations for their children's futures. Traditionally, aspirations have been viewed as an expression of values, whereas expectations have been viewed as a combined expression of values informed by one's social location. We argue that parents' expectations reflect the ubiquitous American cultural frame of hoping their children will do better than they have, as well as what they think is possible for their children, given their proximate social conditions.

Obtaining at least some postsecondary education is now thought of as a necessary part of the credentialing process for successful participation in the labor market and an important part of the process of transitioning to adulthood (Fuglini and Hardway 2004). It is not surprising, then, that an increasing proportion of high school graduates enroll in college (American Academy of Arts and Sciences 2016), which means that a rising proportion of students in higher education are "first-generation students"—students whose parents did not attend college and who therefore are poised to experience social mobility. Given changes in college enrollment patterns and the meaning of a college degree, we explored whether the educational and, perhaps, occupational expectations of working- and middle-class families are more alike than different.

To obtain information on educational and occupational expectations, we asked parents about their adolescents' academic performance in middle school, their expectations for their teens' achievement in high school, and expectations for children's educational attainment. We also solicited their ideas about career paths, as well as their assessment of the likelihood that their expectations would be realized. In doing so, we learned about what parents value for their children's futures as well as the implications of structural realities for their expectations.

EDUCATIONAL EXPECTATIONS

Working- and middle-class parents uniformly articulated an expectation that their children demonstrate high levels of academic performance. Although parents understood that challenges might exist to earning high grades, such as especially difficult courses or demanding teachers, they expected their children to put forth the effort necessary to earn the best grades possible. For most parents, that meant earning grades of B and higher.

Working-class parents connected their expectations regarding academic performance to their children's subsequent opportunities for a good education, a good job, and a good life. Adrienne, an African American working-class mother, viewed good academic preparation in high school as necessary for positioning her son for the future. She described her reaction to a suggestion made by her son's middle school principal that he attend a technical high school: "The principal [said], 'Well, I can get him into Davis High School.' But that's a trade school. He don't need no trade. He needs to be prepared academically for whatever you do in this world, 'cause the computers ruling everything. He needs to be academically ready." Adrienne articulated the need for a solid academic foundation in a changing economy. She hoped her son would obtain the kind of education during high school that would prepare him for college and success in the labor market regardless of how the nature of work changes in the coming years. Juliette, a Haitian working-class mother, was even more explicit in articulating the ways in which future success is predicated on having done well during a prior stage of schooling. She conceptualized her child's educational trajectory as a series of steps that ultimately lead to a good life:

> You got three steps. The kindergarten to 8th grade, this is one. And the 9th grade up to 12th grade, this is the second. And when you finish college, this is the third one. [Then] you could sit down to say, "Oh my God, I'm a nurse or I'm a doctor. I'm gonna make money. I'm gonna drive a good car. I'm gonna buy my house. I'm gonna do this. I'm gonna do that." So, for me, it's a good thing to push the kids to go to school to learn something for tomorrow.

Half of working-class parents in our sample held an expectation that their children would attend college and, in some cases, did so very early on. One parent, Mona, a Latina working-class mother, indicated she had even been thinking about college for her daughter since she was "in the womb." Others were less specific about exactly how much education they expected their children to obtain, using phrases such as "as far as she can go" to communicate that they expected children to continue their education beyond high school. When Joella, an African American working-class mother, discussed the future with her daughter, she believed she was merely explaining "the facts of life" and emphasized that education provides the foundation necessary for success: "The more education you have, the further in life you can go, [and] the better off you'll be later on." This sentiment was prevalent among working-class parents in our sample; they expected that their children would continue with education to the highest level possible. Without having a ceiling in mind, though, they specified floors, such as beyond high school or at least a college degree.

Working-class parents expressed high educational expectations, but they differed from their middle-class counterparts in how far in school they expected their children would go. The size of those differences, however, depends on the granularity with which one views the higher education system. When viewed from the perspective of degree attainment, the expectations of working- and middle-class parents diverged considerably. Table 6.1 shows that the expectations of middle-class parents were concentrated at the top of the educational hierarchy. More than half, 54.5%, of middle-class parents expected their children to obtain graduate degrees, and the remaining 45.5% expected their children to earn bachelor's degrees.[1] In contrast, no working-class parent expressed an expectation that their child would earn a graduate degree, and a little more than half expected their child to earn a bachelor's degree. Thus, at the highest level of degree attainment—graduate degrees—there is a 54.5 percentage-point difference between the expectations of working- and middle-class parents.

If we view the higher education system from the perspective of whether adolescents obtain a bachelor's degree, class differences were smaller. All middle-class parents in our sample expected their children to obtain at least a bachelor's degree, while 53.3% of working-class parents held such an expectation. Furthermore, if we view educational expectations through a lens that simply distinguishes between postsecondary education and secondary education, the expectations of working- and middle-class parents overlapped substantially, given that the vast majority (80%) of working-class parents expected their children to continue their schooling in some way beyond high school. While it is true that working-class parents in our study held lower educational expectations for their children than did their middle-class counterparts, we suggest that it is equally important for our understanding of social reproduction and opportunities for mobility that the vast majority of working-class families desired and expected their children to participate in higher education and that half expected their children to obtain a bachelor's degree.

Working-class parents' narratives gave voice to their expectations for more than secondary education for their children. For example, Mona, a Latina working-class mother, stated, "I talk a lot with her and I make sure that it sinks in, you know, absorbed. From now [on], let it be known that after high school it's automatically college." Joella, an African American working-class mother, also emphasized college in her discussions with her

Table 6.1. Parents' Educational Expectations by Various Views of Higher Education System

Level of Educational Attainment	Middle Class	Working Class
Any Postsecondary Education		
High School Graduate	0.0	20.0
Some College	100.0	80.0
Bachelor's Degree Attainment		
High School Graduate	0.0	20.0
Some College	0.0	26.7
Bachelor's Degree	100.0	53.3
Advanced Degree Attainment		
High School Graduate	0.0	20.0
Some College	0.0	26.7
Bachelor's Degree	45.5	53.3
Graduate Degree	54.5	0.0

daughter. About her daughter's future, she stated, "It's very important. I'm trying to drill it in her head that it's very important." In another example, Josephine, a multiracial working-class mother, wanted to respect the choices her son makes for his life regarding education, but also described her subtle advocacy for college attendance:

> I've always felt that I need to give my kids that right to decide if they want to go to college or not; though, on the back burner, I push them towards it. In conversation I always say, "When you go to college . . ." I keep that instilled in their heads because I want them to go. . . . So again, it goes back to me saying [that] what I didn't have I give to them. I never had no one put [the idea of attending college] in my head. So, I keep that in their heads.

Working-class parents in our sample conveyed to their children the importance of college attendance. And yet, for no working-class parent was college a forgone conclusion as it was for their middle-class counterparts. That all middle-class parents expected their children to earn a college degree and 54.5% expected them to earn a graduate degree signals just how strongly they assumed that their children would go to college. As Kira, a White middle-class mother, explained, "I think it's a given; we never *not* talk about college. I think they know financially that it might be restrictive, but it's like brushing teeth—[it's] just assumed in our family that you're going to college." Paola, a Latina middle-class mother, expressed similar sentiments: "I think that it's a given from the very beginning. It's not something that you bring up, "Oh, by the way. Have you thought about college?" I think that's one of the expectations that's there from 1st grade on. Kindergarten, that's when we talk about going to college." College attendance and degree completion were fully expected by middle-class parents.

In sum, both working- and middle-class parents in this study expected their children to be achievement-oriented and to earn good grades. Middle-class parents were more uniform in their educational expectations than their working-class counterparts, given that all expected at least a bachelor's degree and the majority expected a graduate degree. Only a small minority of working-class parents expected their teens to obtain only a high school education; the large majority (80%) expected their children to acquire some college or specialty training, with a little more than half of working-class parents expecting their children to earn a bachelor's degree.

OCCUPATIONAL EXPECTATIONS

Working- and middle-class parents shared a desire for their children to have jobs and careers that would bring them satisfaction. They hoped that their children would have a job they "loved" and one that would make them "happy." Parents also wanted their children to earn a stable income sufficient to support themselves and their future families.

Olivia, a White middle-class mother in an interracial family who is an elementary school teacher, expressed respondents' collective sentiment when she commented on the sheer amount of time spent at work. Given that one spends a substantial portion of adult life at work, she hoped that her child would do something he loved: "Above all, the most important thing is to love what you do because that's where you're going to spend most of your time when you're in your 20s, 30s, 40s. I tell my students, "You spend more time with me than you do with your parents on a given day, and me with [you]. So, you have to really love what you're doing." Mara, a White middle-class mother, hoped that her daughter would have "a job that gives her a reason to get out of bed in the morning, where you just loved what was coming, whatever it was." Mara articulated how love for one's work can be a motivating force regardless of the challenges each day may bring.

Parents' interests in their children's job satisfaction was further illustrated by the distinctions they made among jobs with desirable attributes but that, nevertheless, might not be ones their children love. Gloria, a White middle-class mother, noted, "Obviously, I want her to have a good job, but I'd more want her to have something that she enjoys." Carla, an African American working-class mother, stated about her son, "I want him to do something that he is happy doin'; not something that he's miserable [doing just] because he's makin' money." Barbara, an African American working-class mother, hoped that her daughter would have a job she's not only interested in, but passionate about:

> She loves so [many things] but I keep telling her that it's alright to love a whole bunch [of things], but focus on the thing you love the most, and get your degree or whatever in that. You can always go back and do them little things that you love, but the one thing that's really burnin' [inside] you, that you really enjoy and love, go for that first 'cause then you'll know you succeeded in that.

For Barbara, the importance of loving one's work was twofold. First, she felt it would help her daughter choose a field of work; and second, passion for the work would lead to success.

Along with job satisfaction, most parents hoped that their children would have jobs that provided a stable and sufficient income. Erica, an African American middle-class mother, described the kind of job she hoped her daughter would have in the future as "one that pays her enough [so that] she doesn't have to worry about the basics that she needs to live. In all honesty, that's pretty much what it's all about." Another mother, Gail, a White working-class woman, stated, "I've told both my kids that you have to do what you love, but be sensible—you have to make a living." Gail hoped her children would enjoy their jobs, but also cautioned that their choices would need to bring home a liveable income.

Working-class parents, in contrast to their middle-class counterparts, additionally emphasized financial independence, which went somewhat beyond a desire for income sufficiency. Patricia, an African American working-class mother, stressed to her son the importance of being self-sufficient. She stated:

> I'm really on him about it. I'm letting him know, "The world don't owe you nothing because you're here. You gotta take care of yourself. Nobody's gonna take care of you like me. You're my child, but it's time for you to grow up." I'm not gonna raise no son, no man, laying around living off of me. Being a sponge and a leech is not an option.

Carina, a Latina working-class mother, echoed Patricia's sentiments, with an emphasis on her daughter having her own resources. She stated:

> I tell [my daughter], "You know you have to pick something that will give you work. That way, when I'm no longer here, or Daddy's no longer here, you won't have to depend on a brother or an uncle."

That she do it on her own. [And] if she gets married, not to have to wait for her husband to give her two or three bucks, if he gives her money at all.

Sarah, an African American working-class mother, shared Carina's desire for financial independence for her daughter. She stated:

I'm trying to show my daughter not to ask anybody for anything if you can help it. I'm talking about finances. She's a girl, so I don't want her to depend on no guy, unless that's your husband and y'all depend on each other. I want to show her how to really be independent when it comes down to things that you need or you want.

Sarah tried to model financial independence for her daughter and believed it was one of the most important ways she could prepare her daughter for the future.

In sum, then, parents hoped that whatever their children's occupation, they would enjoy their work, be happy doing it, and earn a dependable living, while working-class parents also stressed the importance of financial independence.

Specific Jobs Versus Characteristics of Work

In the presence of shared desires that their children find work that they love, working- and middle-class parents differed in how they articulated the kind of work they expected their children to have. When asked about the careers they thought their children would pursue, working-class parents were more likely to name specific jobs than their middle-class counterparts, who often responded by describing work characteristics.

Rosalinda, a Latina working-class mother, discussed her daughter's interest in becoming a mortician. Rosalinda was very supportive of her daughter's plans and expected she would succeed in this career. She explains:

She's been saying for about 2 years now that she wants to be a mortician when she grows up. I know. Weird, right? Nothing freaks her out. She's not afraid and she's got a strong stomach. She's very petite but she's strong. That's my sweetie. . . . She wants to be a mortician. It would be awesome if she could do that. It's so cool. . . . It's like when there are funerals, she wants to go to all of them. I'm serious. This is really off the wall. This is what she wants to do. . . . Being a mortician, if that's where she was to go. . . . She would have to go somewhere [out-of-state] for school. I've even spoken with someone a while ago about being a mortician. There are no schools anywhere close by. She would have to go away. We'd see. This is something she said and she hasn't wavered from it for years.

Rosalinda recognized that her daughter's interest in becoming a mortician was a bit unusual, but felt that since "nothing freaks her out" and that her daughter has a "strong stomach" in combination with her persistent interest in funerals and the mortuary business, there is a strong possibility of her succeeding in the field. Rosalinda also investigated possible options for advanced schooling in support of becoming a mortician, effectively linking her daughter's future career to a clear educational path.

Polly, a White working-class mother, exhibited similar thinking when it came to her daughter's future. Polly described in detail the way her daughter cared for a sick relative and believed it to be an illustration of her daughter's potential as a nurse. She stated:

> I can see her being a nurse, and see her doing it, because she did a lot of helping me with my mom when my mom was sick, taking care of her wounds. She learned how to do the IV, so I could see her doing it. . . . I think it's pretty likely. I think it's pretty likely. She didn't get grossed out. . . . And, it wasn't the best experience. I mean, cleaning an open wound is not a pleasant thing. It's gross. And she turned around and she had no problem doing it. As a matter of fact, even if I was home, she's like, "Mom, you want me to go up and take care of Grandma's belly for her?" Or, "I know it's time for you to do the IV. Do you want me to go up and do it?" I'm looking at her like, "OK." . . . She was 11, 12 years old at the time, and she's having no problem doing it. And there ain't too many out there that are gonna be like, "Can I?" So, I think she's got a pretty good chance at it.

Polly, like Rosalinda, discussed her expectations for her daughter's future in the context of her daughter's demonstrated interest. In addition, Polly and her daughter, Robin, have discussed the possibility of Robin pursuing either a military scholarship for college and then working as a nurse in the military, or going straight into the military after high school and then returning to nursing school on the GI bill. Polly, like Rosalinda, identified an educational path that can help her daughter achieve her career goals.

Stacy, an African American working-class mother, grounded her occupational expectations in her daughter's interest in computers. Stacy explained:

> I told her to go for computers, like when you design programs and things like that. I tell her [that because] she goes on the computer all the time. I be like, "Tasha, you should go design a website," you know? Joking with her and stuff. . . . It's a good possibility.

Stacy believed Tasha could transform her current interest in computers into a career in computer technology. Stacy's sister is a college graduate and often talked with Tasha about what it takes to become academically prepared for college, and Stacy also has planned financially for her daughter to attend college. Working-class parents sought educational pathways as a method to actualize their occupational expectations for their children.

Patricia, an African American working-class mother, said that her focus is on helping her son to form career goals. She regularly asked her son, "You think of any goals, boy? I want to know." Patricia added, "I'm gonna stay on him. He is gonna think of somethin' 'cause I'm gonna come at him so much, he's gonna give it some thought." In response to her questions about goals, Patricia's son mentioned he is interested in developing games for Sony's PlayStation console. As a result, Patricia found a technical school she believes may interest her son after he graduates from high school, and, like many working-class parents, emphasized an educational pathway that would steer him toward his career goals.

Josephine, a multiracial working-class mother, identified a special artistic talent in her son and hoped he would cultivate it into a career. Josephine's son was recognized for his artwork with a scholarship to a local art school for a semester of weekend art classes. About the future, Josephine stated:

> I would want Louis to do exactly what he wants to do, and that's art. And I could see him doing that. I could see him web designing and doing his video games or, you know, designing a house on a computer. I see him doin' all of that. . . . I don't try to bombard him with [college]. I try to keep it at a minimum. Whenever we're in conversation about his artwork, or the video games, because that's mainly his world right now . . . he'll talk about his future, and then I'll pop in [and] start talking to him about [art school].

Josephine tried to keep the future in her son's consciousness, along with the possibility of attending college or art school to build on something he enjoys very much, and an educational step that would provide a career pathway.

Reyna, a Latina working-class mother, had already started looking into nursing assistant classes for her daughter. She said:

> Like I said before, I was takin' nursing assistant classes . . . and I found out that you could be 16 and start takin' those classes. So, the minute that she comes in [turns 16 years old], I'm gonna find out what I have to do financially, how I can go about it so I can get her in there because she can go [to nursing school] at night time, and she can go [to high school] during the day time. She wants to be a nurse. So, I'm gonna do whatever I can to keep her in that direction.

Reyna went beyond suggesting a prospective career for her daughter; she had begun to investigate how her daughter could prepare for it through an educational training program.

Working-class parents described careers that they believed their children would do well in and, importantly, ones that were closely linked to an educational pathway. Having a specific and clearly identifiable educational trajectory into a career gave working-class parents confidence that their children had a realistic chance of actualizing their occupational expectations.

Middle-class parents, in talking about their occupational expectations for their children, described work characteristics rather than specific jobs. For example, some hoped that their children would be able to cultivate work–life balance in whatever career they chose. As Erica, an African American middle-class mother and preschool teacher, explained:

> When I come home, I don't have a headache, and Faith sees that. She's seen me at work, and she's like, "I want to do something that when I get off of work, I'm not bothered." My brother, although he makes a heck of a lot more money than me, complains about his job all the time. And she sees that, too. So, for her, it's like, "Is it possible for me to have both?"

For most middle-class parents in the study, having a job that paid a generous salary and allowed for personal time was not realistic. They described a tension between having a high-paying job and one that does not dominate their personal lives. It was a trade-off that they hoped their children would not have to make.

Middle-class parents also wanted their children to have jobs that provide avenues for intellectual engagement and allow them to improve our world in some way. Nancy, a White middle-class mother, said, "I've not thought of a specific profession. But I'd like him to have a job that he finds really interesting." Jacky, a White middle-class mother of twin boys, stated:

> I would really like it if they did something of value in the world. They've received the best of everything, educationally and socially. I think they are really great people, and I think they could do something that would really make a difference in the world. They could invent a more efficient engine, and I've tried to say that's really our job, because we're eating up the world like a bunch of rabid, starved maniacs. I mean, they've been given everything, and then you see the front page of the *New York Times* with that little baby from Darfur, and we're just destroying the planet. So, I think it's really important that they do something that makes a difference. That's what I want.

Jacky hoped that her sons' privileged educational and social experiences would lead them to develop new ideas that create positive social change. And although she was not sure how they would do it, the goal was important to her. Paola, a Latina middle-class mother, also hoped her daughters would do something of social value one day. She explained:

> I want them to find something fulfilling to do as a job. And I also want them to know that there is more in life than a career, and that a job is just a way for you to pay for the utilities and the house. You don't have to have great wealth to be a happy human being, and I want them to see the big picture. I want them to be able to fight for justice. I want them to be able to save the rainforest. I want them, at least, to see that that's the big picture—not how many cars you park in your driveway. You see the little girls, how they're struggling in Africa, the girls who have no way to participate in their life. There are children in India who are starving, but what are you going do about it? What are you going to do to save or to help someone? There is so much we can do and that's what I really want my kids to do.

Paola sought to raise her daughter to keep "the big picture" in mind, which included understanding how privileged she is in comparison to children who are starving, trafficked, or living in abject poverty.

As illustrated by Erica, Jacky, and Paola, middle-class parents hoped that their children would enter professions that provided work–life balance and intellectual engagement. They also hoped that their children would have the opportunity to contribute to the betterment of society. Linking occupational goals to being socially conscious was, in our sample, unique to middle-class parents. In contrast, working-class parents imagined for their children jobs where formal educational pathways existed to provide clear linkages to good jobs and career fields to secure financial indpendence.

Parents' Communication About Occupational Expectations

In addition to asking parents about their occupational expectations for their children, we asked how they communicate these ideas to them. Middle-class and working-class parents differed in how they discussed their career expectations with their children. Middle-class parents did not specifically raise or pursue the topic of occupational attainment with their children. Rather, they used indirect means of communicating about the subject, often through reaction to an interest or question their adolescent expressed. For example, Mara, a White middle-class mother, explained:

> It's more like we'll come across something, and we'll talk about it as a potential something. I don't think I've actually had a conversation

saying, "In order for you to get to college, you'll have to do this" or "What do you want to do after?" or "What do you want to be?" It's more like coming across a person or reading something that generates some conversation about what that might be like. [It's] very much in general terms. We just sort of look at it more closely, seeing if she would have interest; just exploring questions that we both might have about whatever it was.

Mara did not plan the conversations she had with her daughter about the future. Instead, Mara engaged her daughter about possibilities as they spontaneously arose.

Jacky, a White middle-class mother of twin boys, owns a science-based business with her husband. Although she and her family have talked about a time when the children will join her and her husband in their business, she also pursued a method of following up on her sons' interests rather than having direct conversations about the future. She stated: "Liam is really into becoming a neurologist. I know lots of neurologists and I've been trying to get him time in a scanner so he can see what a brain scan is like." Their other son, Kaleb, was interested in art. Jacky described taking him to a museum to encourage his interest: "Kaleb made [Keith] 'Herring-esque' art for like 3 years, so when there was an exhibition in [another city], we took him." Jacky and her husband used their social network to create opportunities for their sons to engage with potential future interests. They strategically provided opportunities and experiences that animated their sons' interests. Middle-class parents had both the knowledge of where to seek such opportunities and the social networks to make such experiences a reality.

Erica, an African American middle-class mother, shared that her daughter has a gift for words and loves to write. To encourage this interest, Erica did her best to give her daughter more information about what a profession in writing is like. She explained: "When we go to the bookstore, I try to take her to the section about writing or editing. If I come across anything that'll help her, or that would give her some idea about what the job is about, I'll expose her to it." Erica, like other middle-class parents, did not specifically talk about her occupational expectations with her daughter, as much as she followed up on her child's interests. This approach, of strategically following up potential occupational interests, was common among middle-class respondents.

In contrast, working-class parents were more specific in their communication with their children about the future. They emphasized forming goals and often initiated conversations about the types of jobs and careers that could afford social mobility for their children. Joella, an African American working-class mother, hoped her daughter would choose an occupation that she enjoyed, but not just any job would do. She stated, "Yeah, whatever is going to make her happy, but not working at McDonald's or anything like that." Joella, like other working-class parents, knew that fast-food and other service jobs might be available to her daughter, but she questioned whether such jobs would advance her daughter in the long run. Rita, a Latina working-class mother, also thought about her daughter's future career in light of its prospects for mobility. She explained, "I'd like her to be a nurse; that she have a good profession. She tells me she wants to be a [fashion] designer . . . but I would like for her to do something more than that." Rita understood that her daughter was interested in the world of fashion, but she did not think of fashion design as a "good profession." She hoped for "something more"—a career that is socially recognized as worthy, such as nursing. Carla, an African American working-class mother, encouraged her son to aim high—for example, to make a career as a supervisor rather than as a worker. She stated:

> If he say he wanted to be a truck driver [or] a person that pick up garbage—they make good money—but I think that you could be the supervisor, not just settle. You could be more. I always try to encourage him to reach for more. He was saying he wanted to work in [a] store. No, be the owner of the store.

Carla hoped her son would advance in his chosen field and be the person in charge rather than the one following orders. Pilar, a Latina working-class mother, hoped that her son would be spared hard manual labor in his future job. She would rather he find "an office job where he doesn't kill himself." She noted: "All work isn't easy. There are always jobs that are harder than others, but [I want for him] a job that teaches him to survive, and that helps him in his life, and that he likes." For Pilar, "an office job" would help her son earn a living without physical hardship and achieve social mobility. Other working-class parents shared Pilar's viewpoint, and their conversations with their children focused on both career alternatives to manual labor and opportunities for social mobility.

To help children move toward their occupational ambitions, some working-class parents stressed the importance of formulating plans well in advance. For example, Tamara, an African American working-class mother, stated: "If you wanna be somebody, most likely you gotta plan 5 years ahead of what you want to do with your life. If you can't plan ahead, you just gonna be right there stuck on stupid." Tamara emphasized the need to think ahead and make plans for the future in order to move ahead. Overall, in their discussions with their children about the future, working-class parents stressed the importance of aiming high, creating goals, making plans, and sustaining effort.

Comparing middle-class and working-class parents' communication with their children about their occupational expectations revealed that middle-class parents focused on nurturing their children's potential career interests rather than explicitly discussing them, while working-class parents openly emphasized the importance of aiming high and expected their children would have goals and plans for advancement.

THE MEANING OF ADOLESCENT "MISTAKES"

The high expectations that working-class parents had for their children came with a caveat, that youth do not make any life-altering mistakes that could derail their social mobility. Middle-class and working-class parents thought very differently about the potential impact of adolescent "mistakes." Although middle-class parents recognized the potential for adolescents to make poor decisions, they did not view them as having lasting ramifications for their children's life trajectories. In contrast, working-class parents worried that even a single bad decision might have life-altering consequences.

For example, working-class parents described the potential for their children's lives to be forever changed by having children too soon, becoming involved with drugs and violence, or making other poor decisions as a result of peer pressure. Carla, an African American working-class mother, shared about her son: "I'm hoping that he's not one of those to have a baby here, here, here, and there. We talk about that all the time. It's like [I tell him], 'When they takin' that child support out ya check, it won't be cute.'" Gail, a White working-class mother, described her concerns about the ways peer pressure could impact her daughter:

> What always concerns me is what the world throws at children. If you could remove the element of "drugs is fun" and "sex is okay," I think Heather would definitely be very successful if she stays on track. I try to tell her, "Stay on track. Follow your road. The things that might look fun today, or might look like what kids are all doing today, in 10 years when you're an adult, none of those things are going to matter. It's never going to matter who drank, who smoked pot, who had sex. It looks important in your teenage years, but when you're an adult and you're amongst adults, it is not going to matter who did what. You're not missing out on anything." A big thing today, too, is kids cutting themselves. I would always be afraid that my children's curiosity would get them. On her own, I think she'll do fine. She'll do excellent. She likes to work. She likes so many good things that, if I could remove the bad element, she'd be fine. She's never gotten in any trouble or tried anything like that, but we never know what they'll decide.

Gail described multiple troublesome behaviors about which her daughter faces pressure. She believed her daughter would do well provided she does not get "curious" about the many "bad elements" her daughter comes across daily in her peer group. Like Gail, Adrienne, an African American working-class mother, was concerned about how her child would deal with peer pressure. Adrienne's concerns also are linked to the many sources of danger in her neighborhood that could have profound consequences for her son, Bobby. In addition to being pressured into engaging in what some may see as typical adolescent misbehavior—cutting classes, smoking cigarettes, and even smoking marijuana—she worries about how Bobby will react to pressure to do things he doesn't want to do and, as importantly, how others will respond to him. She stated:

> Bobby's the type of kid [who], if you say something wrong [to him], his attitude sometimes will flare. He's gonna say what he wants to say to you; he will blow up. But they ain't [satisfied with] fightin' nobody now. They just coming back with guns. I don't want that.
> . . . He don't smoke weed. He don't smoke cigarettes. Thank you, Jesus. I just don't want him to feel like it's alright when he sees his boys [doing it].

Adrienne worried that in a context in which gun violence is used to settle disagreements, Bobby's quick temper could lead to grave consequences for him. Her concerns were quite understandable considering the kinds of violent incidents official crime statistics show and that working-class parents reported occurring in their neighborhoods, as noted in Chapter 1.

Working-class parents' focus on adolescent "mistakes" was driven not only by worries about safety for their children, but also by concerns regarding their social mobility. In particular, much of the concern that parents had about drugs and early sexual debut is about thwarting their children's prospects for social mobility. Recall from Chapter 3 that Tamara, an African American working-class mother, had concerns about her daughter getting pregnant as a teenager. While her daughter assured her that she wants to go to college, Tamara told her daughter, "If you want to go to college, you can't be taggin' a baby along with you."

Middle-class parents, too, discussed worrisome factors in their children's social environments, but overall they expressed confidence in their children's judgment and did not connect errors made during adolescence to their children's future prospects. Middle-class parents did not worry that a few youthful transgressions would alter the trajectory of their children's lives. For example, Paola, a Latina middle-class mother, explained: "I'm not worried at all about her future. I really am not. I'm more worried about day-to-day accidents that could happen to her or a bad judgment that she could make [while] doing something. But I'm not worried at all about her future. She's really a bright kid."

Sophia, a White middle-class mother, described improper behavior her son displayed during a health class in response to an in-class assignment. The assignment asked students to answer a series of questions. She explained:

> His answers were totally inappropriate, and it was for sex education. They were not happy with his answers, but I really think it was because he's immature. The question that sticks in my mind was, "If your parents were not home and you invited your girlfriend/boyfriend over, and your intention was to watch a movie, and their intention was different, how would you handle it?" So, he wrote something ridiculous like he would throw them in the furnace. But I really think it was because he was immature . . . and he didn't know how to answer it. And somewhere in the essays, [he was to explain] how I would react, and he wrote [that] I would slit their throats. And I'm not violent at all! He's tended to want to be a comedian—he realized it helped with his popularity, so he's playing it to the hilt. They were definitely inappropriate answers, but I don't take them as serious.

While Sophia thought that her son behaved immaturely and inappropriately, she did not feel that it signals a lack of readiness for high school or for the future more generally. Although some working-class parents viewed their sons as childlike, just as Sophia did, they expected consequences to flow from such immaturity, which contrasted with the perspectives shared by their middle-class counterparts.

In short, there is a stark difference between working-class and middle-class parents related to their views of adolescence. Working-class parents worried about the long-term effects adolescent mistakes could have on their children's futures, while middle-class parents accepted that it was culturally normative to make mistakes on the way to adulthood; they did not fear long-lasting repercussions.

SUMMARY

In this analysis, we uncovered similar values and norms across social class, or a cultural mainstream, around educational and occupational expectations. Yet this analysis also revealed that beliefs, or expressions aligned with dominant cultural norms, were not enough for working-class parents in our study to feel secure about the future. Indeed, what working-class parents needed to feel secure was capital that inheres within social institutions and social relations, such as schools, neighborhoods, and social networks, alongside dispositions toward the future that they shared with their middle-class peers. Culture and structure each emerge as necessary but insufficient to support high expectations for youth; rather, this analysis illustrates how culture and structure work in tandem in the lives of parents across social class as they seek to actualize their goals for their children. Figure 6.1 illustrates the differences and similarities in parental expectations between working- and middle-class parents.[2]

Among the middle class, there was genuine confidence that children would move through adolescence and into adulthood with high levels of educational attainment and would pursue careers that were personally fulfilling and that allowed them to contribute to society. Even parents whose children exhibited immature and problematic behaviors seemed confident that their children's futures were bright. Due to their parents' resources, middle-class children had the freedom to explore interests and hobbies as preparation for a future career, and safely made mistakes without incurring life-altering consequences. Middle-class parents spent their time, money, and effort to increase their children's exposure to "a potential something." They regularly did things like purchase books of interest, travel, introduce their children to experts in fields of interest, and have extended dialogues about topics that piqued their children's interests. The substantial emphasis that middle-class parents placed on finding a career in which their children could help people also conveyed self-awareness of their many advantages and the privileged space they occupied relative to those who suffered around the world.

Figure 6.1. Overlaps and Distinctions in Middle-Class and Working-Class Parents' Educational and Occupational Expectations for Adolescents

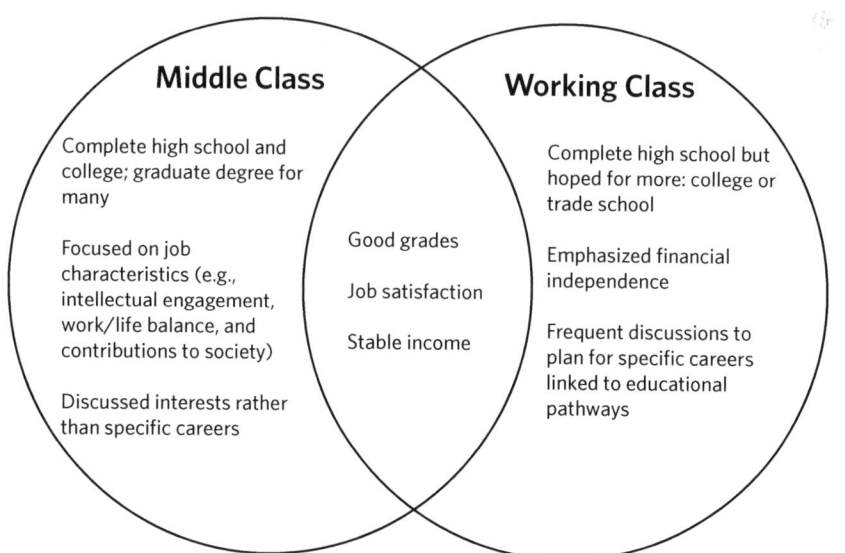

As high and as hopeful as working-class parents' expectations were for their children, their narratives convey their sense of vulnerability as they look to the future. Working-class parents articulated expectations that their children would complete high school and obtain educational credentials necessary for getting a good job. They described plans for their children to secure jobs that could provide financial independence by selecting career fields that were growing or in need of workers. They also emphasized planning ahead, as Tamara's pithy statement conveyed: "If you can't plan ahead . . . you just gonna be right there stuck on stupid." Working-class parents had a deeply internalized conviction that to have a better future meant preparing today. Juliette eloquently stated that children must "learn something for tomorrow."

Yet, working-class parents were aware that the potential to derail their children's futures existed in the contexts of their everyday lives. The precarity of their children's future was visceral, as working-class parents fretted over the many ways their children's trajectories could be altered by teenage childbearing, drug or gang involvement, peer pressure, and violence. Working-class parents knew that their vigilance and best efforts were no guarantee of their adolescents' safe passage into adulthood. Yet, they remained committed to their expectations, thereby resisting a deterministic vision of their children's futures.

Social class differences were quite evident in linkages between educational and occupational expectations. Middle-class parents experienced a true privilege in being able to think about and discuss the future in abstract and amorphous terms, confident that their children would receive good educations and lead meaningful and productive professional lives. Working-class parents, on the other hand, similarly valued educational and occupational success for their children, but in contrast felt the need to craft very specific and concrete pathways just to have a chance to achieve what middle-class parents had the comfort to assume or take for granted. Working-class parents' identification of educational pathways for specific career fields was a way to feel some sense of security that their children would have a successful passage to adulthood. Working-class parents' experiences in imagining and planning for their children's futures are directly related to the conditions and constraints of precarity that characterize everyday life for working-class families.

The findings reported here help us to understand *why* parents' expectations differed by social class. Middle-class parents' robust belief in the potential of their children and the possibilities for their futures was supported by a host of resources. College, graduate school, and interesting and important professional work felt like a natural progression in their walk of life, even if there were bends in the road. This view of children's transition into adulthood, where it is culturally accepted that adolescents make errors and learn from them on the way to adulthood, reflects a predisposition dominant in middle-class culture. In analyzing the narratives of working-class parents, we see that they, too, were predisposed to high and hopeful expectations, yet they did not articulate their expectations with the same degree of confidence about the future. For working-class families in this study, the social contexts in which they lived shaped expectations for their children's futures more than their cultural beliefs about the importance of education and work did alone. In other words, working-class parents were tasked with reconciling their mainstream beliefs with the perils and social constraints experienced in everyday life, causing their pursuit of social mobility for their children to feel, and to be, precarious. Perhaps one of the greatest privileges of middle-class status is the ability to expect the best for one's children with confidence.

CHAPTER 7

The American Shift to Child-Centered Parenting

We've asked our parents about some things, but, you know, [we] find out that a lot of what they say is more relevant to 30, 40 years ago.

—Sal, a White middle-class father

My goal is to use the things that I thought were positive and get rid of the things that I thought were not so positive. And I struggle to do that.

—Anne, an African American working-class mother

In this chapter, we examine how parents think about their own parenting practices in relation to the ways in which they were parented and to the larger society. We asked parents how they parented similarly to and differently from their own parents, their co-parent (if there was one), and other people they know. We also asked parents what or who was their main source of childrearing information and what they felt was most important in parenting an 8th-grade child. We further asked parents how their parenting changed as their child grew older. Perhaps more than in any other endeavor, parenting involves a reflection on one's own personal biography weighed against mainstream norms, allowing parents to modify or preserve the parenting practices by which they were parented themselves. Information about advantageous parenting practices is embedded in the larger society's culture. It is acquired not only by how one was parented as a child and within one's own family of origin, but also by what is deemed acceptable among friends; by child-oriented professionals, such as pediatricians and psychologists; government agencies, such as Child Protective Services (CPS); and by the media (Hays 1996; Lareau [2003] 2011).

Criss and Larzelere (2013) note that "the most important change in recent generations may be the trend away from strict authoritarian parenting to more child-centered discipline" (3). Over time, child care in the United States also has become more time-intensive, with both mothers and fathers spending more time on child care than parents did in the mid-1960s (Sayer,

Bianchi, and Robinson 2004). Hays (1996), in her book *The Cultural Contradictions of Motherhood*, describes a parenting philosophy that she calls "intensive mothering"—one that is "child-centered, expert-guided, emotionally absorbing, labor-intensive and financially expensive"—as having taken hold in the United States (8). This child-centered mainstream parenting approach avoids the use of physical punishment (Hays 1996). While Hays suggests that all mothers operate under the cultural norm of intensive mothering, she indicates there are class differences in "the beliefs and practices" of mothers based on "their financial resources, their reference groups, and their cultural milieux" (86). Lareau ([2003] 2011) similarly argues that this type of parenting philosophy exists in the United States, a parenting philosophy she calls "concerted cultivation," although she argues that this philosophy is limited to the middle class, while working-class parents practice "natural growth," a child-care philosophy marked by unstructured and unsupervised playtime, directives, and corporal punishment. Dow (2019) finds that while middle-class Black mothers engage in forms of middle-class parenting, they take an intersectional approach and emphasize class-, gender-, and race-based strategies to protect their children's comfort, safety, and self-esteem. Ishizuka (2019), in a nationally representative survey of parents, finds that *both* middle- and working-class parents offer support for a parenting philosophy akin to Lareau's "concerted cultivation" and Hays's "intensive mothering"; he also finds that intensive parenting is not limited to just mothers in contemporary society.

A sociological approach to parenting suggests that parenting philosophies emerge from the social conditions in which people live. Contemporary society allows for the proliferation of advice from parenting experts in books, on television, on the Internet, and through social media, which has produced a mainstream culture of child-centered parenting (Hays 1996). We suggest that the discourse of child-centered parenting reaches across social class, not only through the mass media, but also through its dominance in institutions such as Child Protective Services, which can intervene in parenting. We find among *both* middle- and working-class parents an intergenerational shift in parenting to more intensive, child-centered parenting styles supported by the mainstream culture of intensive parenting. Parents are moving from the parenting styles that characterized their own upbringing toward the mainstream of intensive parenting. What this means, however, varies across class. For the middle class, parents are shifting toward being more involved with their children, creating a more educationally enriched environment in the home, and focusing less on chores than their own parents did. Middle-class parents also are seeking ways to diffuse conflict with their children during their adolescent years. Working-class parents are shifting away from corporal punishment as a disciplinary strategy and toward methods based in greater communication or revocation of privileges.

Middle- and working-class parents converge in using open communication as a parenting strategy to learn what their children are involved in, maintaining influence over their children, and avoiding conflict and harsh disciplinary methods. For middle-class parents, mainstream parenting, and in particular their involvement in their children's academic and intellectual lives, may reproduce their class advantage.

CHILD-CENTERED PARENTING

The Value of Open Communication

Key to child-centered democratic parenting is open communication with youth. As a parenting strategy, both working-class and middle-class parents placed a high value on maintaining open communication with their children. Rita, a Puerto Rican working-class mother, said, "You need to be there, understand how they think and how they communicate . . . you have to know how to communicate with them and how to get into their minds." Jayna, a middle-class mother from India, also emphasized the importance of maintaining open communication with her adolescent daughter. She described the ways in which she tries to manage the conversation to keep future lines of communication open:

> I want to be open to her so she can talk to me [about] anything, because even though, sometimes she said so many things and I don't like it, but I listen to her. . . . I tell her my point of view. I don't say, "This is wrong or this is right." I say, "If I were you, I might do these things." So, that might help her because I want to keep the communication link open between us.

Jayna joked that she might have to take an aspirin, but she will still listen to her daughter even if she does not really want to hear what her daughter is talking about.

Monica, a White middle-class mother, also tried to keep the lines of communication with her son, Nathan, open. She said:

> I really feel that Nathan and I have a really open relationship, so that if there's a drug question . . . a lot of these kids are starting to experiment with different things. He tells me about sex, drugs, you know. I want him to be open with me and let me know. And I think that's really important that he knows that he can come talk to me and I'm not going to sit there and punish him or yell at him or anything like that.

Monica felt that open communication was important in her relationship with her son.

Maintaining open communication is a parenting strategy that sometimes marks a departure from the ways that parents were parented themselves. For example, Anne, an African American working-class mother, tried to have open communication when she and her daughter disagreed, which did not occur between herself and her parents when she was growing up. She said, "If she disagrees with a choice that I'll make, I'm like, 'Well, tell me why you feel this way.' And you know . . . it may not matter, but I'll listen to [her] opinion. My mother did not. [She] was not that type." Likewise, Stacy, an African American working-class mother, noted that her emphasis on open communication, and particularly listening to her daughter, was a break from the way she was parented. She said, "I listen to her. My mom, she's not into listening. I always listen. Tasha will be coming to tell me things, I listen, 'cause I want to know what's going on with her and the teenage girls. . . . I give her respect, you know, and try not to talk down to her." Stacy emphasized communication, saying, "'cause once you've lost communication, it is hard." Holly, a White middle-class mother, said that maintaining open communication gave her a different role in her relationship with her son. She said she is "more of a friend to him and more down-to-earth than my mother trying to communicate with him." Some other parents, both middle- and working-class, noted that they needed to sometimes shift the family hierarchy and occupy more of a friend role with their adolescents in order to maintain open lines of communication.

Middle-class parents in our study were more likely than working-class parents to report difficulties in maintaining the open communication that they would like to have with their adolescents, particularly with sons. For example, Holly, mentioned above, described a typical conversation with her son, Ian, about school. She said, "He usually doesn't say too much. I ask him how his day was. He'll grunt." Gloria, a White middle-class mother, noted that her daughter is less open with her than she used to be when she was younger. Gloria said:

> I think when she was younger, I could ask her what she's doing and she would pretty much readily tell me, but now she doesn't tell me. . . . I know people say, "Well, you should talk to your child about these things," . . . but she wouldn't do that. I couldn't sit down and say, "Heidi, well let's talk about sex or, you know, drugs or things like that." She would never sit down with me and talk about those things.

Jerome, an African American middle-class father in an interracial family, described some great conversations with his kids, but also described how "you ask them a question and the answer is always, 'Stuff,' I mean literally the word is, like, 'stuff.'" He said, "That's just kind of what kids do." Even though it is sometimes difficult, Jerome tried to get to what he described as "more meaningful communication" so that he could understand what his son was thinking.

Middle-Class Parents' Involvement in Their Children's Academic and Intellectual Lives

When middle-class parents thought of ways that they parent their own children differently than they were parented, they said that they were more involved in their children's academic and intellectual lives. Monica, whose parents are from Poland, emphasized that she feels more involved with her son than her immigrant parents were with her at his age. She said:

> They had no idea anything that was going on, 'cause they really didn't understand and they couldn't help. Where here I feel I know everything that's going on in terms of his work, what's due, what's not due and if there is anything he needs and if he needs to go shopping for a project, I'm there to help him get all this stuff. And he comes to me and tells me, "This is what's happening in school." I would never come home and tell my mom that the teacher took 10% off. So, I'm more involved with him in terms of school.

Middle-class parents noted that they have a different disposition toward homework than their parents did. Paola, a Latina mother from Brazil, said about her own parents:

> My mom did not value education. My mom and my dad, they were avid readers, too, but they never would ask me, "Is your homework done?" I don't even know if they knew that I had homework. I would put my bag in the corner when I came home and the next day, I would pick it up and go to school. That was pretty much it. So in that sense, it's very different.

Olivia is a White middle-class mother in an interracial family who grew up in foster care because her mother suffered from bipolar disorder. She said that one of the ways she parents her son differently than how she was raised is by helping him with homework. She said:

> I was never helped with homework. Periodically, I ended up in a foster home [and] they have five children of their own. So, typically, they weren't really helping with homework. Like, they might ask once in a while. You know, they never made a big deal out of how important it was to get an education and go to college and so on and so forth. So, in that regard, it's really different, because I've been doing that

since Alex was a baby. I always read to him. You know, just doing silly things . . . sitting in the restaurant [with] a bag of M&M's, "How many yellows? How many blacks?" You know, just playing games like that with him. They never really instilled that importance of an education and what it means to do that and what it can mean for you later in life, which I'm the opposite. I let him know that.

Like Olivia, other middle-class parents broke with their own parents in emphasizing educational material, even in their children's time outside of school. For example, Erica, an African American middle-class mother, said:

When I was young, I had such a hard time understanding how to learn that when I had Faith, I sort of, I don't want to say bombarded her with everything, but that's probably what I did, not really realizing that I was doing it, because Faith had *Hooked on Phonics* when she was 2. Yeah, I was really kind of neurotic about it, because I always felt like had I been taught a different way, I probably would have learned a different way because I didn't really understand how I actually learned until I got to college. So, for me, I thought, "There's no way my kid's gonna be in college before she finds out how to really learn." So, that's when I started, just one-on-one with Faith with everything. She's always been an advanced kid because she's always been exposed to things. Like my brother had her doing long division when she was 6 because for her it was play stuff.

Likewise, Bette, a White middle-class mother, said that one of the ways that she raises her children differently than she was raised is that she is more "intellectually engaged with [her] kids." She explained:

We'll talk about intellectual things at the table. . . . There's a lot more conversation about, not only the academic, but things to do with the world, interesting articles in the newspaper, or things we came across online. Just generally, what's going on in the world and what that means and how we analyze that, and what our values are around that and what other people's values might be around [it] and why there's a difference. Those kinds of conversations are pretty normal, whereas I think in my house of origin they weren't normal. That just didn't happen.

In thinking about these conversations at the dinner table, Bette said, "We've made these choices intentionally. We're lucky we have the education and the wherewithal to follow through in those choices."

Dealing With Disagreements: Middle-Class and Working-Class Perspectives

Middle-Class Parents: Diffusing Conflict. One arena in which a number of middle-class parents were seeking advice was in how to discipline and diffuse conflict with their adolescent children. Many parents sought ways to achieve their parenting goals with less conflict and punishment. Hays (1996) notes that mainstream parenting is "expert-guided" (8), and that seemed to be true for the middle class. Middle-class parents sought out information on discipline by reading parenting books or looking for information in other media (see also Kohn [1969] 1977). Theresa, a White mother, mentioned several parenting books she has consulted for advice, and she talked about what she learned about discipline from the book *Kids Are Worth It: Giving Your Child the Gift of Inner Discipline* by Barbara Coloroso (2002). She said:

> It's about discipline. Really, the goal of discipline is helping your child learn to be disciplined, that it shouldn't be to punish them. . . . It's best to use, where you can, natural consequences. So if you wanna go out with your friends, if you haven't cleaned your room or done the laundry or whatever it is you need to do, you can't go out with your friends. It's not a punishment . . . that's the consequences.

The first time she used this strategy, Theresa was planning to go to the movies with her two daughters, and one daughter, Violet, was supposed to clean her room. She told Violet that if she did not clean her room, she was "making the choice you're not gonna go." In the end, she said, "We had to go without her." She described it as "horrible" because Violet was screaming and saying she would clean her room when they got back, but in the end, Theresa found the advice "very relevant."

Paola, a middle-class Brazilian immigrant, shared some advice on diffusing conflict with young teens that she learned from watching *The Oprah Winfrey Show* and that she has used with her children. She said:

> I learned not to give a response right away. Ask 'em, "Let me think about it." And then, even call my friend and talk about it . . . and tell them: "Right now, I don't have an answer. You need to give me some time. You just brought that up out of the blue, I wasn't expecting it." . . . And I think that teaches me more that whatever they say, if it upsets me, then I'm [not] going to answer in any [beneficial way]. I just want to win the argument. And I learned that that's not good.

Mara, a White middle-class mother, also used techniques that she learned from a book about "dealing with anger or . . . criticizing behavior" as well as "sharing control." Following the strategy of negotiating (Baumrind 2013), she described how she used the advice from books to deal with issues of control when parenting her daughter: "There's a lot more give and take. . . . We really talk a lot more and negotiate things. Sometimes we can negotiate it to death, but I really try not to be fixed unless I have to be, and there's very few times I have to be." A few middle-class parents mentioned guest speakers at McKinley who gave advice on diffusing conflict with adolescents. One parent, Holly, a White middle-class mother, mentioned the speaker's advice to "try to help your kids be involved in decision-making processes and sort of do a role-play kind of scenario instead of just ordering them around." She takes that advice to heart when she gets home from school with the kids and finds herself in "drill sergeant mode," what she described as "badgering without realizing what I was doing."

Wendy, a White middle-class mother, read a lot on the internet and in the paper about limiting access to TV and violent video games. She said, "I think if they don't do it in your house, you're really fooling yourself." She learned that instead of saying "no" to something like a violent movie or music lyrics, "prepare them for how to deal with it instead of telling them 'no.'" She felt that even if she banned something from the house, her son would still have access to it somewhere, such as finding a bootlegged copy or watching a movie at a friend's house. So instead she focused on talking to him about the differences between the movies and the real world. All in all, middle-class parents sought advice on diffusing conflict and used techniques that they learned from books and the media to try to limit the amount of conflict they experience with their adolescents.

A Shift Away From Corporal Punishment Among Working-Class Parents. For some working-class parents, a shift to more mainstream parenting practices meant moving away from their own parents' use of corporal punishment toward other forms of discipline.[1] Rita, a Puerto Rican working-class mother, said that she raises her children in a way that is "totally different" from the way in which she was raised. She specifically cites physical punishment as an example:

> Like in punishment, my dad would hit us with his belt. He would hit us. I don't hit my children. I scold them and tell them, "You're not going to go out until you behave and do your homework." And, well, [my daughter] calms down, doesn't go out, [and] that's it. I don't have to raise my hand. But my dad, back in our day, well, he hit us.

Physical punishment is something about which Rita and the father of her children, who sees them every other weekend, disagreed. She said, "He thinks that you have to hit a child to make them understand and I don't think so. You have to punish them." Their difference of opinion on corporal punishment was the source of arguments between them.

Josephine, a multiracial working-class mother, described the process of moving away from corporal punishment. One of her main influences in changing her style of parenting was a television show on parenting that she watched to learn how to be a better parent. She said:

> When you don't really have anybody to kinda educate you on how to be a parent and you have to do it yourself, you do what you think is best. I can say Louis, as a child, and it took me quite a few years to even forgive myself for this, but when he was a child I used to be really hard on him. I would spank him or I would slap him in the head. Things like that. And I don't know what it was for me, but just out of the blue one day I just took a turn and I broke down and I started crying and I said I can't do this anymore. You know, this isn't what I should do to him. This is not right. But . . . that['s] my upbringing. I used to get hit with hangers wherever the hanger landed [or by] whatever object was in my mom's hand. . . . [S]o, when you come from that and then have your own child and you don't have no one to guide you on the dos and the don'ts, you tend to do what you were taught. And, again, that was something where I said I had to break that cycle because I didn't want him to grow up thinkin' it's okay to hit somebody or slap somebody across the head. So, I had to teach myself, and by watching programs, [I found], a better way.

One of the primary ways that working-class parents shifted to a mainstream style of parenting is by moving away from the physical punishments of their parents' generation toward other kinds of disciplinary techniques, such as revoking privileges. Among the middle-class parents, in contrast, the topic of corporal punishment never even came up.

Shifting from corporal punishment to other disciplinary strategies marks an intergenerational change in parenting practices that incorporates mainstream parenting practices. Harriet, an African American working-class mother, said that she and her husband used to beat their children as a form of discipline. She explained her transition away from corporal punishment, saying, "Now we not beatin' him. We take things . . . because you know with society sayin' 'don't hit your children.' Well, I was raised that you got your behind whooped when you did X, Y, and Z." Although they have transitioned away from corporal punishment, it is more because society frowns on the practice than because Harriet thought that the other methods are better or more effective. Harriet lamented that kids today do not have respect, and says it is "'cause you're not able to discipline your children the way that you would discipline."

Working-class parents' shift away from corporal punishment as a disciplinary tool may have been related to the rise of Child Protective Services and the threat that some parents felt of having their child removed from the home, or being sanctioned in some way by the state for disciplining with corporal punishment. Thus, mainstream parenting is supported by dominant institutions as well as internalized by working-class parents. For example, Tamara, an African American working-class mother, said, "I went through a lot of abuse . . . mentally, and getting my behind beat, but nah, I wouldn't want to raise no child like that." Tamara has drawn on her own experiences as a child in thinking about making a break from corporal punishment for her own children. However, she also cited the increasing role of CPS over time as part of the reason for her shift away from corporal punishment. She said, "These teenagers now is raisin' their parents, because [of] that 1-800 number, you know, you can't touch your kid. They pick up that phone and they call on them and then they come out there and tell 'em well you can't do this and you can't do that." Tamara has some experience in dealing with CPS because of her son's truancy.

Sometimes the state intervenes in parenting when children are perceived to be in danger in the parental home. In some working-class homes, but in no middle-class homes, parents described the intervention of CPS caseworkers into their lives. Sometimes working-class parents made a shift to child-centered parenting through complex sets of events and state intervention. In the following case, CPS became involved and embedded the family in a network of services that transformed Barbara's parenting style into one that was more child-centered and opened up opportunities for her children.

Before her move to the city, Barbara, an African American working-class mother, lived out of state near several relatives in a house with a yard. Then the unthinkable happened. In a whirlwind of misfortune, the house they were renting burned down, forcing them to move to temporary housing, which also burned down. She moved into her current apartment—owned by a friend of her children's father, but away from all of her relatives—because it would allow her to stretch her limited dollars to get a bigger place for less money, albeit with a mouse problem. Previously living in a home with a yard where her children could play, she now lived in a row house with neighbors close on both sides and with the front door opening right onto the street. Soon after her move, her 3-year-old left the house on three occasions when she did not hear him open the door, causing the police to bring him back home. Caseworkers got involved and offered a wealth of services to the family, including behavioral and occupational therapy, and got her son into a Head Start program. Some suggested hyperactivity medication for her son, but Barbara refused; she did appreciate the other services, though. Through Head Start, Barbara became involved in Policy Council, where she attended meetings once a month regarding children's services. Her participation in Policy Council expanded her social network so that she learned about greater opportunities for her children, and exposed her to new research findings on children and new ways of thinking about parenting her 8th-grade child as well as her younger children. About the change in her parenting, she said:

> Before I came here, everything was a scream and a holler and a yell in the house. And it got to the point that they really weren't hearin' me. They were so used to it they weren't hearin' me. So I've learned a lot just bein' in the different organizations that I've been in to just learn how to talk. Wait for a response and then respond to what he's saying. This way he'll feel like he is giving input. Or the kids in general . . . they all give input on what goes on in the household: "Look, we're thinkin' about goin' to such-and-such this weekend. How y'all think about it?" . . . But just giving input, allowing them to talk and allowing them to have input in what's goin' on.

Ultimately in Barbara's case, the intervention by the state into the family had a positive impact on the family as a whole.

Latina Working-Class Mothers Granting Greater Freedoms to Their Daughters

One group of working-class parents, Latina mothers of daughters, particularly emphasized a break with their own family norms of authoritarian rigidity in favor of greater freedoms. While they emphasized being watchful over their children's safety, Latina mothers said that they give their own daughters more freedoms than they had growing up. Allowing freedoms in this way was an explicit rejection of their parents' practice of confining girls to the home, where they were expected to do chores for the rest of the family, limiting the time girls spent with others outside the home, while allowing boys more autonomy to go out and explore the world. Layla, a Puerto Rican working-class mother, for example, said, "My father was very strict, so I had no friends. It was school and home, cook and clean." She continued:

> The way I was raised, I was always in the house. Like I was in jail. I couldn't go nowhere, had no friends, couldn't do anything but go to school and go home. No after-school programs, nothin'. I had to go . . . straight home. So there wasn't much for me to do. I was the only daughter. I had two brothers. My brothers could go out and I couldn't go out I guess.

Similarly, Mona, a working-class mother of Puerto Rican and Arab descent, although still describing her parenting style as strict, allowed her own daughter more freedoms than she had as a child. She said:

I was on my own with my sisters and my mom, I didn't have that many friends, I didn't go out nowhere. It was just basically my sisters were my friends, that's it. She has her own friends, I let her go out and I'm not—my mom was real strict, let's just put it that way. I'm strict, but I let her go out with her friends here and there. And talk with them on the phone; my mom was the type, no friends calling, no going out . . . none of that stuff. And then me being the oldest I was like in charge. Anything that happened in the house was bam, my fault. I don't let that happen to her, I don't want her to go through, "Oh it's your fault."

Although Mona allowed her daughter greater autonomy than she had as a girl, particularly allowing more interaction with friends, she did not allow her daughter to go out with boys or peers that she did not know and approve of. Reyna, a Puerto Rican working-class mother, described a similar experience:

I'm not as strict. My parents were too strict with me. I was 18 and I could just sit in front of the steps. My sister is a chaperone. I couldn't have friends come over. I didn't have friends. . . . With Sabrina, I tell her that I did miss that part of having friends. It's part of life. I did miss it and I didn't want her to miss out on it. So I try to give her a little bit of both.

Reyna emphasized family, but also allowed her daughter to spend time with friends outside the home.

For Latina working-class mothers of daughters, mainstream child-centered parenting meant a shift from their own parents' authoritarian parenting styles to more mainstream styles that involve greater freedoms for their daughters than they had as children.

SUMMARY

A social perspective on parenting suggests that as conditions change in society, parents modify their parenting behavior in response. Over time, the parenting philosophy in the United States has become child-centered, democratic, and time-intensive (Hays 1996; Ishizuka 2019). These changes have occurred with the rise of parenting experts whose advice proliferates in mass media and dominant institutions. While Lareau ([2003] 2011) finds that the child-centered parenting practices she calls "concerted cultivation" apply only to middle-class parents, we find that *both* middle- and working-class parents responded to these societal changes that emphasize intensive parenting by making changes to their own parenting practices, thereby adopting practices that are different from the ways in which they were parented. For both groups, there was an intergenerational transition in parenting practices toward intensive parenting. A key factor in child-centered parenting for both working-class and middle-class parents was open communication with their children. For some parents, this strategy was a break from how they themselves were parented.

Other shifts toward child-centered parenting practices varied by class. Some working-class parents, for example, explicitly rejected the corporal punishment practices of their parents' generation. This may be a form of defensive parenting, given that physical punishment can mean the intrusion of Child Protective Services into the lives of working-class parents. Latina working-class mothers eschewed the authoritarian parenting style in which they were raised and adopted a contemporary mainstream approach with their daughters. While both middle- and working-class parents responded to changing norms about parenting in U.S. society, there are some differences across social class. Middle-class parents also may have transmitted class advantage through their parenting by emphasizing academic and intellectual engagement with their children. Such intellectual engagement may lead to rewards for their children in school and society, thereby reproducing their class advantage. Although working-class parents have shifted to parenting strategies similar to those of their middle-class peers, it is unclear whether this will lighten the burden of social class disadvantage for their children in the future.

Conclusion

Despite the multitude of ways in which social class matters in the United States, middle-class and working-class parents have one essential thing in common—both groups are engaged in a project to raise healthy, happy, independent children who will successfully transition into adulthood. In the pursuit of that shared multifaceted goal, middle- and working-class parents utilize both similar and sharply different parenting strategies, the latter because their resources and social contexts necessitate different approaches and shape what options make sense to employ. When we put the findings of each chapter into conversation with those of the others, a clear picture emerges. Middle-class parents use adolescence as a time to optimize their children's experiences while strategically developing in them the qualities and skills needed to go off to college. Working-class parents use this same period to pursue future opportunities for their children while seeking to protect them from threats in their neighborhoods and schools that may harm them and their prospects for social mobility. Each of the previous chapters illustrates part of the story that unfolded in our study. This chapter presents the integrated picture.

CHILD-CENTERED PARENTING

Both working- and middle-class parents utilized child-centered parenting practices during their children's adolescent years. Doing so strengthens bonds between parents and children, reduces conflict in the home, allows parents to be knowledgeable about the goings-on in children's lives, and permits children to be involved in decisions that affect them. Working-class parents shifted away from corporal punishment to other means of obtaining children's compliance with their standards for behavior and for disciplining them when compliance was not forthcoming. Having received corporal punishment themselves, working-class parents did not use their own experiences to justify continuing the practice. Rather, they were motivated to adopt different forms of engagement based on new information they had received about the negative effects of physical discipline. They also were motivated by affection for their children, an accompanying desire to not hurt them, and, in a limited number of cases, concern about bringing government oversight into their lives via Child Protective Services. In place of corporal punishment, working-class parents restricted their children's privileges and fostered open communication.

Working-class parents also are invested in their children's happiness and development, which is shown most clearly by their approval and support of their children's participation in organized activities. Activity participation can require much from parents, even those activities that are free and take place where children already spend a great deal of time. That is, even free, school-based activities can cost parents in time and effort. Working-class parents supported children's involvement in activities because the activities matched or piqued children's interests, allowed children to socialize with friends, aided children's personal development, provided academic advantages, kept children active, and may lead to future opportunities for them. In short, working-class parents, like their middle-class counterparts, supported children's participation in organized activities because they provided physical, social, and cognitive benefits, but also because they might increase children's prospects for social mobility.

Latina working-class mothers displayed a rather specific shift toward more child-centered parenting practices, one that is informed by their own adolescent experiences with restrictive gender roles. They were clear in not wanting to apply to their children the rules their parents had applied to them, rules that limited their spheres of play and socialization compared with those of their male relatives. Instead, Latina working-class mothers gave their daughters more freedom than they had enjoyed.

Given prior research, it comes as little surprise that middle-class parents described using open communication and other child-centered parenting practices. They also sought to reduce conflict that inevitably arises between adolescents and parents. As we saw in Chapter 4, they invested heavily in their children's participation in organized activities, including non-school activities that required substantial sums of money. And consistent with prior research, middle-class parents in our study attempted to create educationally enriched home environments. Part of that effort involved reducing adolescents' responsibilities at home relative to duties parents were expected to fulfill as children. Middle-class parents reasoned that time spent on household chores would be more productively used on other pursuits, such as participation in organized activities.

Part of the reason working-class and middle-class parents similarly engaged in child-centered parenting practices is because such practices are far less dependent on resources and social contexts than are other parenting strategies. It takes no money to foster open communication with children. Parents can shun corporal punishment no matter the kind of neighborhood they live in. They can work to reduce conflict between themselves and their teenagers no matter how small or expansive their social networks.

Child-centered parenting strategies appear to be more squarely within the control of parents themselves, regardless of how resourced or disadvantaged they may be. Thus, both middle- and working-class parents described such parenting practices to us, even though the two groups vary, to some degree, on implementation.

TO STRATEGIZE AND DEFEND

Although middle- and working-class parents had in common the use of child-centered parenting practices, they differed markedly in other ways. Our data show clearly that middle-class parents used adolescence as a time to make their children "college-ready," not only academically but in all areas of life. And they did so with a set of parenting practices broadly consistent with what Lareau has termed "concerted cultivation," if we imagined that parenting logic applied to early adolescence. For example, middle-class parents taught their children how to manage a demanding schedule comprising multiple commitments and responsibilities. They taught their children how to navigate their city and its public transportation system, with the hope that such lessons would generalize to other places should their children attend college out of state. But in addition to teaching valuable skills, middle-class parents strategically pursued valuable but scarce resources for their children, such as an elite secondary education made affordable through public funds by way of academically selective public high schools. For the working-class parents in our study, in contrast, adolescence was a period during which they sought to move their children toward adulthood unscathed and into a better socioeconomic position than the one in which they had been raised. And they did so with a set of parenting practices that we call "defensive parenting"—an almost frantic use of harm-mitigating interventions designed to protect children from mortal and social threats, paired with the pursuit of social mobility for them. It is an expensive parenting strategy, not in dollars and cents, but in opportunity costs. The time working-class parents spend defending against threats to their children's well-being and social mobility is time that could be spent sharpening their children's skills, enhancing their talents, or developing a closer parent–child relationship.

The differential use of strategic and defensive parenting by social class, we argue, is intricately and inseparably linked to class differences in financial and social resources that middle-class and working-class parents have, along with the neighborhood contexts their respective resources afford them. Relative to most middle-class families, working-class families are more constrained in the quality of the neighborhoods they can buy into, not merely the amount and quality of housing they can afford. Consequently, working- and middle-class families tend to occupy different residential contexts. Indeed, residential segregation by income within metropolitan areas has worsened over time (Reardon and Bischoff 2011; Reardon et al. 2015; cf. Logan et al. 2018), primarily among families with children (Owens 2016). Combined with the unequal residential distribution of amenities (Galster and Killen 1995), segregation by income creates the conditions in which working-class families find themselves in neighborhoods with fewer amenities but with more challenging social forces than their middle-class counterparts. Chapter 1 shows that the neighborhood contexts of the families in our study reflect these social class inequalities.

For reasons directly related to their residential environments, working-class parents are beset with worry, in contrast to their middle-class counterparts. They worry that their children will be killed, will be sexually molested or raped, will be seduced by the informal economy of the street, or will drop out of high school or graduate without skills necessary to earn a living sufficient to support an independent household. Indeed, working-class parents raise their children with a keen sense of the need to defend against myriad negative forces they encounter in their residential and school environments—forces that threaten their children's lives, well-being, and prospects for social mobility. And defend they do; for working-class parents know that veering off course holds more severe consequences for their children than for those from middle-class families. Whereas middle-class families have financial and social network resources needed to strategically attenuate the ramifications of children's missteps, most working-class families do not. Therefore, they engage in defensive parenting with the resources they have—their energy, their time, and their kinship ties.

Defensive parenting is the cornerstone of working-class parents' efforts to get their children to their imagined "finish line." They maintained regular communication with school personnel about their children's behavior and academic performance for fear that teachers and other school personnel might label their children in ways that could steer their education and life trajectory off course. They kept watch over their children in their neighborhoods, some opting to drive or walk their children to and from school even though it was mere blocks from home. They monitored their daughters' clothing, not only to cultivate in them a particular standard of dress, but in a desperate attempt to exercise control over the boys and men their daughters encountered. In this way, working-class parents behaved as lay social psychologists, drawing upon the ways in which we all potentially can influence how others treat us by engaging in impression management (Goffman [1959] 1973). But like the African American professor who is mistaken for a cafeteria worker despite wearing the "costume" of her profession, working-class parents know that presentation of self wields only so much influence over other people's behavior. Thus, they fretted over the prospect that their daughters would be sexually assaulted and derailed from the life hoped for them, due either to pregnancy or the emotional scars an assault can leave. Given that reported rapes in the neighborhoods of working-class parents in this study were, on average, 75.1% more frequent than those in the neighborhoods of middle-class parents, and 67.3% more frequent than in the United States as a whole, there is little wonder why fear of sexual assault loomed so large in the minds of working-class parents and why they sought to defend their daughters against it.[1]

Of course, consensual sexual relations also can result in pregnancy and emotional scars. For this reason, working-class parents were vigilant about monitoring their daughters' voluntary sexual experiences. They also kept an eye on their daughters' peers, fearing that exposure to friends who became pregnant might reduce the stigma attached to teenage childbearing and make it more acceptable to their daughters.

Although working-class parents had relatively little control over threats to children's well-being in their neighborhoods, they could exercise more control over their children's school environments. Therefore, like their middle-class counterparts, they participated in the high school placement process, attempting to match their children with schools that reflected their talents, interests, and career goals. But in addition, working-class parents were motivated by the very real need to avoid a school that was so bad it was officially deemed to be "persistently dangerous" by the school district. Indeed, high school placement had stakes for working-class parents far beyond the type and quality of education their children would receive; it potentially held life or death consequences. Given this knowledge, working-class parents could not leave their children's high school placement to chance, and all but one took action to ensure their adolescent avoided their neighborhood school.

No doubt middle-class parents worried about the many things all parents do; parenting is never carefree. Nor do middle-class families always enjoy high levels of financial and contextual security. Economic recessions, as well as other national and global crises, can undermine it. However, their class-related resources allow them to weather such shocks better than their working-class counterparts.

Relative to the fears and anxieties voiced by working-class parents, middle-class parents exhibited a sense of calmness and security about their children. Middle-class parents were confident their teens would go to college, which presumes that their children would survive their childhoods. Such confidence also presumes that their children would graduate from high school with an education that afforded them college opportunities. That all had children in academically selective high schools signaled that their presumption was well-founded. Thus, many middle-class parents looked beyond college to graduate school with certainty. Given the realistic nature of their children's options, middle-class parents strategically developed in their children the skills they would need to leave home for life at college.

THE PRIVILEGE TO LIVE ONE'S VALUES

To live life in ways consistent with one's values is a privilege. That includes performing socially important roles as we wish to fulfill them or how we think we ought to enact them. Few social roles are as important as that of parent, given society's need to reproduce itself. But shepherding children into adulthood requires substantial financial and social resources, to say nothing of enormous amounts of energy and time. In the United States, the ways in which we enact this particular role are intimately tied to the resources we possess. Thus, the opportunity to parent in ways that tightly cohere with one's values is a privilege that is, in many ways, for sale. Those with sufficient means may parent how they see fit, being limited only by the rule of law and their own capabilities. Such people also can enjoy the cognitive and emotional benefits of behaving in ways consistent with their beliefs, goals, and aspirations—of having such an important part of their lives in alignment with what they desire. In contrast, people with more limited means must settle for doing the best parenting job they can with the resources they have. For some, this means falling only a little short of parenting the way they would like. But for others, it means not coming close to doing what they deem best for their children.

Some may counter that cultural differences between middle- and working-class families weaken the impact and relevance of class inequalities in resources and social contexts. Some may argue that class differences in values, goals, and aspirations foremost inform class differences in parenting perspectives and practices. To be sure, we cannot generalize to working- and middle-class families beyond those in this study. And there is some indication that the working-class parents represented here are more engaged than the general population of working-class families, given that most managed to avoid their neighborhood school. Nevertheless, our findings encourage a reconsideration of such arguments. The social contexts inhabited by working- and middle-class families in our study could hardly be more unequal or their resources more different. These differences matter for whether and how parents are able to actualize their values—that is, to translate their values into social action. The findings from this study ask us to pay more attention to the ways resources and social contexts create and constrain opportunities for parenting practices that facilitate children's development and educational achievement. Indeed, we found social class inequalities in abundance, but not an abundance of class differences in cultural logics about parenting, apart from those clearly informed by class-related advantages and disadvantages, such as strategic parenting and defensive parenting, respectively.

We social scientists have been here before. In 1963, Hyman Rodman argued that people who occupy lower class positions hold society's dominant values and subscribe to middle-class norms. Using Merton's strain theory, Rodman argued that because of disadvantaged circumstances that frustrate mainstream success, people in lower class positions stretch their values to permit alternative forms of success. Critically important is Rodman's emphasis on *stretching* values rather than *replacing* them. Those in the lower classes, he argues, do not toss off or abandon middle-class values. Rather, they respond to disadvantaged circumstances by developing additional values, thereby giving them a larger set of values on which to draw as their circumstances warrant. With a larger set of values comes a lower commitment to all the values held. Rodman refers to this as the "lower-class value stretch." In Ann Swidler's (1986) framework, we might say that people in the lower classes have more tools in their toolkits than others.

Typically, we think it beneficial to have more things that are useful to achieving our goals, but this may not always be true. Although stretching values is a way for working-class people to negotiate their circumstances, having a wider set of values may be yet another difficulty that accompanies disadvantaged class locations. One can imagine a wider set of values feeling burdensome when some of those values are judged harshly by others or when out-group members fail to see or willfully ignore the mainstream values that coexist with alternative ones. If the mainstream values of working-class people were recognized, the country would be forced to confront uncomfortable questions, such as the human costs involved in creating, maintaining, and permitting social contexts to flourish in which parents must struggle to achieve the profoundly important goal they wish to achieve and that society asks them to achieve—the transition of their children into healthy, responsible, and independent adults.

WHAT CAN WE DO? POLICY RECOMMENDATIONS

Below, we recommend policies that target social contexts and institutions, in contrast to ones that act on parents. The recommendations are informed by our findings that class differences in parenting practices emerge primarily from inequalities in family resources and social contexts. We therefore offer policy recommendations that hold the potential to reduce in size, or attenuate in effect, class inequalities in resources and in each of the social contexts in which working- and middle-class families are embedded—neighborhoods, schools, and social networks. These are discussed in reverse order.

Recall from Chapter 2 that working-class families were especially disadvantaged relative to their middle-class counterparts in their discussion networks—the group of people with whom they discussed issues related to parenting and schooling. Ideally, access to information that helps parents make good decisions about schooling would not depend on the size and composition of their social networks. Rather, one could imagine making resources available to parents in a routinized way through institutions with which parents regularly engage. With respect to educationally relevant information, school counselors (and teachers) serve that function. They provide parents and students information and advice about schooling matters, and even wield some measure of influence. However, a national study of the high school counseling system suggests it is ill-equipped in its present form to meet the needs of students and parents (Johnson and Rochkind 2010). Indeed, the national student-to-counselor ratio stood at 482:1 for the 2014–2015 academic year, having changed little over the preceding 10 years.[2] Expanding and substantially strengthening the counseling infrastructure might allow counselors to better perform their role as "mediators of opportunity" (Smith 2011), including mitigating the consequences of class inequalities in social network resources as they play out in the domain of schooling.

Our findings make clear the necessity for increases in socioeconomic school integration. Yet, school attendance patterns have moved in the opposite direction, with school segregation by income increasing over time (Owens, Reardon, and Jencks 2016). Although working- and middle-class adolescents in our study attended different schools because of academic differences, our policy recommendations about schools stem from the ways in which school structures interact with class segregation, no matter its source, to exacerbate inequalities. Recall from Chapter 4 that McKinley and Augusta offered approximately the same number of organized activities to their students, but they differed markedly in the *kinds* of activities in which students could participate. Class differences in the activity choice-sets during middle school become the platform on which class inequalities in participation during high school are constructed. Ameliorating this problem requires making the activity choice-sets at schools that serve primarily working-class students as large and as varied as those at schools that serve their middle-class peers, or reducing levels of school segregation so that working- and middle-class students, more often than not, attend the same schools. If the latter is pursued, attention also would have to be paid to neutralizing opportunity-hoarding efforts that some middle-class families exhibit (Tilly 1998; Lewis-McCoy 2014). Opportunity hoarding, as well as academic tracking (Tyson 2013), can reconstitute inside integrated schools the inequalities that exist between segregated schools.

Policymakers who determine school budgets, and school officials who decide on which activities to offer, should take seriously the relationship between structured activity participation and educational stratification. They also should acknowledge the critical role that schools play in affording participation opportunities to low-income youth. We recognize that school officials must make decisions within constraints: available financial and human resources, educational priorities, space considerations, and the interests of various parties (i.e., those who would be responsible for offering activities, parents, and the students who would express [dis]interest in participating in them). Greater socioeconomic school integration would lessen the impact of how answers to these questions shape working-class adolescents' opportunities to participate in the kinds of activities to which their middle-class counterparts have ready access. And as greater school integration is pursued, we recommend diversifying the activity choice-sets in schools with predominantly working-class students, so that those schools immediately offer more of the kinds of activities that positively influence college attendance and destination.

Local community institutions, beyond schools, also shape the opportunities of young people to participate in structured activities. The relative scarcity of institutions other than religious ones in the working-class neighborhoods in which our respondents lived restricted both the number and type of activities in which their children could participate. Moreover, class differences in children's participation in organized activities were largest for activities away from schools. We recommend that policymakers strengthen the institutional capacity of disadvantaged neighborhoods by creating and supporting entities devoted to children's out-of-school time.

Additionally, policymakers could reduce the amount of time that children are away from school by lengthening the school year and the school day. Doing so would reduce the amount of time during which children are most dependent on the resources of their families for opportunities to participate in organized activities.

The single most far-reaching step we can take to reduce class inequalities in social contexts is to adopt policies that promote socioeconomic *neighborhood* integration. Residential segregation is the primary mechanism through which residential contexts contribute to class differences in parenting practices. To the extent that working- and middle-class families reside in different neighborhoods, they inhabit different geographies of opportunity (Galster and Killen 1995). Their geographic separation translates into their children attending different schools, having access to different community institutions and organizations, and being differentially exposed to crime, violence, and other challenges in their residential environments.

The various chapters in this book have shown that working-class parents have as a primary goal the successful transition of their children into adulthood, a transition they hope will accompany social mobility. It is the same goal sought by middle-class parents. Yet, the two groups pursue it with vastly unequal resources and within vastly unequal social contexts, giving rise to parenting in privilege for some and parenting in peril for others. If these differences were neutral in their effects, we might find them merely an unfortunate consequence of our capitalist economy. That they contribute to social reproduction makes them threats to the American dream.

Sociodemographic Characteristics of Sample[1]

Sociodemographic Characteristic	N	Percent
Social Class[2]		
Working Class	28	56
Middle Class	22	44
Race and Ethnicity[2]		
White	17	34
Black	16	32
Latino	11	22
Asian	2	4
Interracial	4	8
Immigrant Background[2]		
Native Born	40	80
Mixed Status	6	12
Immigrant	4	8
Birth Place[3]		
Mainland	39	78
Puerto Rico	6	12
Outside the United States	5	10

1. N = 50; 2. Family-level classification; 3. Individual-level classification.

List of Occupations Used in the Position Generator

Clerical (For example: bank teller, bookkeeper, secretary, typist, mail carrier, ticket agent)

Craftsperson (baker, auto mechanic, machinist, painter, plumber, telephone installer, carpenter)

Farmer/Farm manager

Full-time homemaker/stay-at-home parent

Laborer (construction worker, car washer, sanitary worker, farm laborer)

Manager/Administrator (sales/office/restaurant manager, school administrator, government official)

Military (career officer, enlisted person in the armed forces)

Operative (meat cutter, assembler, machine operator, welder, taxicab/bus/truck driver)

Professional 1 (accountant, artist, nurse, engineer, librarian, writer, social worker, actor, athlete)

Professional 2 (clergy, dentist, physician, lawyer, scientist, college teacher)

Owner/Proprietor of a small business, contractor, restaurant

Protective service (detective, police officer, guard, sheriff, fire fighter)

Sales (salesperson, advertising or insurance agent, real estate broker)

Schoolteacher (elementary or high school)

Service (barber, beautician, private household worker, janitor, waiter)

Technical (draftsperson, medical or dental technician, computer programmer)

Source: National Center for Education Statistics (1990, 2004).

Appendix C: Selected Characteristics of Individual Study Participants

Pseudonym	Race/ Ethnicity	Family Structure	Num. of Children	Household Income	Educ.	2nd Educ.	Occupation	2nd Occupation	Own Car	Own Home
Adrienne	B	TP	5	<$10k	HS	NR	Teacher's aide	Unemployed	Y	N
Anne	B	TP	1	$50–75k	SC	SC	Welfare Caseworker	Caseworker	Y	Y
Barbara	B	SP	3	$10–15k	GED		Unemployed		Y	N
Bette	W	TP	2	$75–100k	JD	BA	P/T Lawyer	Professional	Y	Y
Carina	L	TP	4	$10–15k	HS	<HS	Homemaker	Laborer	Y	Y
Carla	B	TP	3	$25–35k	HS	HS	Preschool Teacher	Self-Employed	Y	Y
Erica	B	SP	1	$25–35k	BA		Preschool Teacher		N	N
Gabriela	L	TP	3	$10–15k	<HS	NR	Housekeeper	NR	Y	N
Gail	W	TP	2	$50–75k	HS	HS	Homemaker	Technical	Y	Y
Gloria	W	TP	1	$50–75k	BA	JD	P/T Clerical	Lawyer	Y	Y
Grace	M	SP	2	$25–35k	BA		Paralegal		N	N
Gwen	W	TP	2	$35–50k	PhD	BA	Psychologist	Artist	Y	Y
Harriet	B	TP	1	$50–60k	HS	<HS	Drug Counselor	Operative	Y	Y
Holly	W	TP	1	$100–200k	MA	JD	Social Worker	Lawyer	Y	Y
Jacky	W	TP	2	$100–200k	BA	BA	Self-Employed	Self-Employed	Y	Y
Jayna	A	TP	1	NR	BA	MS	Computer Programmer	Engineer	Y	Y
Jerome	B	TP	2	$75–100k	SC	PhD	Consultant/ Writer	Professional	Y	Y
Joella	B	TP	2	$30–40k	GED	HS	Security Guard	Nurse's Aide	Y	N

Josephine	M	SP	4	<$10k	AA	AA	Typist		Y	N
Juliette	B	SP	2	<$10k	NR	NR	Housekeeper		Y	Y
Kira	W	TP	2	$50–75k	BA	BA	P/T Home Business	Manager	Y	Y
Layla	L	TP	4	$60–70k	AA	NR	Court Advocate	Mechanic	Y	Y
Ling	A	TP	4	$50–60k	<HS	AA	Factory Worker	Factory Worker	Y	Y
Mallory	W	TP	1	$35–50k	MA	HS	ESL Teacher	Craftsperson	Y	Y
Mara	W	TP	2	$75–100k	MA	PhD	Nurse	Manager	Y	Y
Marie	B	TP	4	$50–75k	BA	AA	Bond Underwriter	Operative	Y	Y
Mauricio	L	SP	2	$10–15k	HS		Unemployed/Technician		Y	Y
Maxine	B	SP	3	$30–40k	AA	AA	Admin Assistant		Y	Y
Mona	L	TP	2	<$10k	<HS	<HS	Pharmacy Tech	Laborer	N	N
Monica	W	TP	2	$100–200k	MA	BA	Special Ed Teacher	Professional	Y	Y
Nancy	W	TP	2	$100–200k	MA	PhD	P/T Consultant	Scientist	Y	Y
Olivia	W	TP	5	$100–200k	BA	AA	Teacher	Operative	Y	Y
Paige	W	TP	2	<$10k	<HS	GED	In-Home Childcare	Disabled	Y	Y
Patricia	B	SP	3	$20–25k	AA	AA	Unemployed/Disabled		N	N
Paola	L	SP	1	$50–75k	MA	MA	Teacher		Y	Y

continued

Appendix C: Selected Characteristics of Individual Study Participants (continued)

Pseudonym	Race/Ethnicity	Family Structure	Num. of Children	Household Income	Educ.	2nd Educ.	Occupation	2nd Occupation	Own Car	Own Home
Petra	W	TP	2	$200k+	MA	JD	Social Worker	Lawyer	Y	Y
Pilar	L	TP	2	$15–20k	GED	NR	Unemployed	Carpenter	N	N
Polly	W	TP	5	$40–50k	<HS	<HS	Sales Clerk	Laborer	N	Y
Raquel	L	TP	2	$25–30k	GED	<HS	Factory Worker	Factory Worker	Y	Y
Reyna	L	TP	3	$20–25k	SC	HS	Child-Care Worker	Laborer	N	Y
Rita	L	SP	3	<$10k	<HS		Unemployed		Y	Y
Rosalinda	L	SP	4	$50–60k	SC		Admin Assistant		Y	Y
Sal	W	TP	2	$75–100k	BA	BA	Graphic Designer	Professional	Y	Y
Sarah	B	TP	5	NR	<HS	<HS	Housekeeper	Laborer	Y	Y
Sophia	W	TP	2	$200k+	BA	HS	Manager	Self-Employed	Y	Y
Stacy	B	SP	4	$10–15k	HS		Sales Clerk		N	Y
Tamara	B	SP	4	<$10k	<HS		P/T Mail Clerk		N	N
Theresa	W	TP	2	NR	MA	MA	Manager	Homemaker	Y	Y
Wanda	B	SP	5	$15–20k	<HS		Nurse's Assistant		N	N
Wendy	W	TP	1	$200k+	PhD	AA	Professor	Self-Employed	Y	Y

Notes: Y = yes; N = no; NR = not reported; Social class status is indicated by whether at least one parent has at least a bachelor's degree (middle class) or not (working class); *Race/Ethnicity:* W = White; B = Black; L = Latino; A = Asian; M = multiracial; *Household income:* self-reported annual household income; *Educ. (parent's education):* <HS = less than high school diploma; GED = high school equivalency; HS = high school diploma; SC = some college; AA = associate's degree; BA = bachelor's degree; MA = master's degree; PhD/JD/MD = doctorate; *2nd Educ. (education of the second caregiver):* same key as above; *Occupation:* parent's occupation; *2nd Occupation:* occupation of the second caregiver; *Family structure:* SP = single-parent household; TP = two-parent household.

Methodology

There is often curiosity about the process of data analysis in qualitative research studies. Methodological appendixes attempt to elucidate the process by which specific experiences articulated within small samples evolve into an aggregated understanding of the data. For this project, we collected a vast amount of narrative data coupled with survey and social network data. Interviews we conducted, ranging from 2 to 4 hours each, resulted in thousands of pages in transcripts. As our data set grew larger and more complex, so too did our analytic task. If our fieldwork could be translated to a picture, imagine a panoramic portrait of a cityscape where inside of each window of each building lived a story, a life experience, worries alongside hopes and dreams—all moments of meaning, whispers emanating from each window, and together producing a chorus that we sought to identify, explore, and understand.

In the pages that follow, we attempt to address some of the questions we most often are asked about our analytic process, as well as share some of our qualitative research experiences in this project.

WHAT ARE THE TRADITIONS OF QUALITATIVE RESEARCH THAT INFLUENCED YOUR RESEARCH DESIGN?

"Stand on the shoulders of giants," we were advised as graduate students. Throughout the history of sociology, the "giants" rightly have cared deeply about social inequality (as we do), the mechanisms that produce it, and the forces that sustain and reproduce it. In particular, we were very interested in the robust sociological debates around the duality of structure and culture in intergenerational status reproduction and mobility that centrally implicated social institutions and contexts, such as families, schools, neighborhoods, and social networks. To design a study that would address this concern, we knew we would have to collect in-depth data about *how* and *in what ways* parents raised their children within their proximate social conditions and within the larger American cultural milieu. Simply put, a qualitative research design was necessary to attend to our research focus.

Often when we speak of traditions in qualitative research, we hear about germinal work such as grounded theory, the constant comparative method, analytic induction, naturalistic inquiry, the extended case method, as well as a host of variant and hybrid approaches. It is important to note that we do not embrace one tradition in particular, or one over another. There are elements of all these well-known approaches that helped us move our research forward at various stages of the project. Our analytic choices were predicated on an overall understanding of and appreciation for key concepts in qualitative research, such as social constructionism, inductive reasoning, in-depth data collection, as well as thematic and discursive analysis. We are not methodological purists in our research orientation; however, we are steadfast in our commitment to use the most relevant methods to collect data that may answer our theoretically guided research questions, as well as the analytic approaches that may help us to deeply understand each metaphorical window and the panorama produced together.

An important premise of qualitative research rests on social constructionism and an accompanying objective to uncover the constellation of social realities experienced by individuals occupying varying social locations. One approach to achieve this objective is through collecting in-depth information with purposefully selected groups, as opposed to collecting a breadth of information that may be generalizable to a broad population. Our analytic focus remained on capturing variation and searching for a multitude of patterns, not just a specific linear path or set of correlates. In particular, interviews with open-ended questions and follow-up probes allowed us to engage in a transparently inductive research process. We aimed to build an understanding of the lived social experiences that produce social reality, to honor the variation that emerged, and to explore the mechanisms through which these experiences were socially constructed and reproduced.

WHAT IS THE RELATIONSHIP BETWEEN THEORY, DATA COLLECTED, AND THE ANALYTIC PLAN?

The conceptual model for this study, displayed in Figure D.1, reflects our central research question: *How do resources and social contexts mediate the relationship between social class and educationally relevant parenting practices?* Additionally, the model depicts our expectations regarding explanations for class differences in parenting practices, one that allows the influence of cultural elements, structural forces, and their combination to emerge.

Figure D.1. Conceptual Model of Relationship Between Social Class and Educationally Relevant Parenting Practices

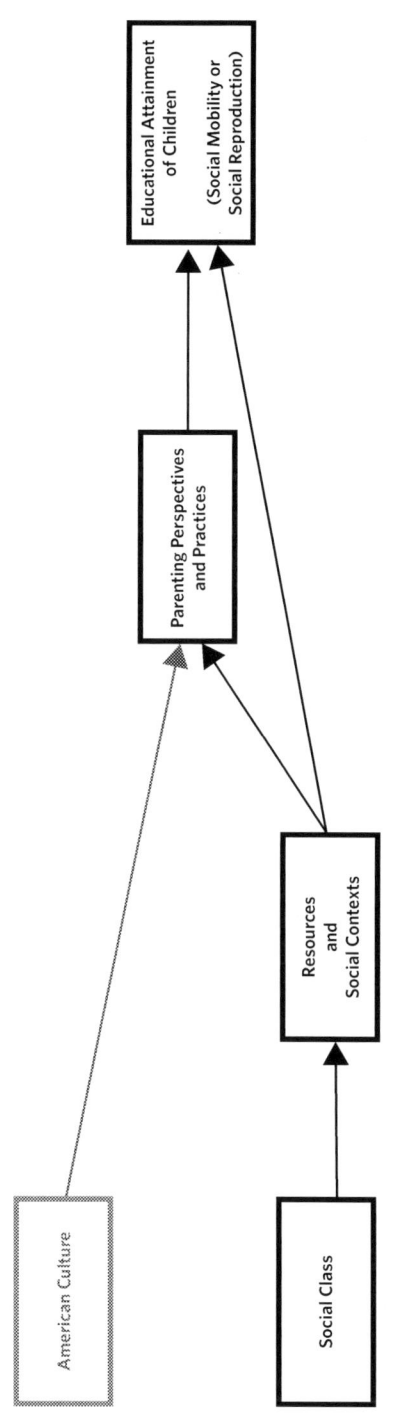

Indicators of Parents' Resources and Social Contexts:
• Household income (Survey)
• Homeownership (Survey)
• Children's schools (Climate survey)
• Neighborhoods
  - Sociodemographic composition (U.S. Census)
  - Reported crimes (Local police reports)
  - Parents' descriptions and experiences (Interview)
• Parents social networks
  - Structure and composition (Interview)
  - Resources (Interview)

Indicators of Parenting Perspectives and Practices:
• Parents' priorities, goals, and motivations (Interview)
• How parenting compares to that of others (Interview)
• Educational expectations (Interview)
• Occupational expectations (Interview)
• Sources of parenting information (Interview)
• Assessments and beliefs about organized activities (Interview)
• Financial outlays for organized activities (Interview)
• Types of activities in which children participated (Interview)
• Institutional linkages to organized activities (Interview)
• Parents' involvement in high school selection process (Interview)
• Mobilization of social networks (Interview)
• Types of network resources utilized (Interview)
• Objectives for which network resources were used (Interview)

During the interviews, we aimed to openly discuss with parents what they believe, value, and find normative, as well as their reasoning for specific choices and actions in the context of both the opportunities and constraints they experience. Thus, we incorporated both structural and cultural elements into our interview protocol. We asked parents about their values, orientations, and expectations. We solicited their perspectives on parenting and schooling. We asked them to reflect on how their parenting was similar to or different from how they were raised. We also designed a structured activity scenario to distinguish between structural influences and cultural ones. We believed our integrated approach, which featured interview methodology in the research design, would allow us to effectively investigate the sources of class differences in parenting practices as well as uncover evidence of both cultural and structural components.

Another important influence on our analytic plan was early engagement with thematic analysis. We did not intend to conduct other types of qualitative research that are possible with interview data, such as discourse analysis, case studies, or phenomenology. Rather we were explicit in our design that our analysis would incorporate a thematic approach because it was particularly important to us to understand *patterns* between groups with distinctly different social backgrounds, as well as the conditions and constraints that undergird these patterns. Additionally, the patterns we wished to investigate were not just similarities and differences between groups, but the interconnections and relationships within and between groups as well.

Finally, we did not anticipate a linear research process in designing this study. Consistent with qualitative research approaches more generally, we expected a discursive one. Between different phases of the research process, we anticipated that we might take a step forward and then back to revise certain concepts or ideas, or move diagonally where we recognized a new emergent direction. A key tradition in qualitative research is to adopt iterative and ongoing analysis, and this thinking centrally influenced our analytic plan as well.

WHAT WAS YOUR FIELD EXPERIENCE LIKE?

Soon after we visited Augusta and McKinley Middle Schools to introduce our study, and parents expressed their interest in participating in the study through postcards and surveys, we began to schedule interviews. It was a process that involved patience, persistence, and often a bit of luck as well to call at the right time. There were many instances when we called and the parent was not home or unavailable. Often it took a few calls to schedule and confirm interviews. Sometimes we got to know all the members of the family in the process of scheduling the interviews, as we talked to whoever picked up the telephone, and by the time of the interview, we often could mentally place each of the family members our respondent mentioned. We share this aspect of our fieldwork to illustrate that the process of building rapport began long before the interview. Rather, the first impression parents had of us was based on our participation at their school meeting, through several pieces of written communication, and then during phone calls to schedule the interview.

We met parents for the interview either in their home or at a nearby hotel. The location of the interview was the parent's choice. Sometimes a parent preferred to meet at the hotel but needed a ride, so the research team picked them up before the interview and dropped them back off at home afterward. When the interviews were at the hotel, we convened in the living room of a suite, and we had snacks and bottles of water on hand. When we went to parents' homes for the interviews, we brought baked goods for the family. At the conclusion of the interview, parents received a gift card.

At the start of the interview, we reviewed consent and requested permission to audio-record the interview. Many parents seemed a bit surprised, and for most of them, it was the first time they had ever been recorded for anything. Rather than feeling uneasy or self-conscious, interestingly, parents seemed to feel respected that we wanted to be sure that we correctly captured everything they said. One of us is a copious note-taker during interviews, and at one point a parent leaned over to ask if we had gotten it all down or if they should say it again! It was empowering for parents to discuss their parenting experiences and they cared that they would be quoted correctly. We took interview notes in OneNote on a Tablet PC where each tab moved us to a new area of questions in the interview guide, and at the conclusion of the interviews we showed parents how we recorded our notes using the tablet. Some asked to try navigating the technology themselves. They were especially interested in the spreadsheets we created to record social network data and density matrices.

When we first sent letters to families, we sent them in both English and Spanish. The postcard that parents sent back to indicate their interest in participating in the study also contained messages in English and Spanish. In follow-up, we mailed family surveys in both English and Spanish, too. We anticipated that the parents who sent their surveys back in Spanish likely would prefer to participate in the interview in Spanish. We, therefore, translated our interview guide to Spanish. All Spanish interviews were conducted by one of us who is fluent in Spanish. One thing we did not anticipate was that some family surveys would be filled out by students in English. We discovered at the time of the interview that the parent preferred to participate in the interview in Spanish. Since we had our interview guide prepared in Spanish, we were able to seamlessly move to Spanish interviews whenever the participant preferred it, even in the unanticipated cases. In one instance, during the course of the interview, we came to learn that the parent had limited literacy in Spanish, which may explain why they had not opted to fill out the survey in Spanish and relied on their child to do so in English instead. We also conducted one interview with a speaker of Chinese. It was a particularly difficult interview to schedule as both parents worked long shifts at a local factory. All of our communication to set up the interview was with their oldest son (not the target child). They were an immigrant Cambodian family, and preferred to participate in the interview in Chinese with their oldest son as their interpreter. This process is not as free-flowing as interviews conducted in a single language. However, we clarified both our questions and their thoughts every step of the way with detailed probes, and we were able to gather rich data about their parenting experiences. These field experiences underscored for us the importance of recognizing language diversity and the need for field methods to remain flexible and accommodating in order to capture the experiences of people who otherwise would not be represented in science.

We often think of research instruments as objective and concrete tools we use to collect information. In qualitative research that involves in-depth interviews, the researcher is known as the research instrument herself, as the quality and depth of data collected during an interview often hinge on the rapport that is built between the interviewer and participant. The greater sensitivity, transparency, and positive affect shown by the interviewer, the greater the interpersonal connection that develops, resulting in more reliable data. We began each interview with the same question, asking parents to tell us about their day "yesterday" so we could gain a sense of the daily dynamics their family experienced. We followed this question by asking how typical this day was; that was also very revealing in allowing us to quickly assess the relative stability versus unpredictability that characterized their family life. Our next question was about how they spent the past weekend as well as how typical that was for them. This series of questions helped establish rapport very quickly. After just the first few questions, we knew a lot about parents' routines, the important people in their lives, the kinds of time constraints and work–life balance they regularly experienced, as well as what they did for fun and leisure. Almost everything that was discussed in the rest of the interview could be connected back to some item mentioned early on in response to these questions. Asking such foundational questions was very helpful in establishing rapport because the participant could speak more freely after that, and in more detail, as we could quickly relate to the people, places, and priorities in their lives without much additional explanation. In other words, we were all on the proverbial same page.

We took several other measures to help participants feel comfortable during the interviews. We offered water and snacks, took breaks as requested, and gladly answered any questions they had for us. We listened attentively using both verbal and nonverbal cues, and expressed genuine reactions and emotions in response to their narrative. We allowed participants to speak as long as they liked without cutting them off, and assured them we would simply move to a different question without explanation if they preferred not to answer.

Positionality, and the potential power imbalance between the interviewer and participant, has been scrutinized by field researchers as integrally important to the discussion of rapport. As part of the academy, we were acutely aware of our privilege by way of our educational credentials and affiliation with a research university. Yet we also found commonalities with many of the parents we interviewed through shared racial, ethnic, and language identity; being of similar age; and our mutual interest in schooling issues. We went by our first names, dressed as we normally do in our individual styles, and enjoyed casual conversation with participants, too. Many different topics came up, but one that especially generated interest occurred when one of us was nearing the end of pregnancy, and the participants excitedly asked many questions (When are you due? Have you picked a name yet? How are you feeling?) and fondly remembered their own children's arrival to the world. We found concerns related to positionality were best addressed through a qualitative research axiom where we identified our respondent as the subject of the research (rather than an object), thereby centering the locus of knowledge on their lived experiences as parents (rather than on academic knowledge). Epistemologically, we recognized parents as "the knower" or expert, and viewed "what can be known" and knowledge production as borne out of our discussions rather than external to them.

A discussion of our fieldwork would be incomplete without mentioning the experience of conducting qualitative research as a team. On the way to one of our interviews, as we were driving on the interstate to meet a family, we heard a loud pop and flapping sound and pulled over to discover a flat tire. Unfortunately, we were near an exit without a clear shoulder on the road, so we were forced to stop in a relatively dangerous spot in between the highway and exit lane. Luckily, one member of our research team had serious automotive skills and expertly changed the flat tire to the spare (although with injury to her thumb) while another member looked out for speeding cars on both sides of us. Somehow, we still made it to the interview on time! This anecdote serves as a metaphor for the many challenges we have experienced and overcome together as well as all the ways we supported one another throughout this qualitative research endeavor, which had its share of ebbs and flows. Our years of discussion, reflection, debate, and collaboration culminated in an analysis where the end result is much greater than each of our individual parts. The synergy we developed while doing our fieldwork was a formative experience that grew, developed, and sustained our collaboration, and allowed us to engage in deep and critical analysis together to produce this book.

HOW DID YOUR DATA ANALYSES DEVELOP?

Our data analysis began with transcription of the audio recordings of our interviews. We transcribed several of the interviews ourselves and completed transcription of the dataset with the help of two assistants. The transcription process brought us much closer to the data. The Spanish interviews were first transcribed in Spanish and then translated to English. We also found substantive importance in ensuring that the punctuation in transcripts correctly described the respondent's intentions. A stray or absent comma could change meaning. We removed false starts and repeated words and phrases. We also inserted words in brackets to add clarity or context. The transcripts also recorded pauses, laughter, and times when the participant's voice grew louder or softer, which also provided affect for our interpretive task.

Once the transcriptions were complete, we decided to begin the analysis with a specific topic (structured activities). We commenced a process of open-coding together as a team, based on the major topics covered in our interview guide, as well as our fieldnotes. We then loaded our transcripts into a qualitative data analysis software program, MAXQDA. To facilitate easy identification of several respondent attributes, such as parent's social class position and child's school, we created an alphanumeric identifier for respondents and transcripts in MAXQDA. We coded the same transcript together, applying the open-codes we previously had developed. We did this several times until our coding practices were consistently aligned. We also added coding categories as necessary during this phase to capture ideas that were not part of the original open-coding phase. To keep track of our joint coding process, we developed a glossary where we kept a running definition of what each primary code and subcode meant to us.

The use of a qualitative data analysis software program was helpful in organizing and indexing the data. However, after completing the coding for just one topic covered in our interviews, we had hundreds of coded segments to further analyze. To make sense of the ideas, patterns, and intra-connections within each coding family, we began writing analytic memos. In this way, the data analysis developed very organically and inductively, and allowed us to create a refined coding system. Not only was writing essential in identifying saturation of particular ideas in the data; it was imperative for understanding variation as well. Ultimately, we completed this process of coding and writing analytic memos for all major topics covered in the interviews (such as parenting philosophies and expectations, experiences with their child's school, structured activities, the transition to high school, neighborhoods, as well as social network and financial resources). It took multiple passes through the data by all three of us. Our coding process shares similarity with "flexible coding" (Deterding and Waters 2018) and "cycles of coding" (Saldana 2015). Moving from the open-coding phase, to memo writing, to developing a refined coding system resulted in 27 primary coding categories with 41 supporting subcodes.

The next phase of our analysis involved identifying emerging themes in the data. This step during thematic analysis is closely tied to further investigation of the relationships between subcodes within a coding category, as well as relationships between the major coding categories. In particular, we aimed to uncover the context of these interrelationships and the specific contexts that enjoined as well as separated the various codes and subcodes. To develop our thinking about emerging themes, we began to experiment with different figures, diagrams, tables, and matrices in order to organize important interconnections and overlapping ideas in visual ways. Our first attempt at a data matrix yielded nine domains where working-class and middle-class parents reported both overlapping and distinctly different ideas: expectations, parenting practices, homework, high school destination, vigilance, structured activities, local social context, social capital, and financial capital. As we worked through the similarities and differences between social class groupings, we began to see important patterns developing around two broad categories—resources and social contexts, and specifically those associated with neighborhoods, schools, and social networks—where we saw stark differences between the working and middle class. By amplifying these patterns, we could specifically connect the supporting ideas within each of the nine domains to a context of either *security* or *precarity*. Creating a new table with this information yielded an emerging understanding of parenting practices, which we labeled *strategic* and *defensive*, that were associated with contexts of security and precarity within neighborhoods, schools, and networks.

Returning to our conceptual model, our emerging understanding of the data certainly addressed the ways that resources and contexts mediated a relationship between social class and parenting practices. But we were yet to incorporate the influence of culture on parenting practices into our emerging understanding. We returned to our coding system, analytic writing, data matrices, tables, and figures, and identified a few areas where the broader cultural milieu influenced parents—related to structured activity participation, child-centered parenting, and expectations for postsecondary education and future careers—and recognized these dimensions as areas where working-class and middle-class parents converged in their beliefs.

In other words, analysis of resources and contexts revealed *divergence* between working- and middle-class parents, while cultural norms and beliefs conveyed *convergence* between the two groups. The final analysis incorporates the influence of both culture and structure on parenting practices, with contexts and resources emerging as more critically defining. Table D.1 summarizes the emerging parenting strategies shown by our data.

To summarize this discussion of how our analyses developed, we began with an inductive open-coding process that grew to a comprehensive

Table D.1. Major Findings Related to Parents' Contextual Precarity and Security Informing Engagement of Defensive and Strategic Parenting

	Context of Precarity	Context of Security
Neighborhoods	Contain threats to physical and psychological well-being and social mobility	Are relatively safe
Schools	• Reduced sense of safety in and around middle school • Inconsistent partners with respect to keeping children safe • Heavily influences level of participation in organized activities • Limited opportunity to participate in elite activities that colleges and universities value • Parents seek to avoid a persistently dangerous high school; charter schools are acceptable	• Adolescents feel safe in and around middle school • Broad opportunities to participate in elite activities valued by colleges and universities • Parents seek academically elite public high schools
Social Networks	• Not socioeconomically advantaged • Used for immediate financial and material needs (e.g., funds for transportation; computer); may suppress use to help realize college aspirations	• Socioeconomically advantaged • Used to support children's academic achievement and long-term goal of college attendance (e.g., entry into elite public schools; contributions to college funds)
American Cultural Milieu	• Child-centered parenting • High educational expectations • Active pursuit of social mobility	• Child-centered parenting • High educational expectations • Active pursuit of social reproduction
Financial Resources	Insufficient to need	Abundant or sufficient to need
Emerging Parenting Practice	Defensive parenting	Strategic parenting

coding system that reflected an array of primary and secondary codes fully describing our data. The key element that produced this coding system was a series of collaborative analytical writings and discussions. Over the next several phases, we categorically aggregated the data to identify areas of similarity and difference. We also incrementally developed an understanding of the interrelationships between structure, culture, and parenting practices, and utilized data matrices, tables, charts, and figures to aid this process. Throughout this time, the research team stayed in close contact, and documented the evolution of each part of the analysis in great detail. In conducting qualitative research, Weiss (1995) describes a four-step analytic plan: (1) coding, (2) sorting, (3) local integration, and (4) inclusive integration. While coding and sorting are the initial phases of the analysis, local integration refers to developing a "mini-theory" to make sense of the coded and sorted data. Inclusive integration is the aggregation of all the mini-theories, and in the end, "tells the story" of the data. Our analytic process aligns with Weiss's recommended analytic plan as well.

DESCRIBE THE METHODOLOGICAL RIGOR OF THE STUDY

There are several aspects of this study that illustrate the rigor and robustness of the research process. First, we pilot tested our interview protocols with both an African American working-class parent and a middle-class parent of Asian immigrant background. We learned a lot from these interviews and streamlined our questions, developed an understanding of anticipated probes, and identified instances where our questions were confusing or complicated. The pilot also allowed us to test the various technological tools we planned to use in the field. By the time we went to the field to conduct the interviews, we had reviewed and incorporated all of the feedback we had collected from pilot testing.

Second, we applied methods of analytic induction, which emphasizes the search for the "negative case." This type of inquiry emphasizes not only identification of saturated themes within the data, but rigorous interrogation of the exceptions as well. Such a focus on the negative case(s) allows for more inclusive conclusions to be drawn that capture not only the saturated theme but conditions under which the emerging theme may not hold. For example, while our work focused primarily on social class, we also noted that Latina working-class families did not always fit the pattern emerging among working-class parents overall—that is, although they were working class, their narrative did not fully fit with the themes expressed by other working-class parents. Reporting the negative case in qualitative research is important to establishing validity. In quantitative analysis, the concept of validity establishes that the survey instrument in fact is measuring what it is intended to measure. Qualitative researchers, on the other hand, utilize analysis of the negative case to provide credibility for the saturated themes. By being able to articulate when the interpretation of the data does not fit, we have greater trust that the findings reported are saturated in the data minus the exception, or negative case, as noted.

Third, we triangulated our conclusions through analysis of multiple types of data (about neighborhoods, schools, and social networks). Ultimately, our overall convergent mixed-methods research design allowed us to bring together different types of data and analyses to holistically examine and investigate our stated research problem. Using this methodology involved a multistep research process. We first analyzed each type of data (qualitative and quantitative) separately within their respective research traditions. The various analyses were then independently and collectively interrogated in relation to specific research questions. By triangulating our interpretation of one set of findings with an accompanying set of findings, the resulting analysis improves the validity of the study and advances the possibility of capturing and conveying the array of saturated patterns of social experiences and contexts our study participants described. Triangulation involving both qualitative and quantitative data sources is found in several chapters, including those about neighborhoods, social networks, and structured activities.

Finally, we conducted member-checks with the working class and middle class. We shared drafts of various analyses and the entire book manuscript with people of various social backgrounds to assess whether and in what ways they agreed with our interpretation of the data. This feedback gave us confidence in the robustness of the findings.

Re-Analysis of Social Class Differences in Structured Activity Participation Using a Multidimensional Measure of Social Class

For our investigation of social class differences in educationally relevant parenting practices, we employ class categories that are common in the literature so that we can be in conversation with prior work. However, social class can be defined in various ways. We, therefore, explore whether and how our conclusions regarding the sources of class differences in structured activity participation would change if we were to adopt an alternative measure of social class. To do so, we rely on the work of sociologist Erik O. Wright (1985), who defines social class locations with respect to "three principal dimensions of exploitation relations—exploitation based on control of capital, organization [of labor,] and credential/skills—combined in various ways" (148). Wright's approach identifies four class categories.

First, owners are distinguished from nonowners by their control of capital, ability to hire workers, and/or ability to work for themselves (e.g., bourgeoisie, small employers, and petty bourgeoisie). The cross-classification of exploitation of organizational and credential assets with three levels of possession and control (high, some, little-to-none) yields nine specific class locations among nonowners. These nine locations are then grouped into three class categories—middle class, marginal working class, and working class. The middle class comprises those who have high-level educational credentials, who hold jobs that require such credentials, and who exercise control over labor assets within an organization. The marginal working class includes individuals who possess moderate credentials and exercise moderate control over labor. Finally, the working class comprises individuals who have neither credentials nor control over labor. This classification maintains the Marxist distinction between owners and workers. However, it also acknowledges diversity among workers by distinguishing among them along dimensions widely accepted as important to life chances, such as credentials and skills (Weber 1947). Reclassifying the respondents in this study would result in 10 members of the petty bourgeoisie (those who are self-employed or are owners of small businesses with one or two employees), 11 members of the middle class, 11 members of the marginal working class, and 19 members of the working class.[1]

Wright's multidimensional classification identifies a group (the marginal working class) that can be thought of as a kind of "lower middle class" or an "upper working class." We anticipate that the contrasts in activity participation between working- and middle-class families will be sharpened by treating members of Wright's marginal working class as a distinct group. Below we investigate: (1) whether the conclusions we reach with the education-based measure of class we use throughout the book will hold under a different measurement of class, and (2) how the marginal working class compares with the middle class and how it compares with the working class. We also examine whether and how members of the petty bourgeoisie are similar to and different from the middle class.

MIDDLE-CLASS AND WORKING-CLASS FAMILIES

Adolescents from middle-class families participated in more activities than did their working-class counterparts—3.9 compared with 2.3 activities per child (see Table E.1, Panel B). However, schools narrow the class gap in participation. For non-school activities, the class gap stands at 2.0 activities per child in favor of middle-class youth, whereas the gap is 0.4 activities per child in favor of working-class youth for activities that are organizationally tied to schools. The distribution of adolescents' activities across school and non-school contexts underscores the ways in which schools reduce class inequalities in participation by giving working-class youth opportunities to participate. Almost two-thirds (62.2%) of all the activities in which working-class adolescents participate are school-based activities, whereas the reverse is true for middle-class youth; three-quarters (74.4%) of their activities are non-school activities.

Types of Activities in Which Youth Participated

Focusing on activities the literature indicates are most related to college-going opportunities—cultural, sports, school-service, and hobby club activities (Kaufman and Gabler 2004; Gabler and Kaufman 2006)—shows that both working- and middle-class adolescents participate in such activities, with substantial involvement in cultural and sports activities. However, in all but school-service activities, working-class youth evidence

Table E.1. Mean Number of Activities by Social Class Location

Activity Location	Petty Bourgeoise	Middle Class	Marginal Working Class	Working Class
Number of Children	12	11	11	20
Panel A. Number of Activities				
All	64	43	37	45
School	31	11	21	28
Non-School	33	32	16	17
Panel B. Mean No. of Activities				
All	5.3	3.9	3.4	2.3
School	2.6	1.0	1.9	1.4
Non-School	2.8	2.9	1.5	0.9
Panel C. Distribution of Activities				
School	48.4	25.6	56.8	62.2
Non-School	51.6	74.4	43.2	37.8

less participation than the middle class in activities that may pay the highest educational dividends. The working class is most different from their middle-class counterparts in the percentage of religious activities in which they participate; the working class has the highest percentage of activities in this category.

Our investigation of the role that schools play in class differences in the kinds of activities in which youth from different social classes participated is limited to those types of activities that exist in both contexts: cultural, sports, hobby club, academic, and youth-development activities. We confront the problem of small cases once we divide the sample by Wright's four social class positions, distinguish activities by location (school vs. out-of-school), then separate them into various activity types. To avoid placing too much emphasis on findings based on very small numbers of cases, we limit our discussion to cultural, sports, and academic activities. With that caution in mind, Figure E.1 shows that the activity profile of working-class youth is more favorable relative to that of their middle-class counterparts for activities that are organizationally tied to schools compared with non-school activities. This pattern is clear with respect to cultural and sports activities. For example, the gap between working- and middle-class youth in cultural activities exists only in non-school activities; their participation in cultural activities organizationally tied to schools is virtually identical. The class gap in sports activities is wholly reversed when the comparison moves from non-school to school activities. For non-school sports activities, there is a class gap of almost 20 percentage

Figure E.1. Distribution of School and Non-School Activities Across Activity Types by Social Class Location

points in favor of middle-class youth; yet, the gap in school sports activities is just as large (19.8 percentage points) but favors working-class youth. These findings are consistent with those we previously reported.

Responses to Structured Activity Scenario

Our findings on parents' responses to our structured activity scenario are also consistent with our original analysis. First, a substantial percentage of both social classes indicated they thought the level of participation described in our scenario was good without articulating caveats—36.4% and 36.8% for the middle class and working class, respectively. Combining all forms of positive responses together indicates that 54.6% of middle-class parents were supportive of the participation depicted in the scenario, whereas 52.6% of working-class parents were positive about it. Likewise, a similar percentage of parents in both social classes thought the level of participation for our fictional child was too high—36.4% of the middle class and 31.6% of the working class. We again find a concern among the working class (15.8%), but much less so among the middle class (9.1%), regarding whether an active participation schedule affords sufficient time for and attention to schoolwork.

There is one finding from this sensitivity analysis that departs significantly from the results we report in Chapter 4 and our published paper—that regarding the concern among some parents that a participation schedule should be evaluated in light of the child's capabilities. In the original analysis, this was expressed exclusively by middle-class parents. However, only a single parent in our new group of middle-class families did so. Using Wright's classification, we find that this concern is expressed primarily among the petty bourgeoisie (or small business owners).

Parental Support for Children's Participation in Structured Activities

As in our original analysis, both middle-class and working-class parents express support for their children's participation in structured activities. Parents of both groups indicate that they see these activities as beneficial on the basis of their child's interest (seven middle class, seven working class), personal development (six middle class, five working class), socializing and meeting new kids (three middle class, three working class), keeping active (five middle class, three working class), and academic knowledge (two middle class, three working class). Of the parents who indicated that they supported activity participation to keep their children active, four middle-class parents specifically mentioned physical exercise in addition to general busyness, while no working-class parent mentioned physical exercise. Some working-class parents, but no middle-class parents, indicated that they support their child's participation on the basis of keeping the child safe and off the streets (nine working-class parents) or that activities offered children future opportunities (four working-class parents).

Participation in Elite and Non-Elite Activities

Using Wright's class schema, differences between middle- and working-class adolescents in the distribution of activities across elite, secular, and religious activities are approximately the same as those we observed under our original measure of class (see Figure E.2). The only difference between the two sets of results is that the under-involvement of working-class youth in elite activities relative to the middle class is somewhat larger under Wright's classification.

MARGINAL WORKING-CLASS FAMILIES

We find that the marginal working-class evince patterns that are, in some respects, similar to those of the middle class, but that are mostly in line with those of the working class. The marginal working class resembles the middle class in level of participation and in the kinds of activities in which youth became involved. However, they resemble the working class in greater participation in school-based activities, responses to the structured activity scenario, and participation in elite versus non-elite activities.

Levels of Participation and Type of Activities in Which Youth Participated

Youth from the marginal working class were rather similar to the middle class in their level of activity participation; they participated in an average of 3.4 activities per child compared with 3.9 for the middle class. Additionally, the activity profile of marginal working-class youth is similar to that of the middle class. For example, the share of activities that are cultural, school service, hobby, and religious for the marginal working class matches or exceeds that for the middle class. The only activity in which the marginal working class substantially trails the middle class is in participation in sports activities. This is in contrast to the working class, which is disadvantaged relative to the middle class in all but academic and school-service activities. In sum, then, the marginal working class is similar to the middle class with respect to the number and kinds of activities in which they participated.

Figure E.2. Distribution of Non-School Activities Across Elite, (Non-Elite) Secular, and (Non-Elite) Religious Activities by Social Class Location

Petty Bourgeoise

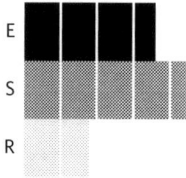

Middle Class

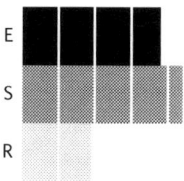

Marginal Working Class

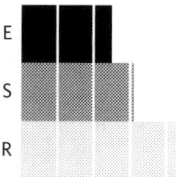

Working Class

Categories

E: Elite
S: (Non-Elite) Secular
R: (Non-Elite) Religious

Effects of Schools on Participation

Like the working class, the marginal working class participated in more school activities than did the middle class (1.9 versus 1.0, respectively), but fewer non-school activities (1.5 versus 2.8, respectively). Consequently, the gap in participation in school activities between the marginal working class and middle class is 0.9 activities per child in favor of the former, but reverses to a 1.3 disadvantage in non-school activities. Moreover, the activity profile of marginal working- and working-class youth with respect to activity types is more favorable relative to that of middle-class youth for school versus out-of-school activities. We again base that judgment on patterns for cultural and sports activities, as other types of activities that occur in both contexts have very small numbers for all social classes.

Responses to Structured Activity Scenario

The marginal working class is similar to both the middle and working class in its all-around support for the level of participation depicted in our scenario (54.6%, 54.6%, and 52.6%, respectively). The marginal working class shares with the working class a concern about the consequences that an active participation schedule may have for children's ability to do homework. In fact, a larger proportion of marginal working-class parents raised this issue than any other group.

Parental Support for Children's Participation in Structured Activities

Like other parents, those in the marginal working class offered overwhelming support for children's participation in activities. Some parents within this class category, like those in other classes, base this support on their child's interest, personal development, socializing, keeping active, and academic knowledge. Of those who support the idea of keeping their child active, three marginal working-class parents specifically mentioned physical exercise (like four middle-class, but no working-class, parents). In terms of supporting activity participation on the basis of safety or future opportunities, only one respondent who offered each of these reasons was from the marginal working class, while all others who mentioned these themes were from the working class.

Participation in Elite and Non-Elite Activities

As is the case for the working class, religious activities are the mode for the marginal working class, and elite activities are least represented. However, youth from the marginal working class are involved in substantially more elite activities relative to working-class youth. In this way, they appear somewhat closer to the middle class than to the working class. Yet, the overall shape of the distribution of their activities is closer to that of the working class.

PETTY BOURGEOISIE

In level of participation and type of activities in which children participated, the petty bourgeoisie resembles the middle class, but with a somewhat better profile overall. For example, youth from the petty bourgeoisie participated, on average, in 5.3 activities, the highest of all social classes. We do not observe the equalizing effect of schools among these two relatively privileged groups. The types of activities in which youth from petty bourgeoisie families participate are very similar to those of the middle class, with the exception that the former participate in relatively more hobby activities and fewer religious ones. The petty bourgeoisie and middle class also have strikingly similar patterns of participation in elite, non-elite secular, and non-elite religious activities.

Responses to Structured Activity Scenario

Although a substantial share of both the petty bourgeoisie and middle class approved of the level of participation described in our scenario, there are some notable differences in their responses to it. The majority of middle-class families (54.6%) thought the level of participation in our scenario was good (although a very small number of middle-class parents offered caveats); a smaller proportion of petty bourgeoisie parents (40.0%) thought so. However, it is not the case that more petty bourgeoisie than middle-class parents thought the level of participation in the scenario was too much (10.0% vs. 36.4%, respectively). Rather, the distinction between the two groups appears to be driven mostly by self-employed individuals' and small business owners' desire to evaluate the activity schedule in light of the capabilities of the child in question. Recall that this represents one of the findings that differs substantially from that of the original analysis—that this expression of a desire to customize the level of activity participation to the child's capacities does not describe the middle class in general, but more specifically middle-class parents who are self-employed or owners of small businesses.

Parental Support for Children's Participation in Structured Activities

Both the petty bourgeoisie and middle class indicate substantial support for children's participation in structured activities. Parents from both classes express benefits in terms of their children's interest, socializing, and academic knowledge. Only half as many petty bourgeoisie parents express benefits of structured activity participation in terms of personal development, and only two petty bourgeoisie parents (the lowest of any social class) express support in terms of keeping children active, perhaps because they are involved in so many activities. They also have the largest number of parents who express concerns about the amount of time activities take away from other things, like homework, family time, relaxing, and travel; about rushing; and about coordination associated with travel to and from activities.

CONCLUSIONS

The objective of this sensitivity analysis is to assess whether our conclusion regarding class differences in structured activity participation is robust to an alternative measure of social class. Results indicate that it is. Findings on the relationship between social class and activity participation from analyses based on Wright's multidimensional measure of class are consistent with our original analysis. Whether we distinguish between the working class and middle class using a bachelor's degree or with a combination of control of capital, organization of labor, and education and credentials, we arrive at the same conclusion. In light of few differences between working- and middle-class parents in their dispositions toward structured activity participation, and given that the activity profiles of the two groups are substantially alike with respect to school versus non-school activities, understanding the structural conditions in which members of different social classes are embedded is critically important to understanding why youth from working-class backgrounds participate in fewer and different activities than their middle-class counterparts.

NOTE

1. This analysis originally was conducted for our published article in *Sociology of Education* (see Bennett, Lutz, and Jayaram 2012), which is based on a sample of 51 parents (and 54 children, given the presence of three sets of twins), whereas all analyses in this book are based on a sample of 50. For the book, we excluded one respondent for whom information relevant to other chapters is missing.

Notes

Introduction

1. See Alesina, Stantcheva, and Teso (2017).

2. See Alexander, Entwisle, and Olson (2014) for a particularly effective example.

3. All names of persons, organizations, and institutions other than those of colleges and universities are pseudonyms.

4. Schools are described in more detail in Chapter 1.

5. Some of the ways in which social contexts are relevant to class differences in parenting practices are through the presence and quality of social institutions in those contexts. That working- and middle-class parents were recruited primarily from different schools does not prevent us from considering whether and how social institutions meaningfully factor into class differences in parenting because we consider institutions beyond the schools attended by the adolescents of our parent-respondents. For example, in Chapter 4, on class differences in participation in structured activities, we consider neighborhood institutions in addition to the schools adolescents attended. In Chapter 5, on parents' participation in the high school selection process, we consider all the schools in the district in which our parents lived.

6. Presently, multiple terms describe populations with origins or identities based in Latin America. They include "Hispanic," "Latino," "Latinx," and "Latine." We use the terms "Hispanic" and "Latino" interchangeably. When referring to an individual man or woman with origins or an identity in Latin America, we use the terms "Latino" and "Latina," respectively.

7. We conducted a sensitivity analysis to determine whether we would reach different conclusions with a different measure of social class. To do so, we repeated the analysis of class differences in children's involvement in organized activities that is presented in chapter 4 using a multidimensional measure of social class based on "three principal dimensions of exploitation," as defined by sociologist Erik Olin Wright (1985, 148). Results are consistent with those we report in Chapter 4 and in the journal *Sociology of Education*. See Appendix E.

8. Women constitute the majority of respondents in this study. That fact may suggest that we ought to use the terms *mothers* and *mothering* rather than *parents* and *parenting*. Although women provide most of the intellectual, emotional, and physical work to which the term *parenting* refers, we use "parenting" instead of "mothering" because the latter connotes a substantive and analytical attention to matters that differ from those with which we engage. Studies that claim to analyze mothering require, at

a minimum, a framework that attends to gender, if not to gender, race, and class. On the former, scholar Evelyn Nakano Glenn (2016, 3) notes that "mothering and gender are closely intertwined: each is a constitutive element of the other." On the latter, scholar Patricia Hills Collins (1991) notes the necessity of understanding mothering as informed by the simultaneous influences of race, class, and gender. Given that our focus is centered on how social contexts inform class differences in parenting practices, we use the term *parenting* to avoid signaling that this study is situated in a literature that it is not. Our use of the term *parenting* is not intended to obscure women's central role in this study. Indeed, doing so is impossible, given that we describe and quote parents individually throughout our presentation of evidence. Therefore, women's involvement, labor, and contributions are found everywhere in this book. For an intersectional analysis of mothering, see Jayaram (2009).

9. The school climate survey was developed by the Center for Social Organization of Schools at the Johns Hopkins University.

Chapter 1

1. See Appendix C for selected characteristics of individual study participants.

2. The neighborhood for one working-class respondent is unidentifiable; thus, the number of neighborhoods for working-class parents could be as high as 11.

3. Robert Sampson, Jeffrey Morenoff, and Thomas Gannon-Rowley (2002), in their review of the neighborhood effects literature, conclude that empirical findings are relatively consistent across studies that use census tracts and those that use block groups. The consistency of results is due to the fact that "place stratification of local communities in American society by factors such as social class, race, and family status is a robust phenomenon that emerges at multiple levels of geography" (Sampson, Morenoff, and Gannon-Rowley 2002, 446–47). In contrast, Hipp (2007) argues that the choice among areal units should be a theoretically informed one. After estimating effects of neighborhood characteristics measured at both the census tract and block levels, he concludes that "there is no one single 'appropriate' level of aggregation." Instead, he suggests that "some constructs work at different geographic levels depending on the outcome being studied" (674).

4. See Xie and Baumer (2019) on the underrepresentation of crime in official crime statistics.

5. The Federal Bureau of Investigation defines violent crime as "offenses which involve force or threat of force" (U.S. Federal Bureau of Investigation 2013).

6. Citywide crime rates are provided by the U.S. Federal Bureau of Investigation, (2005, 2006, 2007). We do not report crime rates for the city to maintain the anonymity of study participants. National crime rates for the same period are 0.1 for homicide, 0.3 for rape, 2.3 for assault, and 1.4 for robbery (UU.S. Federal Bureau of Investigation 2007).

Chapter 2

1. If respondents knew more than one person in a given occupation, we asked them to identify the first person who came to mind.

2. The 16 occupations come from the National Center for Education Statistics (NCES), which paired them with Duncan SEI scores. NCES used these occupations

to measure parents' socioeconomic status in large, nationally representative surveys of U.S. students (for example, the National Educational Longitudinal Study of 1988 [NCES 1990] and the Education Longitudinal Study of 2002 [NCES 2004]).

3. Limiting the number of alters a respondent can name may contribute to bias toward less diverse networks (Campbell, Marsden, and Hurlbert 1986, but also see Merluzzi and Burt 2013).

4. Recall that we asked each parent whether the person named for an occupation knew any of the other persons named in response to the position generator. If the parent had ties to two or more occupational categories, then we calculated density based on the degree to which there were ties among those named individuals. For example, if a parent named someone in response to 11 occupational categories, then density was calculated based on the degree to which there were ties among those 11 individuals. Likewise, if a respondent named someone in response to four categories, we calculated density based on the degree to which there were ties among those four persons.

5. Note that the class disparity in network size is not merely a function of the relative number of working- and middle-class parents with no or one network member. Among parents with two or more network alters, middle-class parents reported, on average, 5.9 alters while working-class parents reported 3.4 alters.

6. The IQV is a measure of dispersion for nominal or qualitative variables. It is defined as $(1 - \Sigma p2_i)/(1 - 1/k)$, where k is the number of categories in the qualitative variable (e.g., race) and p is the proportion of observations in the ith category (Agresti and Agresti 1978, 208). It ranges from 0 to 1, where 0 indicates that all observations belong to the same category and 1 indicates that observations are evenly distributed across all categories. We measure diversity across six categories of race and ethnicity—White, Black, Latino, Asian, American Indian, and multiracial—and multiply the value by 100 so that it can be expressed in percentage terms.

7. There is debate as to whether low-income groups benefit from weak ties. Granovetter (1983) cautions that "in lower socioeconomic groups, weak ties are often not bridges but rather represent friends' or relatives' acquaintances; the information they provide would then not constitute a real broadening of opportunity" (208). However, Lin and Dumin (1986) articulate a clear expectation that weak ties are beneficial to individuals who occupy lower positions in the social hierarchy, stating that "a low-status person's weak ties should provide better social resources than his/her strong ties provide. Consequently, the lower the initial position, the greater the effect of weak ties over strong ties on the [instrumental] action" (367).

8. For some research questions, it is desirable to distinguish between instances when respondents sought help from their network and those when network members provided assistance whether or not it was sought. However, it is not possible to maintain this distinction in our analysis because respondents did not always make it clear whether the assistance they received was the result of their help-seeking behavior or not.

9. The qualitative analysis of network utilization is based on 47 of 50 respondents. Two respondents, one middle class and one working class, reported no network utilization. Additionally, the interview for one working-class respondent

could not be transcribed verbatim due to audio issues. Although interview notes document that the respondent utilized her network, we do not rely on these notes as a complete representation of network utilization described by the respondent. We include these respondents in the quantitative analysis of social networks presented in Tables 2.1 and 2.2, because data on the existence of social network members and their characteristics were collected via tools that were not dependent on audio recordings of interviews.

10. Participation in structured activities is also part of concerted cultivation. We examine parents' utilization of networks to support activity participation separately from their use of networks to intervene, customize adolescents' experiences, and develop their skills and talents via other means because prior work suggests strong structural influences on participation in organized activities, and because we take up this question in Chapter 4.

Chapter 3

1. Shedd's (2015) work also emphasizes that getting to school safely is a concern for working-class youth in Chicago.

2. Our findings are very different from those of Edin and Kefalas (2005), who find that for working-class single mothers having children is a joy and something they do not want to postpone. Our findings may not necessarily contradict their results, however, but rather may reflect a different perspective. Edin and Kafalas focus on single mothers *who already have children*, whereas we interviewed *parents* of young adolescents who do not have children. The children of the parents in our study are also younger, just finishing middle school, than the parents in Edin and Kefalas's work.

3. Hamilton's (2016) work describes class and parenting styles among parents of college women. While we do not find examples of the helicopter parents she describes, the middle-class parents in our study are similar to her description of "hybridized" parents for whom children's autonomy was important.

Chapter 4

1. This chapter is based on our paper published in *Sociology of Education* (see Bennett, Lutz, and Jayaram 2012). Because of missing information for one respondent that bears on the analyses of other chapters, we omit that respondent from all analyses in the book, including this one, which results in a sample of 50 rather than 51 used for the article.

2. Lareau ([2003] 2011) also uses a scenario, but our use of it differs from hers in important ways. First, our scenario is designed to elicit parents' values toward structured activity participation only, whereas Lareau's scenario includes activity participation and other parenting practices, such as restrictions on TV watching and required reading time. Second, our scenario is silent on the fictional child's attitude toward activity participation, whereas Lareau's child dislikes one of his activities but is forced to participate in it by his parents. As a result, parents' responses to our scenario are about the level of activity participation in contrast to forced participation.

3. Church/synagogue/temple/mosque attendance qualifies as an organized activity under our definition. Additionally, attendance at religious services is treated as an organized activity by other scholars (see Barber, Eccles, and Stone 2001; Barber, Stone, and Eccles 2005; Lareau and Weininger 2008b). To exclude church/synagogue/temple/mosque attendance, which is a voluntary although not universal activity, would artificially lower the reported level of participation by working-class respondents. Thus, we include it and categorize it with all other religious activities. Note, however, that our conclusions do not rest on treating religious services as organized activities. In fact, their presence in the analysis makes our conclusions more conservative than they would be otherwise. That is, removing religious services would widen the reported class gap in participation in out-of-school activities, which would provide even greater evidence for the importance of social institutions in class differences in activity participation. We discuss this issue more thoroughly later in the chapter.

4. These mean values are very similar to those reported by Lareau ([2003] 2011, Table C4), who documented, on average, 4.9 activities for her middle-class respondents and 2.0 activities for her working-class and poor respondents combined.

5. We report the major themes present in the data. We observe in our data many of the same themes reported in other studies (e.g., Lareau [2003] 2011), such as "child's interest" and "personal development," but also others that, to our knowledge, are not reported elsewhere.

6. It is noteworthy that no middle-class parent in our study explicitly linked participation in structured activities with future opportunities for their child or with their child's social mobility. There is now a body of research that suggests that middle-class families use activity participation to improve their children's chances of being admitted to elite colleges (Stevens 2007; Friedman 2013). We cannot know for certain the reasons why middle-class parents did not speak to this link. However, one reason may be related to the high levels of confidence they appear to have regarding the educational expectations they hold for their children. We explore this topic in Chapter 6.

7. Most of the previous research on cultural differences in parenting across class has been limited to Black and/or White participants. Given that we employ a more diverse sample in our research, one that is better reflective of contemporary metropolitan demographics, one might ask how our findings relate to those of prior studies. To address this question, we conducted a sensitivity analysis to determine whether our results would vary if we limited our study to Black and White participants. The findings are the same as those reported for the full sample.

8. See Downey, von Hippel, and Broh (2004) for discussion of schools as both contributors to and levelers of social inequality.

9. See also Friedman (2013) for middle-class children's involvement in elite, competitive activities.

10. Following Gilbert (2003), we use $75,000 as an income division between lower-middle-class and upper-middle-class families.

11. Although we cannot be certain that we identified all available activities, based on our search it appears that structured activities that are not organizationally

tied to schools or religious institutions are relatively scarce in the neighborhood of our working-class respondents.

12. Although not mentioned by the working-class parents in this study, one can imagine that constraints on parents' abilities to transport their children, or arrange transportation for them, to secular activities located beyond their neighborhoods also contribute to lower levels of participation by working-class adolescents.

Chapter 5

1. Despite parents' assumptions that prestigious public high schools will lead to entrance into selective colleges and universities, Attewell (2001) finds that students at elite public high schools who are not in the top of their class are actually less likely to go to prestigious colleges than their peers at less selective high schools due to the use of class rank in admissions. He also finds that students at elite public schools are less likely to take advanced math and science courses compared with their peers who are not in elite schools.

2. States that receive federal funds through the Elementary and Secondary Education Act (ESEA) were required to establish criteria for identifying "persistently dangerous schools." Through the No Child Left Behind Act, students who were victims of crime at school or who attended schools classified as persistently dangerous were permitted to transfer to a different school within the same district (U.S. Department of Education 2004).

3. Although most of the school choice literature focuses on academic outcomes, our findings mirror those of Pattillo, Deale-O'Connor, and Butts (2014), who find that safety is a particular concern for low-income African American parents during the high school selection process in Chicago.

Chapter 6

1. About two thirds (63.7%) of middle-class families in the sample have graduate degrees. Holding an advanced degree, however, is not correlated with an expectation that children will obtain such degrees. Only half of highly educated parents expected their children to earn an advanced degree, while 62.5% of middle-class parents without graduate degrees expected their children to attain one.

2. Latino working-class parents differed from other working-class parents in two important ways: (1) they were less likely to name specific occupational expectations and, rather, wanted their children to choose, and (2) they were optimistic about bright futures for their children regardless of the precarity they experienced.

Chapter 7

1. One may ask whether a shift away from corporal punishment is a strategy parents undertake as their children grow older. The parents in our study did not speak to how the child's age factored into their approaches, but related to us a clear shift in parenting philosophy in terms of corporal punishment.

Conclusion

1. See Endnote 6 in Chapter 1 for nationwide crime rates.

   2. See p. 6 of *State-by-State Student-to-Counselor Ratio Report: 10-Year Trends* published by the National Association for College Admission Counseling (n.d.), which presents data from the Common Core data. The report can be accessed at https://www.nacacnet.org/globalassets/documents/publications/research/ratioreportdr3.pdf.

References

Archbald, Douglas. 2004. "School Choice, Magnet Schools, and the Liberation Model: An Empirical Study." *Sociology of Education* 77: 283–310.

Adams, James Truslow. 1931. *The Epic of America*. Boston: Little, Brown & Co.

Agresti, Alan, and Barbara F. Agresti. 1978. "Statistical Analysis of Qualitative Variation." *Sociological Methodology* 9: 204–37.

Alesina, Alberto, Stefanie Stantcheva, and Edoardo Teso. 2017. "Intergenerational Mobility and Preferences for Redistribution." Working Paper 23027. NBER Working Paper Series. Cambridge, MA: National Bureau of Economic Research.

Alexander, Karl L., Doris R. Entwisle, and Samuel D. Bedinger. 1994. "When Expectations Work: Race and Socioeconomic Differences in School Performance." *Social Psychology Quarterly* 57: 283–99.

Alexander, Karl, Doris Entwisle, and Linda Olson. 2014. *The Long Shadow: Family Background, Disadvantaged Urban Youth, and the Transition to Adulthood*. New York: Russell Sage Foundation.

American Academy of Arts and Sciences. 2016. *A Primer on the College Student Journey*. https://www.amacad.org/multimedia/pdfs/publications/researchpa persmonographs/PRIMER-cfue/Primer-on-the-College-Student-Journey.pdf.

Attewell, Paul. 2001. "The Winner-Take-All High School: Organizational Adaptations to Educational Stratification." *Sociology of Education* 74 (4): 267–95.

Barber, Bonnie, Jacquelynne S. Eccles, and Margaret R. Stone. 2001. "Whatever Happened to the Jock, the Brain, and the Princess? Young Adult Pathways Linked to Adolescent Activity Involvement and Social Identity." *Journal of Adolescent Research* 16 (5): 429–55.

Barber, Bonnie L., Margaret R. Stone, and Jacquelynne S. Eccles. 2005. "Adolescent Participation in Organized Activities." In *What Do Children Need to Flourish? Conceptualizing and Measuring Indicators of Positive Development*, edited by Kristin A. Moore and Laura H. Lippman, 133–46. New York: Springer.

Baumrind, Diana. 2013. "Authoritative Parenting Revisited: History and Current Status." In *Authoritative Parenting: Synthesizing Nurturance and Discipline for Optimal Child Development*, edited by Robert E. Larzelere, Amanda Sheffield Morris, and Amanda W. Harrist, 11-34. Washington, DC: The American Psychological Association.

Bennett, Pamela R., Amy Lutz, and Lakshmi Jayaram. 2012. "Beyond the Schoolyard: The Role of Parenting Logics, Financial Resources, and Social Institutions in the Social Class Gap in Structured Activity Participation." *Sociology of Education* 85 (2): 131–57.

Bennett, Pamela R., and Katrina McDonald. 2013. "Assessing Military Service as a Pathway to Early Socioeconomic Achievement for Disadvantaged Groups." In *Life Course Perspectives on Military Service*, edited by Janet M. Wilmoth and Andrew S. London, 119–43. New York: Routledge.

Blau, Peter M., and Otis Duncan. 1967. *The American Occupational Structure*. New York: Wiley.

Bourdieu, Pierre. 1986. "Forms of Capital." In *Handbook of Theory and Research for the Sociology of Education*, edited by John G. Richardson, 241–58. New York: Greenwood Press.

Bourdieu, Pierre, and Jean Claude Passeron. 2000. *Reproduction in Education, Society and Culture*. 2nd ed. London: Sage Publications.

Bronfenbrenner, Urie. 1979. *The Ecology of Human Development: Experiments by Nature and Design*. Cambridge, MA: Harvard University Press.

Bureau of Labor Statistics. 2021. "CPI Inflation Calculator." https://www.bls.gov/data/inflation_calculator.htm.

Burt, Ronald S. 1992. *Structural Holes: The Social Structure of Competition*. Cambridge, MA: Harvard University Press.

Burton, Linda M., Kevin Allison, and Dawn Obeidallah. 1995. "Social Context and Adolescence: Perspectives on Development Among Inner-City African-American Teens." In *Pathways Through Adolescence: Individual Development in Relation to Social Contexts*, edited by Lisa J. Crockett and Ann C. Crouter, 119–38. Mahwah, NJ: Lawrence Erlbaum.

Burton, Linda M., and Robin L. Jarrett. 2000. "In the Mix, Yet on the Margins: The Place of Families in Urban Neighborhood and Child Development Research." *Journal of Marriage and the Family* 62: 1114–35.

Byrnes, Hilary F., Brenda A. Miller, Meng-Jinn Chen, and Joel W. Grube. 2011. "The Role of Mothers' Neighborhood Perceptions and Specific Monitoring Strategies in Youths' Problem Behavior." *Journal of Youth and Adolescence* 40: 347–60.

Calarco, Jessica McCrory. 2018. *Negotiating Opportunities: How the Middle Class Secures Advantages at School*. Oxford: Oxford University Press.

Campbell, Karen E., Peter V. Marsden, and Jeanne S. Hurlbert. 1986. "Social Resources and Socioeconomic Status." *Social Networks* 8: 97–117.

Chaiken, Jan M., and Marcia R. Chaiken. 1990. "Drugs and Predatory Crime." *Drugs and Crime* 13: 203–39.

Chin, Tiffani, and Meredith Phillips. 2004. "Social Reproduction and Child-Rearing Practices: Social Class, Children's Agency, and the Summer Activity Gap." *Sociology of Education* 77: 185–210.

Chudacoff, Howard P. 2007. *Children at Play: An American History*. New York: New York University Press.

Cochran, Moncrieff M., and Jane Anthony Brassard. 1979. "Child Development and Personal Social Networks." *Child Development* 50 (3): 601–16.

Cochran, Moncrieff M., Mary Larner, David Riley, Lars Gunnarsson, and Charles R. Henderson Jr. 1990. *Extending Families: The Social Networks of Parents and Their Children*. Cambridge: Cambridge University Press.

Coleman, James S. 1988. "Social Capital in the Creation of Human Capital." *American Journal of Sociology* 94 (Supplement): S95–120.

Collins, Patricia Hill. 1991. *Black Feminist Thought: Knowledge, Consciousness, and the Politics of Empowerment*. New York and London: Routledge.

Collins, Randall. 1979. *The Credential Society: An Historical Sociology of Education and Stratification*. New York: Academic Press.

Coloroso, Barbara. 2002. *Kids Are Worth It: Giving Your Child the Gift of Inner Discipline*. New York: Quill HarperResource.

Condron, Dennis. 2009. "Social Class, School and Non-School Environments, and Black/White Inequality in Children's Learning." *American Sociological Review* 74: 685–708.

Conley, Dalton. 1999. *Being Black, Living in the Red: Race, Wealth, and Social Policy in America*. Berkeley: University of California Press.

Connell, James P., J. Lawrence Alber, and Gary Walker. 1995. "How Do Urban Communities Affect Youth? Using Social Services to Inform the Design and Evaluation of Comprehensive Community Initiatives." In *New Approaches to Evaluating Community Initiatives: Concepts, Methods, and Contexts*, edited by James P. Connell, Arne C. Kubish, Lisbeth B. Schorr, and Carol H. Weiss, 93–125. New York: The Aspen Institute.

Criss, Michael M., and Robert E. Larzelere. 2013. "Introduction." In *Authoritative Parenting: Synthesizing Nurturance and Discipline for Optimal Child Development*, edited by Robert E. Larzelere, Amanda Sheffield Morris, and Amanda W. Harrist, 3–8. Washington, DC: The American Psychological Association.

Crosnoe, Robert. 2011. *Fitting In, Standing Out: Navigating the Social Challenges of High School to Get an Education*. New York: Cambridge University Press.

Cullen, Jim. 2003. *American Dream: A Short History of an Idea That Shaped a Nation*. Oxford, UK: Oxford University Press.

Deming, David J., Justine S. Hastings, Thomas J. Kane, and Douglas O. Staiger. 2014. "School Choice, School Quality, and Postsecondary Attainment." *American Economic Review* 104 (3): 991–1013.

Denise, Patrick, and Bethany Gross. 2016. "Choice, Preferences, and Constraints: Evidence from Public School Applications in Denver." *Sociology of Education* 89 (4): 300–20.

Deterding, Nicole M., and Waters, Mary C. 2018. "Flexible Coding of In-Depth Interviews: A Twenty-First-Century Approach." *Sociological Methods & Research*, 1–32.

Donato, Katharine M., Charles Tolbert, Alfred Nucci, and Yukio Kawano. 2008. "Changing Faces, Changing Places: The Emergence of New Nonmetropolitan Immigrant Gateways." In *New Faces in New Places: The Changing Geography of American Immigration*, edited by Douglas Massey, 75–98. New York: Russell Sage Foundation.

Dow, Dawn Marie. 2019. *Mothering While Black: Boundaries and Burdens on Middle Class Parenthood*. Oakland: University of California Press.

Downey, Douglas B., Paul T. von Hippel, and Beckett A. Broh. 2004. "Are Schools the Great Equalizer? Cognitive Inequality During the Summer Months and the School Year." *American Sociological Review* 69 (5): 613–35.

Dumais, Susan. 2006. "Elementary School Students' Extracurricular Activities: The Effects of Participation on Achievement and Teachers' Evaluations." *Sociological Spectrum* 26: 117–47.

Eccles, Jacquelynne S., and Bonnie L. Barber. 1999. "Student Council, Volunteering, Basketball, or Marching Band: What Kinds of Extracurricular Involvement Matters?" *Journal of Adolescent Research* 14 (1): 10–43.

Edin, Kathryn. 1991. "Surviving the Welfare System: How AFDC Recipients Make Ends Meet in Chicago." *Social Problems* 38 (4): 462–74.

Edin, Kathryn, and Maria Kefalas. 2011. *Promises I Can Keep: Why Poor Women Put Motherhood Before Marriage.* Berkeley: University of California Press.

Edin, Kathryn, and Laura Lein. 1997. *Making Ends Meet: How Single Mothers Survive Welfare and Low-Wage Work.* New York: Russell Sage Foundation.

Elliot, Delbert S., Scott Menard, Bruce Rankin, Amanda Elliot, William Julius Wilson, and David Zuizinga. 2006. *Good Kids From Bad Neighborhoods: Successful Development in Social Context.* Cambridge, MA: Cambridge University Press.

Entwisle, Doris R., and Karl L. Alexander. 1992. "Summer Setback: Race, Poverty, and School Composition, and Mathematics Achievement in the First Two Years of School." *American Sociological Review* 57: 72–84.

Finn, Jeremy D. 1989. "Withdrawing From School." *Review of Educational Research* 59 (2): 117–42.

Friedman, Hilary Levey. 2013. *Playing to Win: Raising Children in a Competitive Culture.* Berkeley and Los Angeles: University of California Press.

Fuglini, Andrew J., and Christina Hardway. 2004. "Preparing Diverse Adolescents for the Transition to Adulthood." *The Future of Children* 14 (2): 98–119.

Furstenberg, Frank. 2001. "Managing to Make It: Afterthoughts." *Journal of Family Issues* 22 (2): 150–62.

Furstenberg, Frank, Thomas D. Cook, Jacquelynne S. Eccles, Glen H. Elder Jr., and Arnold Sameroff. 1999. *Managing to Make It: Urban Families and Adolescent Success.* Chicago: University of Chicago Press.

Gabler, Jay, and Jason Kaufman. 2006. "Chess, Cheerleading, Chopin: What Gets You Into College?" *Contexts* 5: 45–49.

Galambos, Nancy L., and Jennifer L. Maggs. 1991. "Out-of-School Care of Young Adolescents and Self-Reported Behavior." *Developmental Psychology* 27 (4): 644–55.

Galster, George C., and Sean P. Killen. 1995. "The Geography of Metropolitan Opportunity: A Reconnaissance and Conceptual Framework." *Housing Policy Debate* 6 (1): 7–43.

Gamoran, Adam, and Eileen C. Hannigan. 2000. "Algebra for Everyone? Benefits of College-Preparatory Mathematics for Students With Diverse Abilities in Early Secondary School." *Educational Evaluation and Policy Analysis* 22 (3): 241–54.

Gilbert, Dennis. 2003. *The American Class Structure in an Age of Growing Inequality.* 6th ed. Belmont, CA: Wadsworth.

Glenn, Evelyn Nakano. 2016. "Social Constructions of Mothering: A Thematic Overview." In *Mothering: Ideology, Experience, and Agency,* edited by Evelyn Nakano Glenn, Grace Chang, and Linda Rennie Forcey, 1–29. London and New York: Routledge.

Goffman, Erving. (1959) 1973. *The Presentation of Self in Everyday Life.* Woodstock, NY: The Overlook Press.

Goldstein, Derrick J. 2003. "The Drugs/Violence Nexus: A Tripartite Conceptual Framework." In *Crime: Critical Concepts in Sociology,* edited by Philip Bean, 96–111. New York: Routledge.

Goyette, Kimberly, and Yu Xie. 1999. "Educational Expectations of Asian American Youths: Determinants and Ethnic Differences." *Sociology of Education* 72 (1): 22–36.

Granovetter, Mark. 1973. "The Strength of Weak Ties." *American Journal of Sociology* 78 (6): 1360–80.

Granovetter, Mark. 1983. "The Strength of Weak Ties: A Network Theory Revisited." *Sociological Theory* 1: 201–33.

Hamilton, Laura T. 2016. *Parenting to a Degree: How Family Matters for College Women's Success*. Chicago: University of Chicago Press.

Harding, David J. 2009. "Violence, Older Peers and the Socialization of Adolescent Boys in Disadvantaged Neighborhoods." *American Sociological Review* 74: 445–64.

Harding, David J. 2010. *Living the Drama: Community, Conflict, and Culture Among Inner City Boys*. Chicago: University of Chicago Press.

Hays, Sharon. 1994. "Structure and Agency and the Sticky Problem of Culture." *Sociological Theory* 12: 57–72.

Hays, Sharon. 1996. *The Cultural Contradictions of Motherhood*. New Haven: Yale University Press.

Hipp, John R. 2007. "Block, Tract, and Levels of Aggregation: Neighborhood Structure and Crime and Disorder as a Case in Point." *American Sociological Review* 72 (October): 659–80.

Hofferth, Sandra. 2008. "Linking Social Class to Concerted Cultivation, Natural Growth and School Readiness." In *Disparities in School Readiness: How Families Contribute to Transitions Into School*, edited by Alan Booth and Ann C. Crouter, 199–205. New York: Lawrence Erlbaum.

Hofferth, Sandra L., and John F. Sandberg. 2001. "How American Children Spend Their Time." *Journal of Marriage and Family* 63 (2): 295–308.

Holloway, Susan D., and Bruce Fuller. 1992. "The Great Child Care Experiment: What Are the Lessons for School Improvement?" *Educational Researcher* 21 (7): 12–19.

Horvat, Erin McNamara, Elliot B. Weininger, and Annette Lareau. 2003. "From Social Ties to Social Capital: Class Differences in the Relations Between Schools and Parent Networks." *American Educational Research Journal* 40 (2): 319–51.

Hsin, Amy, and Yu Xie. 2014. "Explaining Asian Americans' Academic Advantage Over Whites." *Proceedings of the National Academy of Sciences* 111 (23): 8416–21.

Hughes, Diane. 2008. "Cultural Versus Social Class Contexts for Extra-Curricular Activity Participation." In *Disparities in School Readiness: How Families Contribute to Transitions Into School*, edited by Alan Booth and Ann C. Crouter, 189–98. New York: Lawrence Erlbaum.

Ishizuka, Patrick. 2019. "Social Class, Gender, and Contemporary Parenting Standards in the United States: Evidence from a National Survey Experiment." *Social Forces* 98 (1): 31–58.

Jarrett, Robin L. 1999. "Successful Parenting in High-Risk Neighborhoods." *The Future of Children* 9 (2): 45–50.

Jayaram, Lakshmi. 2009. "Social Reproduction Reconsidered: A Critique of Bourdieu's Concept of Habitus Based on Mothering Urban Youth." PhD diss., Johns Hopkins University. ProQuest (AAT 3392316).

Jessor, Richard. 1993. "Successful Adolescent Development Among Youth in High-Risk Settings." *American Psychologist* 48 (2): 117–26.

Johnson, Jean, and Jon Rochkind. 2010. "Can I Get a Little Advice Here? How an Overstretched High School Guidance System Is Undermining Students' College Aspirations." New York: Public Agenda (A Report for the Bill and Melinda Gates Foundation). https://eric.ed.gov/?id=ED508672.

Karabel, Jerome. 2005. *The Chosen: The Hidden History of Admissions and Exclusion at Harvard, Yale, and Princeton*. Boston and New York: Houghton Mifflin Company.

Kaufman, Jason, and Jay Gabler. 2004. "Cultural Capital and the Extracurricular Activities of Girls and Boys in the College Attainment Process." *Poetics* 32 (2): 145–68.

Kena, Grace, Lauren Musu-Gillette, Jennifer Robinson, Xiaolei Wang, Amy Rathbun, Zhang Jijun, Sidney Wilkinson-Flicker, Amy Barmer, and Erin Dunlop Velez. 2015. *The Condition of Education 2015*. NCES 2015-144. Washington, DC: U.S. Department of Education, National Center for Education Statistics.

Kimelberg, Shelley McDonough. 2014. "Middle-Class Parents, Risk, and Urban Public Schools." In *Choosing Homes, Choosing Schools*, edited by Annette Lareau and Kimberly Goyette, 207–36. New York: Russell Sage Foundation.

Kling, Jeffrey, Jeffrey B. Liebman, and Lawrence F. Katz. 2005. "Bullets Don't Got No Name: Consequences of Fear in the Ghetto." In *Discovering Successful Pathways in Children's Development: Mixed Methods in the Study of Childhood and Family Life*, edited by Thomas S. Weisner, 243–281. Chicago: University of Chicago Press.

Kohn, Melvin L. (1969) 1977. *Class and Conformity: A Study in Values, 2nd ed With a Reassessment*. Chicago University of Chicago Press.

Kotchick, Beth A., and Rex Forehand. 2002. "Putting Parenting in Perspective: A Discussion of the Contextual Factors That Shape Parenting Practices." *Journal of Child and Family Studies* 11 (3): 255–69.

Kozol, Jonathan. 1992. *Savage Inequalities: The Children in America's Schools*. New York: HarperPerennial.

Kozol, Jonathan. 2005. *The Shame of the Nation: The Restoration of Apartheid Schooling in America*. New York: Crown Publishers.

Krivo, Lauren J., Christopher J. Lyons, and María B. Vélez. 2020. "The U.S. Racial Structure and Ethno-Racial Inequality in Urban Neighborhood Crime, 2010–2013." *Sociology of Race and Ethnicity*, 1–19. https://doi.org/10.1177/2332649220948551.

Kusserow, Adrie. 2004. *American Individualisms: Child Rearing and Social Class in Three Neighborhoods*. New York: Palgrave Macmillan.

Lareau, Annette. 2002. "Invisible Inequality: Social Class and Childrearing in Black Families and White Families." *American Sociological Review* 67 (5): 747–76.

Lareau, Annette. (2003) 2011. *Unequal Childhoods: Class, Race, and Family Life, With an Update a Decade Later*. 2nd ed. Berkeley: University of California Press.

Lareau, Annette, and Elliot B. Weininger. 2008a. "The Context of School Readiness: Social Class Differences in Time Use in Family Life." In *Disparities in School Readiness: How Families Contribute to Transitions Into School*, edited by Alan Booth and Ann C. Crouter, 155–87. New York: Lawrence Erlbaum.

Lareau, Annette, and Elliot B. Weininger. 2008b. "Time, Work, and Family Life: Reconceptualizing Gendered Time Patterns Through the Case of Children's Organized Activities." *Sociological Forum* 23 (3): 419–54.

Lauen, Douglas Lee. 2007. "Contextual Explanations of School Choice." *Sociology of Education* 80 (3): 179–209.

Lee, Valerie E., and David T. Burkam. 2003. "Dropping out of High School: The Role of School Organization and Structure." *American Educational Research Journal* 40 (2): 353–93.

Lee, Valerie E., Robert G. Croninger, and Julia B. Smith. 1996. "Equity and Choice in Detroit." In *Who Chooses? Who Loses? Culture, Institutions, and the Unequal Effects of School Choice*, edited by Bruce Fuller, Richard F. Elmore, and Gary Orfield, 70–94. New York: Teachers College Press.

Lewis-McCoy, L'Heureaux. 2014. *Inequality in the Promised Land: Race, Resources, and Suburban Schooling*. Stanford, CA: Stanford University Press.

Liebow, Elliot. 1967. *Tally's Corner: A Study of Negro Streetcorner Men*. Boston: Little, Brown and Company.

Lin, Nan. 1982. "Social Resources and Instrumental Action." In *Social Structure and Network Analysis*, edited by Peter Marsden and Nan Lin, 131–45. Beverly Hills, CA: Sage Publications.

Lin, Nan. 2001. *Social Capital: A Theory of Social Structure and Action*. Cambridge: Cambridge University Press.

Lin, Nan, and Mary Dumin. 1986. "Access to Occupations Through Social Ties." *Social Networks* 8 (4): 365–85.

Loeber, Rolf, and Per-Olof H. Wikström. 1993. "Individual Pathways to Crimes in Different Types of Neighborhoods." In *Integrating Individual and Ecological Aspects of Crime*, edited by David P. Farrington, Robert J. Sampson and Per-Olof H. Wikström, 169–204. Stockholm: National Council for Crime Prevention.

Logan, John. 2014. *Diversity and Disparities: America Enters a New Century*. New York: Russell Sage Foundation.

Logan, John R., Andrew Foster, Jun Ke, and Fan Li. 2018. "The Uptick in Income Segregation: Real Trend or Random Sampling Variation?" *American Journal of Sociology* 124 (1): 185–222.

Loury, Glenn C. 1977. "A Dynamic Theory of Racial Income Differences." In *Women, Minorities, and Employment Discrimination*, edited by Phyllis A. Wallace and Annette M. LaMond, 153–86. Lexington, MA: Lexington Books.

Luster, Tom, and Lynn Okagaki. 2005. *Parenting: An Ecological Perspective*. Mahwah, NJ: Lawrence Erlbaum.

Marsden, Peter V. 1987. "Core Discussion Networks of Americans." *American Sociological Review* 52 (1): 122–31.

Marsh, Herbert W. 1992. "Extracurricular Activities: Beneficial Extension of the Traditional Curriculum or Subversion of Academic Goals?" *Journal of Educational Psychology* 84 (4): 553–62.

Marsh, Herbert W., and Sabin Kleitman. 2009. "Extracurricular School Activities: The Good, the Bad, and the Nonlinear." *Harvard Educational Review* 72 (4): 464–514.

Marshall, Gordon. (1994) 1998. *Oxford Dictionary of Sociology*. Oxford: Oxford University Press

Maslow, Abraham H. 1943. "A Theory of Human Motivation." *Psychological Review* 50: 370–96.

Massey, Douglas S. 1994. "Getting Away With Murder: Segregation and Violent Crime in Urban America." *University of Pennsylvania Law Review* 143: 1203–32.

Massey, Douglas S. 1999. "The Age of Extremes: Concentrated Affluence and Poverty in the Twenty-First Century." *Demography* 33 (4): 395–412.

Massey, Douglas S., and Chiara Capoferro. 2008. "The Geographic Diversification of American Immigration." In *New Faces in New Places: The Changing Geography of American Immigration*, edited by Douglas S. Massey, 25–50. New York: Russell Sage Foundation.

McFarland, Joel, Bill Hussar, Jijun Zhang, Xiaolei Wang, Ke Wang, Sara Hein, Melissa Dilibert, Emily Forrest Cataldi, Farrah Bullock Mann, and Amy Barmer. 2019. "The Condition of Education 2019." NCES 2019-144. Washington, DC: National Center for Education Statistics, Institute of Education Sciences, U.S. Department of Education.

McNeal, Ralph B. 1998. "High School Extracurricular Activities: Closed Structures and Stratifying Patterns of Participation." *The Journal of Educational Research* 91: 183–91.

McNeal, Ralph B. 1999. "Participation in High School Extracurricular Activities: Investigating School Effects." *Social Science Quarterly* 80 (2): 291–309.

McPherson, Miller, Lynn Smith-Lovin, and Matthew E. Brashears. 2001. "Birds of a Feather: Homophily in Social Networks." *Annual Review of Sociology* 27 (1), 415–444.

McPherson, Miller, Lynn Smith-Lovin, and Matthew E. Brashears. 2006. "Social Isolation in America: Changes in Core Discussion Networks Over Two Decades." *American Sociological Review* 71 (3): 353–75.

Merluzzi, Jennifer, and Ronald S. Burt. 2013. "How Many Names Are Enough? Identifying Network Effects with the Least Set of Listed Contacts." *Social Networks* 35: 331–37.

Morenoff, Jeffrey D., Robert J. Sampson, and Stephen Raudenbush. 2001. "Neighborhood Inequality, Collective Efficacy, and the Spatial Dynamics of Urban Violence." *Criminology* 39 (3): 517–59.

National Association for College Admission Counseling. n.d. *State-by-State Student-to-Counselor Ratio Report: 10-Year Trends*. https://www.nacacnet.org/globalassets/documents/publications/research/ratioreportdr3.pdf

National Center for Education Statistics. 1990. "National Education Longitudinal Study: Base Year: Student Component Data File User's Manual." NCES 90-464. Washington, DC: U.S. Department of Education.

National Center for Education Statistics. 2004. "Education Longitudinal Study of 2002: Base Year Data File User's Manual." NCES 2004-405. Washington, DC: U.S. Department of Education.

Nelson, Margaret K. 2010. *Parenting out of Control: Anxious Parents in Uncertain Times*. New York: New York University Press.

O'Connor, Alice. 2001. *Poverty Knowledge: Social Science, Social Policy, and the Poor in Twentieth-Century U.S. History*. Princeton, NJ: Princeton University Press.

Oliver, Melvin L., and Thomas M. Shapiro. 1995. *Black Wealth/White Wealth: A New Perspective on Racial Inequality*. New York: Routledge.

Orfield, Gary, and Susan E. Eaton. 1996. *Dismantling Desegregation: The Quiet Reversal of* Brown v. Board of Education. New York: The New Press.

Owens, Ann. 2016. "Inequality in Children's Contexts: Income Segregation of Households with and without Children." *American Sociological Review* 81 (3): 549–74.

Owens, Ann, Sean F. Reardon, and Christopher Jencks. 2016. "Income Segregation Between Schools and School Districts." *American Educational Research Journal* 53 (4): 1159–97.

Park, Robert, Ernest Burgess, and Roderick D. McKenzie. (1925) 1967. *The City: Suggestions for Investigation of Human Behavior in the Urban Environment*. Chicago: University of Chicago Press.

Pattillo, Mary, Laurie Deale-O'Connor, and Felicia Butts. 2014. "High-Stakes Choosing." In *Choosing Homes, Choosing Schools*, edited by Annette Lareau and Kimberly Goyette, 237–267. New York: Russell Sage Foundation.

Peterson, Ruth D., and Lauren J. Krivo. 2010. *Divergent Social Worlds: Neighborhood Crime and the Racial-Spatial Divide*. New York: Russell Sage Foundation.

Pittman, Robert B., and Perri Haughwout. 1987. "Influence of High School Size on Dropout Rate." *Educational Evaluation and Policy Analysis* 9 (4): 337–43.

Planty, Michael, William Hussar, Thomas Snyder, Grace Kena, Angelina Kewal-Ramani, Jana Kemp, Kevin Bianco, and Rachel Dinkes. 2009. "The Condition of Education 2009." NCES 2009-081. Washington, DC: National Center for Education Statistics, Institute of Education Sciences, U.S. Department of Education.

Quane, James M., and Bruce H. Rankin. 2006. "Does It Pay to Participate? Neighborhood-Based Organizations and the Social Development of Urban Adolescents." *Children and Youth Services Review* 28: 1229–50.

Ream, Robert K., and Russell W. Rumberger. 2008. "Student Engagement, Peer Social Capital, and School Dropout Among Mexican American and Non-Latino White Students." *Sociology of Education* 81 (2): 109–39.

Reardon, Sean F., and Kendra Bischoff. 2011. "Income Inequality and Income Segregation." *American Journal of Sociology* 16 (4): 1092–1153.

Reardon, Sean F., Lindsay Fox, and Joseph Townsend. 2015. "Neighborhood Income Composition by Household Race and Income, 1990–2009." *The ANNALS of the American Academy of Political and Social Science* 660: 78–97.

Rich, Meghan Ashlin. 2009. "'It Depends on How You Define Integrated': Neighborhood Boundaries and Racial Integration in a Baltimore Neighborhood." *Sociological Forum* 24 (4): 828–53.

Roda, Allison, and Amy Stuart Wells. 2013. "School Choice Policies and Racial Segregation: Where White Parents' Good Intentions, Anxiety, and Privilege Collide." *American Journal of Education* 119 (2): 261–93.

Rodman, Hyman. 1963. "The Lower-Class Value Stretch." *Social Forces* 42 (2): 205–15.

Saldana, Johnny. 2015. *The Coding Manual for Qualitative Researchers*. 3rd ed. SAGE Publications.

Sampson, Robert J. 2012. *Great American City: Chicago and the Enduring Neighborhood Effect.* Chicago: University of Chicago Press.

Sampson, Robert J., and John H. Laub. 1992. "Crime and Deviance in the Life Course." *Annual Review of Sociology* 18: 63–84.

Sampson, Robert J., Jeffrey D. Morenoff, and Thomas Gannon-Rowley. 2002. "Assessing 'Neighborhood Effects': Social Processes and New Directions in Research." *Annual Review of Sociology* 28: 443–78.

Sampson, Robert J., Stephen Raudenbush, and Felton Earls. 1997. "Neighborhoods and Violent Crime: A Multilevel Study of Collective Efficacy." *Science* 277: 918–24.

Sayer, Liana C., Suzanne M. Bianchi, and John P. Robinson. 2004. "Are Parents Investing Less in Children? Trends in Mothers' and Fathers' Time With Children." *American Journal of Sociology* 110 (1): 1–43.

Scott, John G., and Peter J. Carrington. 2011. *The SAGE Handbook of Social Network Analysis.* London and Thousand Oaks, CA: SAGE Publications.

Sewell, William H., Archibald O. Haller, and Alejandro Portes. 1969. "The Educational and Early Occupational Attainment Process." *American Sociological Review* 34: 82–92.

Shaw, Clifford R., and Henry D. McKay. 1929. *Delinquency Areas: A Study of the Geographic Distribution of School Truants, Juvenile Delinquents, and Adult Offenders in Chicago.* Chicago: University of Chicago Press.

Shedd, Carla. 2015. *Unequal City: Race, Schools, and Perceptions of Injustice.* New York: Russell Sage Foundation.

Small, Mario Luis. 2013. "Weak Ties and the Core Discussion Network: Why People Regularly Discuss Important Matters With Unimportant Alters." *Social Networks* 35: 470–83.

Smith, Sandra S. 2007. *Lone Pursuit: Distrust and Defensive Individualism Among the Black Poor.* New York: Russell Sage Foundation.

Smith, Vicki. 2011. "Mediators of Opportunity: High School Counselors in the 21st Century." *Sociology Compass* 5 (6): 792–806.

Soares, Joseph A. 2007. *The Power of Privilege: Yale and America's Elite Colleges.* Stanford, CA: Stanford University Press.

Social Explorer. 2002. Technical Documentation. Census of Population and Housing, Summary File 3, U.S. Census Bureau.

Stack, Carol. 1974. *All Our Kin.* New York: Basic Books.

Staff, Jeremey, and Derek A. Kreager. 2008. "Too Cool for School? Violence, Peer Status and High School Dropout." *Social Forces* 87 (1): 445–71.

Steffensmeier, Darrell, Emilie Andersen Allan, Miles D. Harer, and Cathy Streifel. 1989. "Age and the Distribution of Crime." *American Journal of Sociology* 94 (4): 803–31.

Stevens, Mitchell. 2007. *Creating a Class: College Admissions and the Education of Elites.* Cambridge, MA: Harvard University Press.

Stevenson, Harold W., and James W. Stigler. 1992. *The Learning Gap: Why Our Schools Are Failing and What We Can Learn From Japanese and Chinese Education.* New York: Simon & Schuster.

Stiglitz, Joseph E. 2012. *The Price of Inequality: How Today's Divided Society Endangers Our Future.* New York: W. W. Norton & Company.

Stiglitz, Joseph E. 2015. *The Great Divide: Unequal Societies and What We Can Do About Them.* New York: W. W. Norton & Company.

Sutherland, Edwin. (1924) 1955. *Principles of Criminology*, 5th ed., revised by Donald R. Cressey. Philadelphia, PA: J. B. Lippincott Company.

Sutherland, Edwin. 1940. "White-Collar Criminality." *American Sociological Review* 5 (1): 1–12.

Swidler, Ann. 1986. "Culture in Action: Symbols and Strategies." *American Sociological Review* 51 (2): 273–86.

Teachman, Jay D., Kathleen Paasch, and Karen Carver. 1996. "Social Capital and Dropping out of School Early." *Journal of Marriage and Family* 58 (3): 773–83.

Teske, Paul, Jody Fitzpatrick, and Gabriel Kaplan. 2006. "The Information Gap?" *Review of Policy Research* 23 (5): 969–81.

Teske, Paul, and Mark Schneider. 2001. "What Research Can Tell Policymakers About School Choice." *Journal of Policy Analysis and Management* 20 (4): 609–31.

Tilly, Charles. 1998. *Durable Inequality.* Berkeley and Los Angeles: University of California Press.

Tyson, Karolyn. 2013. "Tracking, Segregation, and the Opportunity Gap." In *Closing the Opportunity Gap: What America Must Do to Give Every Child an Even Chance*, edited by Prudence L. Carter and Kevin G. Welner, 169–80. Oxford: Oxford University Press.

Ulmer, Jeffery T., and Darrell Steffensmeier. 2014. "The Age and Crime Relationship: Social Variation, Social Explanations." In *The Nature Versus Biosocial Debate in Criminology: On the Origins of Criminal Behavior and Criminality*, edited by Kevin M. Beaver, J. C. Barnes, and Brian B. Boutwell, 377–96. Newbury Park, CA: SAGE Publications.

U.S. Census Bureau. 1994. *Geographic Areas Reference Manual.* https://www.census.gov/programs-surveys/geography/guidance/geographic-areas-reference-manual.html

U.S. Census Bureau. 2002. "Census 2000 Summary File 3." https://www.census.gov/prod/cen2000/doc/sf3.pdf.

U.S. Department of Education. 2004. "Unsafe School Choice Option: Non-Regulatory Guidance." https://www2.ed.gov/policy/elsec/guid/unsafeschoolchoice.pdf

U.S. Federal Bureau of Investigation. 2005. "Crime in the United States, 2004." http://www2.fbi.gov/ucr/cius_04/documents/CIUS2004.pdf

U.S. Federal Bureau of Investigation. 2006. "Crime in the United States, 2005." http://www2.fbi.gov/ucr/05cius/data/table_08_pa.html

U.S. Federal Bureau of Investigation. 2007. "Crime in the United States, 2006." http://www2.fbi.gov/ucr/cius2006/data/table_08_pa.html

U.S. Federal Bureau of Investigation. 2013. "Crime in the United States, 2012." http://www.fbi.gov/about-us/cjis/ucr/crime-in-the-u.s/2012/crime-in-the-u.s.-2012/violent-crime/violent-crime

van der Gaag, Martin, Tom A. B. Snijders, and Henk Flap. 2008. "Position Generator Measures and Their Relationship to Other Social Capital Measures." In *Social Capital: An International Research Program*, edited by Nan Lin and Bonnie Erickson, 27–48. Oxford: Oxford University Press.

Wacquant, Loïc. 2008. *Urban Outcasts: A Comparative Sociology of Advanced Marginality*. Cambridge: Polity Press.

Weber, Max. 1947. *Max Weber: The Theory of Social and Economic Organization*. Edited by Talcott Parsons. Translated by A. M. Henderson and Talcott Parsons. New York: Oxford University Press.

Weininger, Elliot B. 2014. "School Choice in an Urban Setting." In *Choosing Homes, Choosing Schools*, edited by Annette Lareau and Kimberly Goyette, 268-294. New York: Russell Sage Foundation.

Weiss, Robert S. 1995. *Learning From Strangers: The Art and Method of Qualitative Interview Studies*. Free Press.

Wellman, Barry. 1983. "Network Analysis: Some Basic Principles." *Sociological Theory* 1: 155–200.

Wellman, Barry, and Scot Wortley. 1989. "Brother's Keepers: Situating Kinship Relations in Broader Networks of Social Support." *Sociological Perspectives* 32 (3): 273–306.

Wellman, Barry, and Scot Wortley. 1990. "Different Strokes From Different Folks: Community Ties and Social Support." *American Journal of Sociology* 96 (3): 558–88.

White, Michael J. 1987. *American Neighborhoods and Residential Differentiation*. New York: Russell Sage Foundation.

Wilson, William Julius. 1987. *The Truly Disadvantaged: The Inner City, the Underclass and Public Policy*. Chicago: University of Chicago Press.

Wilson, William Julius. 1996. *When Work Disappears: The World of the New Urban Poor*. New York: Vintage Books.

Wright, Erik Olin. 1985. *Classes*. London: Verso.

Wright, Erik Olin. 2008. "Logics of Class Analysis." In *Social Class: How Does It Work?* edited by Annette Lareau and Dalton Conley, 329–49. New York: Russell Sage Foundation.

Xie, Min, and Eric P. Baumer. 2019. "Crime Victims' Decision to Call the Police: Past Research and New Directions." *Annual Review of Criminology* 2: 217–40.

Zhou, Min, and Susan Kim. 2006. "Community Forces, Social Capital, and Educational Achievement: The Case of Supplementary Education in the Chinese and Korean Immigrant Communities." *Harvard Educational Review* 76 (1): 1–29.

Index

The letter f or t following a page number indicates a figure or table, respectively.

About the Authors

Pamela R. Bennett is an associate professor in the School of Public Policy and faculty affiliate in Language, Literature, and Culture at the University of Maryland, Baltimore County. She received her doctorate in sociology from the University of Michigan in Ann Arbor. Her research and writing center on social inequality as it relates to education and operates through racial and ethnic residential segregation. Her research has received support from the National Science Foundation, the Russell Sage Foundation, the Spencer Foundation, the American Sociological Association, and the Poverty & Race Research Action Council. Her work on race and higher education has focused on the experiences of Black students, both African Americans and Black immigrants, revealing the dimensions of what she has termed the "net black advantage" in college attendance. In other research, she explores the implications of changes in affirmative action for racial and ethnic disparities in access to and graduation from selective colleges and universities. Combining her interests in education and segregation, Bennett has written on whether and how lessons from affirmative action can be applied to the persistent problem of residential segregation.

Amy Lutz is an associate professor of sociology in the Maxwell School of Citizenship and Public Affairs at Syracuse University. Her research interests include sociology of education, racial and ethnic inequality, and immigration. Her work has been funded by the National Science Foundation, the Social Science Research Council, the Spencer Foundation, the Russell Sage Foundation, and the Poverty and Race Research Action Council. Her work has recently appeared in *City and Community*, *Ethnic and Racial Studies*, *Ethnic Studies Review*, *Journal of Ethnic and Migration Studies*, and *Sociology of Education*. Her recent work includes a study with Pamela R. Bennett and Rebecca Wang of the impact of affirmative action bans and the *Grutter* Supreme Court case on students' application to, enrollment in, and completion from selective colleges. Her current research includes collaborative research with Dalia Abdelhady on the school and early labor market experiences of children of immigrants in the United States, France, and Germany. She is also currently working on a collaborative project with

Sujung (Crystal) Lee and Baurzhan Bokayev on mothers' experiences of remote schooling during the Covid-19 pandemic.

Lakshmi Jayaram is president of the Inquiry Research Group LLC, and affiliated with the University of Central Florida, the University of South Florida, the University of Tampa, and the School of Public Policy at the University of Maryland, Baltimore County. She received her doctorate in sociology from the Johns Hopkins University and specializes in qualitative and mixed methods research, with a focus on social disparities, intersectionality, and policy-relevant studies. Her grant-funded projects span education, human services, children and families, and politics. Prior to working in academia, Jayaram received her master's degree in public policy from the University of Chicago and worked at The White House, the U.S. Department of Justice, and the U.S. Senate Foreign Relations Committee as a Presidential Management Fellow.